MILTON'S RABBINICAL
READINGS

PUBLISHED BY THE

UNIVERSITY OF ILLINOIS PRESS

URBANA, ILLINOIS, U.S.A.

1930

FRONTISPIECE
The Hebrew Title-page of Buxtorf's Rabbinical Bible,
Basel, 1618-19.

MILTON'S RABBINICAL
READINGS

BY

HARRIS FRANCIS FLETCHER, 1892-

URBANA
UNIVERSITY OF ILLINOIS PRESS
1930

500 10 30 7351

UNIVERSITY
OF ILLINOIS
:: PRESS ::

'the flower of great art blooms only where the soil is deep, . . . it takes a great deal . . . to produce a little literature, . . . it needs a complex . . . machinery to set a writer in motion.'

—HENRY JAMES

'. . . there is no short cut to the great thoughts of great thinkers. We can only assimilate them by grappling with their works and work and lifting ourselves by slow degrees to the level at which truth as revealed to them reveals itself to us also.'

—ANON.

TABLE OF CONTENTS

FACSIMILES

FOREWORD

Some years ago, Professor James Holly Hanford suggested to me that it might be worth while to investigate systematically the possibility of arranging our knowledge of Milton's indebtedness to Semitic sources. Just after that, there appeared Saurat's article on 'Milton and the *Zohar*,' supplying detailed information lacking in his more general *La Pensée de Milton* in which he had, however, suggested the heading 'Hebrew Sources' as part of his schematic survey of the sources on which Milton drew. As I worked on the general subject of the Semitic literary influences on Milton and finished my thesis on it, I discovered that, in reality, definite knowledge of Milton's connections with Semitic literature was almost entirely lacking. Generalities abounded, and as in the work of Saurat, parallels alone were enough to warrant the inference or conjecture that because an idea was found both in Milton and in the *Zohar* for instance, therefore Milton had taken the idea direct from that work. This to me seemed unsatisfactory. I wanted to know more of the form in which Milton would have known not only the *Zohar*, but other rabbinical works. I found little or no account being taken of such a problem. For some time, I worked with the cabbalistic material, finding much that was interesting, even fascinating, but little that I was able in any way to connect directly with Milton except by the dubious method of pointing out parallels to which as a method I had originally objected. It very soon thereafter became apparent to me that such a manner of working was basically profitless, although superficially productive of much that was vaguely attractive. I became convinced that the field was worth cultivating, however, if the proper method of work could be found. This was easy to find, once I realized fully the significance of what I had learned from my previous study. For it became clearer and clearer that what was needed most was not mere collections of parallels, but actual connection with Milton of various rabbinical works. This gave me, moreover, the basic principle on which my work has gone forward now for a number of years: parallels alone are useless except perhaps to suggest the location of possible material. But the only valid basis on which to work toward the rabbinical materials Milton knew and used is the establishment of connections between him and definite rabbinical works. As I have stated in the body of the present work, the start must be from Milton and not from the rabbis themselves. So important is this principle that I risk the charge of repetition by again pointing it out here. It is no longer of much value to point out parallels: we know enough now to see that Milton's reading of rabbinical works has definite limits; that the more important fact is to connect him with individual rabbinical works rather than further to accumulate collections of parallels. In other words, we have passed the stage when it was either necessary or desirable to treat rabbinical material as a general source for his poetic ideas and details. It is now possible to show how he drew on individual rabbinical works. In general there are two ways in which Milton may be shown to have used a rabbinical work: either he himself has somewhere referred to it directly or in a recognizable manner, as in the case of Maimonides's *Doctor Perplexorum;* or it may be pointed out how a particular rabbinical work was so extremely well-known to his age that certain statements of his are strongly indicative that it was to such a work he was referring. Now I should be the last person in the world to deny the possibility of connecting Milton with many rabbinical works, which he has never been even suspected of having used. But, on the other hand, I wish to emphasize the very real limitations imposed by the basic principle of investigation and study I have just mentioned. There *are* limits to Milton's rabbinical reading, and even more restrictive limits to our reconstruction of it. If it is true that it is possible to discover a great deal about his rabbinical reading, it is equally true that as much, perhaps more of it can never be completely reconstructed. The reason for this is obvious from my present study. One ever-present characteristic of rabbinical writings in general is the amount of repetition they contain. The same ideas will be repeated with minor variations, omissions, or expansions, in many, many different works. One rabbi will include and explain all or nearly all of the work done by an earlier rabbi. It is then impossible to tell inferentially in which form Milton knew the idea. If he has mentioned one of such works, that one he certainly knew. But did he know the others? We cannot say definitely that he did not; nor can we blandly assume that he did. Thus, it is impossible to determine whether he knew the material in any other form than the single one he has actually mentioned, or possibly the one that is found to have been most largely circulated among Christian scholars of his time and best known to them. I have tried to stress this fact in the case of several points made in the body of this work, but it is difficult to do so adequately for those who are unacquainted with rabbinical writings. However, this has had a distinct effect on my work, for in many cases it may seem strange that I have not listed *all* the rabbinical works in which occur the particular idea or image being discussed. I have deliberately refrained from doing this in most cases, and in none have I endeavored to cite every rabbinical work in which the idea occurs. I have, on the contrary, pointed out the occurrence of the idea only in rabbinical works I could connect definitely with Milton; if other works contained it and could even inferentially be connected with him, I have mentioned them. But in the case of some of the ideas the poet has used that clearly belong to rabbinical lore, unless they are found in a work known to be connected with him or capable of being so connected, I have omitted all discussion of them. The result is that this study becomes almost exclusively a study of Milton's use of rabbinical commentaries on Scripture, largely because I have found it possible indubitably to connect him with such material. The scope of the work is thus almost automatically indicated, and, if it seems to be limited thereby, I would suggest as a corrective to such an idea, a glance at a translation of a single work, Rashi on the Pentateuch, for an adequate conception of the magnitude and nature of such literature.

So many persons have been interested in this study and helpful to its continuation, that I must first thank everyone who in any way came in contact with my work, if for nothing more than encouragement. My colleagues, Professors Thomas Whitfield Baldwin and Clarissa Rinaker, read manuscript for me that was in the very throes of composition. Moses Jung, at present of the School of Religion of the State University of Iowa and formerly of the Hillel Foundation of the University of Illinois, afforded me great aid with the text and translation of the various rabbis. Professor Marjorie Nicolson of Smith College kindly read an enormous mass of manuscript and made many helpful suggestions. The encouragement and criticism of Professor David Harrison Stevens of the University of Chicago were very valuable and constant over a period of several months. In addition, my thanks are due to the patience and helpfulness of my many friends who endured the formative period of much of the material. In partic-

ular, Professor Robert Francis Seybolt was the source of
constant suggestion, unflagging interest, and impartial
judgments. Professor William Abbott Oldfather read the
manuscript for publication and offered many suggestions.
My thanks are due to him for pointing out errors of all
kinds in the Latin quotations. Professor Jacob Zeitlin is
really responsible for the form in which the finished work
appears, and without his helpfulness, publication would
have been greatly delayed, if not impractical. Many were
the letters from various persons throughout the country
containing suggestions and corrections. I must also thank
various libraries for their generosity and courtesy, especially the Harvard College Library, the Library of the Hebrew Union Seminary, the Harper Memorial Library of
Chicago, the Library of Congress, and that of the Union
Theological Seminary.

However, the whole work was made possible only through
the liberality of the University of Illinois, represented
chiefly by the Dean of the Graduate School, Arthur Hill
Daniels, and the Librarian, Phineas Lawrence Windsor.
Access to books and manuscripts necessary for the continuation of the work was always a serious problem, and
Dean Daniels's generosity and ready support were essential
and unfailing. To Professor Windsor and his Library staff
in general, especially to Willia Kathryn Garver, the as-
sembling of most of the necessary material was due.
Without their aid, the entire project, if it had not been
made impossible, would have been delayed for years.

The printing of the Hebrew calls for some explanation.
It is much more difficult to print Hebrew with English or
any other European language than to print it alone, as is
indicated by the refusal of some presses to accept work
containing untransliterated Hebrew characters. Biblical
quotations appear herein without vowel points, it being

certain that those persons who can read Hebrew will not miss the points, and to others their omission will make no difference. It was very early decided to use square characters throughout, although the material quoted from the rabbis in Buxtorf's Bible appears always therein in the so-called 'Rashi' type, the Italian *literae rabbinicae*. The best modern critical editions of rabbinical material are usually printed in square characters, and it seemed advisable to follow this practice.

Textual variations in rabbinical works are very difficult to indicate adequately. In general, all quotations from the commentaries are direct from Buxtorf's text, except for abbreviations of words which, as always, are arbitrary. The few quotations from the *Midrashim* are from the great Wilna edition.

The 'translations' of the rabbis are paraphrastic renderings of the original. Usually the meaning is clear enough, but sometimes, especially with Ibn Ezra, only a paraphrase is possible. So-called 'translations' of rabbinical works provide little or no idea of the cryptic and often turbid style of the original. This is especially true of Ibn Ezra, who deliberately sought to obscure many of his meanings. There is, perhaps, no other field of medieval texts that so urgently needs attention from the trained textual scholar as the Jewish writings of the Middle Ages.

CHAPTER I

MILTON'S REFERENCES TO THE RABBIS IN HIS PROSE WORKS

This work is intended to form an introduction to the study of those special branches of Milton's Semitic learning which may be called his rabbinical readings, or his readings of rabbinical materials. In general, the phrase 'rabbinical readings' may be taken to include his readings in all non-Biblical Jewish literature, from that produced in pre-Christian times up to and including the writings of the medieval rabbis. As a matter of fact, limitations and restrictions on the great mass of material thus indicated will become apparent almost at once. Indeed, it will be quite largely the function and purpose of my present work to make the actual nature and limits of such readings as precise and definite as possible.

Heretofore, no adequate account of Milton's rabbinical browsings has existed, and none at all that was in the nature of a survey of his use of such material. But his connections with rabbinical literature have been hinted at by all his biographers and commentators, from Phillips to Hanford.[1] That is, it has long been recognized that he drew on rabbinical and other Jewish material not included in the Old Testament. But nothing has been known of the amount or the nature of such material available to him, nor of the forms in which he knew it. Needless to say, without such a knowledge, almost nothing whatever has been known of how he used it, especially in his poetry. In

[1]Allusions to his use of Semitic materials may be found especially in Phillips's *Life*, in Milton's own autobiographical statements, in the anonymous biography, in Hume's notes to *Paradise Lost*, in Toland's *Life*, in Johnson's *Life*, in Todd's *Life* and notes, in Keightley's *Life* and observations, in Masson's *Life* and notes, and in Hanford's *Handbook*. See also my own *Milton's Semitic Studies*.

order, therefore, to become acquainted with the possibilities involved in Milton's rabbinical readings, considerable preliminary work has been necessary. Thus, it has been found imperative to investigate fully his knowledge and use of the Bible, especially of the Old Testament in its original Hebrew. The reading of rabbinical writings in their original implies, indeed demands, a thorough knowledge of the Hebrew Old Testament and of the Aramaic Targums. Such a knowledge Milton is commonly known to have possessed, although the extent and nature of his Semitic studies in general and of his Biblical learning in particular have only recently been examined in detail.[1] Throughout his prose works are scattered many evidences of his close acquaintance with Torah and Targum in their respective originals, and with the necessary Biblical critical and theological literature of his day.[2] Thus it was necessary to examine his knowledge and use of such critical apparatus and theological literature, although none of this material is presented here. This in turn involved some consideration of the Biblical learning of his time, in order to determine the contemporary state of rabbinical knowledge among Christian scholars. Then in order to secure definite information concerning Milton's contacts with such learning, a complete investigation of his own references to rabbinical literature has been made. Following this, I have considered the implications of such citations.

[1] Cf. my thesis, *Milton's Semitic Studies*, Chicago, 1926; and more recent 'The Use of the Bible in Milton's Prose,' *University of Illinois Studies in Language and Literature*, vol. XIV (1929).

[2] Milton's knowledge and use of the Bible constitutes an independent study in itself and I have so presented it elsewhere. Too long and detailed a work to be included here, nevertheless it constitutes one of the two main bases on which rests Milton's use of the rabbis, the only other one being his actual citation of them. The monograph referred to in the foregoing footnote examines in detail his acquaintance with the text of Scripture and affords proof of his constant use of the original texts of תנך and Targum.

With the Hebrew text sufficiently at his command to permit his paraphrasing it in Latin or in English apparently whenever he so desired, and with his knowledge of Biblical Aramaic firmly assured together with his actual use of the *Targumim*, there is every reason for assuming that he could and did read at least some forms of the works of the rabbis. It is the purpose of the present chapter, as it is of the whole of the present work, to put Milton's use of the rabbis definitely beyond the status of assumption.

The amount of Christian scholarly study of Semitic and rabbinical literatures during the sixteenth and seventeenth centuries was enormous. Milton's knowledge of this activity, indicated by his citations of portions of it, therefore becomes of great importance in this work. But the difficulties surrounding the problem of his contacts with such a stream of learning are numerous. No adequate histories or accounts exist of the Christian studies of Semitic and rabbinical materials during the two centuries just mentioned. These centuries are too late for the medievalist to have investigated in connection with the development within them of Semitic studies in general, and they are slightly too early for consideration with the rise and development of the modern school of Biblical scholarship. Such studies as exist of Semitic learning in these centuries are chiefly isolated monographs, often difficult of access and providing a very inadequate view of the whole status of Gentile Semitic scholarship during that period.

The result is that this study is divided between the task of opening up the whole field of Milton's knowledge and use of the rabbis in the light of the rabbinical learning among Christians of his day, and the further task of exploring the detailed studies suggested by that investigation. In order to make my work as pointed as possible under these circumstances, I have aimed directly at presenting a full account of the bases of Milton's rabbinical readings. Having done this, I have then proceeded to investigate particularly his connection with and use of one distinct branch of rabbinical literature, namely, rabbinical commentary on Scripture. In the investigation of his connections with this literature there appear suggestions of his use of other rabbinical materials. But in general such materials must await further study. I wish at this time to point out particularly my deliberate exclusion from this study of the entire subject of Milton's use of the Talmud. Fascinating as that use appears to be, it must await special investigation. In order to perform any valuable service with it, a much fuller knowledge of the Christian Talmudical learning of his time must be acquired than is readily accessible.

I shall, therefore, attempt in this work to provide a basis for the fullest consideration of Milton's readings in rabbinical commentaries to Scripture, thereafter presenting the influence on his work, especially his later poetry, of some of those readings. My present work is in a sense incomplete, being intended rather to present a way into the subject than to furnish an exhaustively complete scrutiny and evaluation of all that is involved in the phrase 'Milton's rabbinical readings.' It is, therefore, with further studies in mind that I include in this some account of the basic apparatus and equipment of which such studies must make use.

At first glance, the possibilities suggested by the phrase 'rabbinical readings,' may seem only confusing. The amount of such material is large. Consequently, the problem that arises first is one of procedure. How should one proceed to discover what rabbinical material is to be investigated with special reference to Milton? Until this question is adequately answered, disaster is constantly imminent for the unwary investigator, the pitfalls being many and the irrelevant byways innumerable.

One might begin by employing an omnibus method, which would examine all or almost all of the rabbinical material available. Then, on the basis of parallels between portions of such material and portions of Milton's works, a process of selection might be applied which would eventually result in affording us an estimate, but never more than that, of the amount and nature of Milton's reading in rabbinical literature. This method has been used almost entirely in the past; but the results from it have been relatively negligible because of the necessarily uncertain character of such work. The definite results from it have been almost entirely accidental. Consequently, aside from the slow accumulation of what are at best rather dubious parallels, little has been accomplished because not enough has been known of actual connections between Milton and definite rabbinical works.[1] A more informative and closely knit treatment of the problem of Milton's rabbinical readings is, therefore, necessary. If we begin with the rabbis, as has been done almost exclusively in the past, and work toward Milton, the problem is almost hopeless because of the enormous amount of material involved. The first great need here is therefore to point out the limitations and guides that are clearly indicated and defined. Thus, if we pose the question, 'What did Milton know and conse-

---

[1] In 1695 Patrick Hume published his annotated edition of *Paradise Lost*. This contained much important material for the investigation of Milton's whole relationship with Semitic literature in general, and his knowledge and use of the Hebrew Old Testament and rabbinical works in particular. But Hume did not follow up his excellent beginning, probably feeling that the whole matter was clear enough to an age that generally made much more use of such materials than our own. Appearing nearly two hundred years later, Thomas Keightley's *Life* was the next work of consequence that added anything to our knowledge of Milton's Semitic studies. Keightley, after all, added but little to Hume's suggestions, but did set forth several important hints and even a few new facts, which, however,

quently what could he have used of the writings of the rabbis?' decided limitations immediately begin to operate which soon reduce the whole problem to more easily manageable dimensions. In fact, it seems obvious that the start must be from Milton, and not from the rabbinical material. Only by constantly referring to Milton and conditions existent for him may any real advance be made in our knowledge of his rabbinical readings.

The first limitation is set by the rabbinical material itself, viewed from the standpoint of Milton's time. Milton was virtually a contemporary of a number of England's pioneer rabbinical scholars, such as Cartwright, Drusius, Selden, Pococke, Whitgift, and the others who were in a sense the product of the intense interest in Semitic study induced by the labors of the translators of the King James Version of the Bible. This interest in the translation of Scripture was itself an outgrowth of the attempts of Protestant scholars to maintain the Protestant position wholly on the basis of Scripture. Systematic attack upon Jewish literature by Gentiles was one of the great contributions of Milton's own century, flowering in the work of Lightfoot, Reland, and others of the generation just following his. Throughout the seventeenth century, however, rabbinical material was very narrowly circulated, as it still is today. Gentile interest in such material was then and is now con-

he seemed to have misunderstood and did not himself appreciate, for he made no use of them. Masson appears to have realized the importance of Milton's Semitic and rabbinical contacts, but apparently was unable to do more than accord them generous if unexplored recognition. Still more recently, Saurat has advanced several stimulating if unconfirmed suggestions. A remarkable collection of parallels has appeared in an article by E. C. Baldwin (*Journal of English and Germanic Philology*, July, 1929). The difficulty with all of these treatments of the subject is that none of these writers has been able to give us actual facts concerning Milton's definite connections with such literature. It is true that Keightley did so; but nevertheless for some reason he was unable to see the implications of such connections and in no way followed out their possibilities. Consequently, the whole state of our knowledge of Milton's use of the rabbis has been ambiguous and uncertain.

fined to scholars. Even though, owing to the great and often extreme reverence in which Scripture was held with a corresponding attention to scriptural commentary and exegesis, the appeal of such material in Milton's day was very large, yet only the occasional scholar possessed sufficient equipment to use rabbinical material in its original language. In addition to this, the English scholar who was desirous of access to rabbinical material and who was more or less capable of using the Biblical tongues, was largely dependent upon continental printing presses for texts of the original. True rabbinical material, with its peculiar letter formations, has never been printed in England to any appreciable extent, even to this day. All of these facts must be kept in mind in connection with the problem of Milton's rabbinical readings, for that problem is inextricably bound up with the history of the development of Semitic and rabbinical study in England. We shall return to the consideration of this point in the next chapter, but it is pointed out here because it marks out a most important limitation on Milton's rabbinical reading. These facts simplify the matter of connecting Milton with rabbinical materials, for obviously, they limit the amount of such material available to him, and also somewhat determine its nature.

But to turn to the consideration of the direct problem of whether Milton did or did not employ the rabbis. We shall turn directly to his works and investigate his actual citations or references to rabbinical writings. Did he ever directly cite the rabbis? To answer this question, it is only necessary to examine his works and find out. If, as is actually the case, we find him directly referring to rabbinical commentary on Scripture for instance, no better evidence of his knowledge and use of such material could be produced. The bases, therefore, of any account of his knowledge and use of the rabbis must consist of Milton's own citation and employment of them.

In his works, where has Milton cited or used the rabbis, particularly their scriptural commentaries? What passages in his works refer to the rabbis? Do any of these passages refer to rabbinical commentary upon Scripture? The answers to these questions will furnish considerable information concerning Milton's ability to use the rabbis, and afford all the knowledge necessary to an understanding of how he employed them.

Milton's earliest reference to rabbinical commentary on Scripture, in fact his earliest direct and unmistakable reference to any form of the rabbis, occurs in *An Apology against a Pamphlet against Smectymnuus*, which appeared early in 1642. This tract was largely made up of a defence of himself from the attack of the Halls, whom he had himself attacked through the father, Bishop Hall, in the *Animadversions upon the Remonstrant's Defence against Smectymnuus* of the previous year, 1641.

Because the *Apology* contains so much defence of himself, it forms an important document in his *biographia*. He defended, among other matters, his personal character, and then turned to a defence of the violence of his invective in his earlier tract which the younger Hall had attacked. Milton also defended his use of the undignified, even indecent language he had employed in the *Animadversions*. He based the justification of his use of the objectionable language contained therein, first, upon reference to like use by Luther and even Christ himself. He alleged that 'the example of Luther may stand for all: · · · who not of revelation, but of judgement writ so vehemently against the chiefe defenders of old untruths in the Romish Church, that his own friends and favourers were many times offended with the fiercenesse of his spirit; yet he being cited before Charles the fifth to answer for his books, and having divided them into three sorts, whereof one was of those which he had sharply written, refus'd though upon deliberation giv'n him to retract or unsay any word therein; as we may reade in Sleiden.'[1] He then ferociously turned to the defence of his manner of writing in the *Animadversions* by direct appeal to Scripture itself. He continued:

And this I shall easily averre though it may seeme a hard saying, that the Spirit of God who is purity it selfe, when he would reprove any fault severely, or but relate things done or said with indignation by others, abstains not from some words not civill at other times to be spok'n. Omitting that place in Numbers at the killing of Zimri and Cosbi done by Phineas in the heigth of zeal, related as the Rabbines expound, not without an obscene word, we may finde in Deuteronomy and three of the Prophets, where God denouncing bitterly the punishments of Idolaters, tels them in a terme immodest to be utter'd in coole blood, that their wives shall be defil'd openly. But these, they will say were honest words in that age when they were spok'n. Which is more then any Rabbin can prove, and certainly had God been so minded, he could have pickt such words, as should never have come into abuse. What will they say to this. David going against Nabal, in the very same breath when he had just before nam'd the name of God, he vowes not *to leave any alive of Nabals house that (mingentem ad parietem).* But this was unadvisedly spoke, you will answer, and set downe to aggravate his infirmity. Turne then to the first of Kings where God himselfe uses the phrase; *I will cut off from Ieroboam him that (mingentem ad parietem).* Which had it beene an unseemely speech in the heat of an earnest expression, then we must conclude that Ionathan, or Onkelos (*sic*) the Targumists were of cleaner language then he that made the tongue; for they render it as briefly, *I will cut off all who are at yeares of discretion,* that is to say so much discretion as to hide nakednesse. Whereas God who is the author both of purity and eloquence, chose this phrase as fittest in that vehement character wherein he spake... Which the Masoreths and

---

[1] *The Works of John Milton in Verse and Prose.* [edited by] John Mitford (Pickering, London, 1851, 8 vols.), vol. III: 280. Milton found this defence of Luther ready at hand in Sleiden's *de Statu Religionis et Reipublica Carolo quinto Caesare.* cf. *Commonplace-Book*, p. 76, 'Nec acerbitate, nec scommatis abstinuit Lutherus interdum etiam parum verecundis. *Sleidan.* l. 16. p. 261.'

Rabbinicall Scholiasts not well attending, have often us'd to blurre the margent with Keri, instead of Ketiv, and gave us this insuls rule out of their Talmud, *That all words which in the Law are writ obscenely, must be chang'd to more civill words.*[1]

Here is a peculiar passage. The general meaning is, perhaps, clear enough; but it is not so easy to understand the details contained in all the statements Milton has made here. In order to understand these details, it is first necessary to sort out the various elements contained in the passage. Milton stated that he could justify the violence of his language by appeal to Scripture. He went on to say that he would pass over that place in Numbers, the eighth verse of the twenty-fifth chapter, in which Phinehas killed Zimri and Cosbi in a zealous frenzy.[2] He next stated that the rabbis explain this passage with a more obscene word than the text itself contains. In other words, there is no mistaking the precise and rather objectionable treatment of the text.

Taking no more of Milton's quoted passage than this, we must first determine just what it was to which he was referring. Obviously, he was concerned here with a portion of the text of the book of Numbers and the comment upon it of certain rabbis. But we must determine what text it was to which he referred and where he secured the

---

[1] *ibid.*, vol. III: 281-282.

[2] The whole of the passage is (Numbers 25:5-8):
'And Moses said unto the judges of Israel, Slay ye every one his men that have joined themselves unto Baal-peor. And behold, one of the children of Israel came and brought unto his brethren a Midianitish woman in the sight of Moses, and in the sight of all the congregation of the children of Israel, while they were weeping at the door of the tent of meeting. And when Phinehas, the son of Eleazar, the son of Aaron the priest, saw it, he rose up from the midst of the congregation, and took a spear in his hand; and he went after the man of Israel into the pavilion, and thrust both of them through, the man of Israel, and the woman through her body.' The 14th and 15th verses give the names of the man and woman who were slain, 'Now the name of the man of Israel that was slain, who was slain with the Midianitish woman, was Zimri, the son of Salu, a prince of a fathers' house among the Simeonites. And the name of the Midianitish woman that was slain was Cozbi, the daughter of Zur.' [Amer. R. V.]

rabbinical comments. No translations of the Old Testament will aid us here. The English translations, including his favorite, the Authorized Version, in neither text nor in commentaries, provides an explanation of what Milton has said here. Nor will any Latin text clarify his statements. Tremellius, in neither text nor notes furnishes any clue to these. If Latin commentaries are invoked, and Milton has elsewhere suggested a number of them,[1] they yield nothing to the point here. But Milton did not say that some commentators or other had explained the passage, 'not without an obscene word.' He specifically stated that he was speaking of 'rabbis.'

The fact is that no translation of the text will explain his point. No translation suggests that there is any particular reason for an obscene explanation, as, aside from the entire incident in Numbers having been of a sordid nature, no words are needed to tell of it which are particularly obscene. There is but one form of the text in which there is a possibility for obscenity, and this is the Hebrew original. To this we must therefore turn for an explanation. The Hebrew for the eighth verse of the twenty-fifth chapter of Numbers reads as follows:

ויבא אחר איש ישראל אל הקבה וידקר את שניהם את איש ישראל ואת האשה אל קבתה

In the Hebrew, there appears the phrase אל הקבה, which causes some difficulty. The chief reason for this difficulty is that this verse contains two very similar expressions. The first of these, אל הקבה, clearly means 'into the pavilion.'[2]

---

[1] *de doctrina*, p. 454, 'Bucerum, Calvinum, Martyrem, Musculum, Ursinum, Gomarum, aliosque.'

[2] This is the reading of the American Revised Version, with footnote, 'or *alcove*.' Brown, Driver, and Briggs (*A Hebrew and English Lexicon of the Old Testament*, Boston, 1907, p. 866b) explain the word, which occurs only here in the Old Testament, as meaning *large vaulted tent*. They add that it means *Zimri's princely tent*, also pointing out that Gesenius and others take the word to mean *large tent* used as *lupanar*.

The second phrase, אל קבתה, is very similar to the first in
spelling and appearance, and may have been connected
with it in derivation. It denotes the precise part of the
anatomy of Cozbi into which the spear was thrust. There
is but one other occurrence of the word in the Old Testament.[1] Its meaning in Numbers is not at all ambiguous,
unless there is a connection between it and the first phrase.
The whole passage is disturbed by the occurrence of these
two very similar phrases, and the Syriac version of the
passage has attempted to make the second clear by adding
אל הקבה *in the tent*, after the second expression, אל קבתה.[2]
But the Hebrew alone does not offer sufficient basis for
Milton to have called attention to its obscenity. The passage is not particularly offensive, even in the Hebrew. The
point of Milton's statement is that the comments of the
rabbis are more offensive than the passage itself, and even
make it itself offensive. This is an important point for us,
because it enables us to find the clue to Milton's whole discussion of the passage. With this in mind, we can attempt
to find a form of the Hebrew text with rabbis commenting
upon it. Of course the bare Hebrew text itself supplies no
indication of any explanation by rabbis or others. In order
to secure rabbinical explanations, it is necessary to discover in what form Milton could have had access to their
comments. How would he or any other Englishman of his
day have secured rabbinical commentaries to Scripture?
The answer to this question is about the same as it is for
anyone who wishes to study such commentaries today.
The most logical place to find them is in a rabbinical Bible,
which usually surrounds its text with comments by various rabbis.

[1] Deut. 18:3.
[2] Brian Walton, *versio syriaca secundum editionem Polyglottam Londoniensem*,
1654 sequentes.

In Milton's time there was but a single printed form of such a Bible, which was the Bomberg. Being a Gentile, Milton presumably would have used the edition of this Bible printed by Buxtorf and already mentioned as a possible form in which he read the Hebrew text in the original.[1]

Assuming for the moment that Milton had access to a rabbinical Bible, the rabbis who commented on this verse in Numbers should determine whether he actually used their commentaries or not. His statement concerning their comment was of such a nature that unless he read them, what he said of their comment would betray the fact. But if what he has said of them agrees with their comment, he must have read that comment.

The Numbers passage, which Milton discussed, is commented upon in Buxtorf's Rabbinical Bible by two rabbis, Rashi (Solomon ben Isaac) and Ibn Ezra. Rashi's comment is as follows:

אל קובתה' כמו הלחיים והקיבה כיון בתוך זכרות של זמרי ונקבות שלה וראו כולם
שלא לחנם הרגם'

Translation: in the stomach: as (Deut. 18:3) 'the two cheeks and the maw' (so American Revised Version, but Brown, Driver, and Briggs, *stomach*). Exactly in the middle of the male genitals of Zimri and the female genitals [of the woman], so that all saw that he had not killed them for no cause.

Ibn Ezra's comment is much less explicit and contains no objectionable details. He does, however, contribute a

---

[1] I have already called attention to the probability of Milton's use of this Bible. I shall throughout the present work assume always that he used it for Hebrew reading. Buxtorf's text followed that of the third Bomberg, and so far as the rabbis are concerned, it makes but little difference whether Milton was actually using Buxtorf or an earlier edition of the rabbinical Bible. The presumption that he used Buxtorf is all but certainty, for Buxtorf's work as author, printer, and editor, including the rabbinical Bible, the Lexicon written to accompany it, and his grammar, was, perhaps, among Gentiles the best known work of its kind. Buxtorf was mentioned by Milton as the editor of Maimonides's *Doctor Perplexorum, Doctrine and Discipline of Divorce*, vol. IV:34.

statement concerning Phinehas which helps explain Milton's statement about Phinehas having acted 'in the heigth of zeal.' After explaining that the killing took place in the tent, Ibn Ezra continues:

יש דרך דרש שנעשו י׳ נסים לפנחס רק הכתוב לא הזכירם

Translation: there is also the matter of explaining the wonders which Yahweh did to Phinehas (or, *through Phinehas*) but the Text does not mention them.

It is now clear as to what Milton's statement about the passage in Numbers really means. He has cited Numbers 25:8 as a passage in the Old Testament in which God did not hesitate to relate in a plain-spoken manner a certain rather terrible event. Not content with that, Milton has next called attention to the fact that Rashi has explained the verse in such a detailed manner that the explanation is more objectionable than the text itself.

Rashi's words זכרת של זמרי ונקבות specifically naming the male and female pudenda are, as Milton stated, much more obscene than the text itself. Apparently he took a hint from Ibn Ezra in attributing to Phinehas a 'zealous frenzy,' for Ibn Ezra's statement clearly implies that Phinehas was that day possessed.

To understand Milton's statement about the Numbers passage is, therefore, to realize that he was here using a rabbinical Bible, and, what is more, to connect him with the commentaries of two rabbis, Rashi and Ibn Ezra. As he himself pointed out, the exposition of the two rabbis has no direct bearing upon his argument; but the evidence afforded by realizing the significance of what he said at this point, is clearly indicative of the fact that Milton was employing the rabbinical commentary of a rabbinical Bible. Contact with the commentaries, as found in Buxtorf, of these two rabbis is now afforded him, his ability to read their peculiar jargon in its original being attested by his citation.[1]

But the previously quoted passage from the *Apology* contains more information than this. Milton's next statement, dealing with Deuteronomy and three of the prophets, is equally enlightening in connection with his use of rabbinical material, and shows even more clearly than the portion just examined that he was using a rabbinical Bible and rabbinical commentaries. In the remainder of the passage quoted, Milton stated that there is a verse in Deuteronomy which contains an expression too indecent to be uttered in cold blood. This same expression, he further stated, occurs also in three of the prophets. But, he said, this expression is softened or somehow modified, and the rabbis explain that such a process is necessary because the expression belongs to another and more primitive period of the language.

His whole discussion at this point becomes meaningless unless it is clearly understood that Milton was here referring to the Hebrew text itself, and this in a particular form. The expression itself exists only in the Hebrew text, but for the remainder of Milton's statement, the text alone will not suffice. He referred to a form of the text which offers indications of an attempt to soften the original Hebrew with explanations by rabbis of why this was done. Only one form of the Hebrew text will provide for such a case, and that is the form found in a rabbinical Bible.

The expression which Milton discussed as 'too immodest

---

[1]The possibility that he had access to these commentaries in translation is completely negligible. Even today rabbinical commentary has been but little translated into any language. It is perhaps true that more of it exists in Latin than in any other language, and that some of this had been translated in Milton's day. But such translations consisted only of excerpts, and the best evidence against the possibility of Milton's having known this commentary in translation is contained in the remainder of the passage quoted from the *Apology*.

to be utter'd in coole blood' is the Hebrew word ישגלנה,
which occurs in the thirtieth verse of the twenty-eighth
chapter of Deuteronomy. Only on the basis of this word
in the Hebrew can the passages in the prophets which contain it be located at all. But by means of the Hebrew
word, it is relatively a simple matter to discover what passages Milton referred to as 'the prophets.' They are, respectively, the sixteenth verse of the thirteenth chapter
of Isaiah; the second verse of the fourteenth chapter of
Zechariah; and the second verse of the third chapter of
Jeremiah. In order fully to explain all that his statement
implied, it is necessary at this point to trace the steps by
which he arrived at the complicated arguments contained
in it. Beginning with the thirtieth verse of the twenty-
eighth chapter of Deuteronomy, the expression which he
stated to be objectionable is ישגלנה. The word is from the
root שגל meaning *ravish* or *violate*. Milton's paraphrase is
to the point, 'that their wives shall be openly defil'd.'
In neither the Authorized nor the Revised Versions may
the reason for Milton having selected this passage be detected. Nor will any other translations such as Tremellius
or the Vulgate indicate any irregularity. But in the text
of the Hebrew Bible, the word ישגלנה carries an indication
of a marginal reading. This occurs often in the Hebrew
text for various reasons. The margins of most Hebrew
Bibles exhibit variant readings, which were the work of
various times and schools of rabbinical exegetical experts.[1]
These variants are called קרי, *to be read*, and vary for different portions of the Bible according to the opinion of the
rabbinical critics who first inserted them. These critics

---

[1]For a brief but adequate account of the rise and development of the קרי, cf.
Gesenius's Hebrew Grammar, edited by A. E. Cowley (Oxford, 1910), p. 19. For a
more complete account, see C. D. Ginsburg, *Introduction to the Massoretico—
Critical Edition of the Hebrew Bible* (London, 1897), pp. 183-186, *et passim*.

felt that the marginal variants indicated were preferable to the כתיב, that is, what is *written* in the text, and were actually to be read instead of the word in the text itself. A small circle or asterisk in the text always refers to the marginal reading. These marginal readings appear, however, with no explanation whatever. As they are noted, it becomes apparent that they are there for various reasons, and they form a body of variants, which may or may not be explained.

In the case before us, the word ישגלנה in the Deuteronomy text carries a sign of a marginal reading in the text, and the קרי is present in the margin. It was this which Milton first noted.[1] But the reason for its being there which he discussed came, not from the קרי itself, but from the commentaries of the rabbis, in a rabbinical Bible also accompanying the text. It is not obvious in the present case that the קרי is indicated for purposes of softening the vigor of the text. The קרי for the word in question is ישכבנה, *to lie with*. Milton indicated that the commenting rabbis point out that this is actually a softening of the vigor of the original expression in an attempt to refine the text. But, he says, this is 'more then any Rabbin can prove.'

The point he raises may be disputable; but the evidence his statement affords as to what he had done here, is perfectly clear.

Milton's statement is evidence that he had read, not only the קרי of the margin for the textual כתיב, for any person able to read Biblical Hebrew could at least point this out; but also, what is for us much more important, the rabbinical commentaries to the passage. He exclaimed

---

[1] This is not the only place in his works that Milton mentioned the קרי of the Hebrew Bible. In the *Areopagitica*, vol. IV:412, he also called attention to it in the following manner, 'ask a Talmudist what ails the modesty of his marginal Keri, that Moses and all the Prophets cannot perswade him to pronounce the textuall Chetiv.'

against the explanations of the commenting rabbis of the reason for the presence of the קרי. Let us look at the comments of the rabbis on this passage.

The same two rabbis comment on this passage who did on the passage in the book of Numbers. Rashi explained the reason for the קרי to the word ישגלנה as follows:

ישגלנה׳לשון שגל פלגש והכתוב כינהו לשבח ישכבנה ותיקון סופרים הוא זה

will ravish her: from the root שגל *concubine,* Nehem. 2:6. But the margin substitutes as a softening an emendation of the Sof'rim (stylistic refiners).

Ibn Ezra's comment is much more brief, but is of the same nature:

ישגלנה׳ כנוי לשכיבה

will ravish her: substituting לשכיבה *to lie with.*

It was to these rabbinical softenings of the original, as explained by Rashi and Ibn Ezra, that Milton objected. He objected on the grounds that the text is sacred and can say what it pleases. But his expostulation affords clear evidence that he read the Hebrew text, noted the קרי of the margin, and then read the rabbinical explanations of why the קרי was there. He then proceeded to deny the need of tampering with the text, and wrapped the whole discussion up in a characteristically perplexing sentence to hurry on to another just like it. But he has left his evidence of what he was doing, nevertheless.

Those passages in the prophets to which he referred use the same verb שגל. They are, as already stated, Isaiah 13:16; Zechariah 14:2; and Jeremiah 3:2. The passage carrying the rabbinical explanations of the *qere* to which Milton most objected was in Deuteronomy. The passage in Isaiah has but little comment from the rabbis. In Buxtorf's Bible, there are two rabbis commenting on this passage, Rashi and David Kimchi. Rashi omitted mention of the expression here. Kimchi merely alluded to it by mentioning the *qere* as follows:

ותשכבנה' כתוב ותשגלנה קרי

be ravished: written, and *lain with:* read.

That is, Milton here found only that there was a *qere* for the same word for which the *qere* was explained in the Deuteronomy passage. He could not quarrel with the explanations of the rabbis here, for there is but one, which merely repeats the *qere* of the margin. But he had the Deuteronomy passage in mind, and mentioned this one in Isaiah for that reason.

The Zechariah passage contains the same verb in the same form as in Isaiah. It means precisely the same thing as before, and carries the same *qere*. But neither of the two rabbis commenting on this prophet mentions the word at this point. The word in Jeremiah is in the form שגלת, a *pual* perfect, derived from the *qal*, in the second person, feminine singular. It carries the same *qere*, in its proper form, as the other forms of the word carried in the other passages. Both Rashi and Kimchi comment on the word שגלת. Rashi said only:

לא שגלת' לשון פלוש

not been ravished by: from the root שלו.

Kimchi's comment is longer and much more concerned with the explanation of the *qere* and why it is there, the process which Milton derided, than was Rashi's. Kimchi said:

שגלת'כתוב שכבת קרי כמו ישגלנה ישכבנה לשון נקיה וכבר פירשנו כי לשון הזנות

והשכיבה הוא ענין הע"ז

been ravished by, written. *couched with,* read. Thus the original expression is purified. And already we have explained (Deut.

28:30) that the expression is unchaste. And *couched with* conveys the idea of wickedness.

Kimchi's explanation of the reason for the *qere* here is the kind of rabbinical explanation against which Milton was exclaiming.

Let us now continue the examination of Milton's statement. He went on to discuss the nature of a passage containing a threat by David, and another threat in the same words by God himself:

What will they say to this. David going against Nabal, in the very same breath when he had just before nam'd the name of God, he vowes not *to leave any alive of Nabal's house that mingentem ad parietem.* [1 Sam. 25:22] But this was unadvisedly spoke, you will answer, and set downe to aggravate his infirmity. Turne then to the first of Kings where God himselfe uses the phrase; *I will cut off from Ieroboam him that mingentem ad parietem.* [1 Kgs. 14:10] Which had it been an unseemely speech in the heat of an earnest expression, then we must conclude that Ionathan, or Onkelos the Targumists were of cleaner language then he that made the tongue; for they render it as briefly, *I will cut off all who are at yeares of discretion*, that is to say so much discretion as to hide nakednesse.

Milton's general attitude here is about the same as it was in the first part of his statement. He has seized upon the passage concerning David and the other concerning God's own threat. These two passages provide instances of what he wished to illustrate. He has not for either of them employed the commentary of rabbis, but he has used the passages nevertheless. There is no *qere* for either passage, but he has here used more of the equipment found in the rabbinical Bible. This time it is neither *qere* nor commentary that has engaged his attention, but the text of the Targum which parallels the Hebrew. Both of the passages to which Milton has referred are softened in the Targum. He referred in the second instance to the change

from the Hebrew *mingentem ad parietem* to the Aramaic
'who are at years of discretion,' and this change actually
occurs in the two texts mentioned, the Hebrew reading
משתין בקיר and the Aramaic ידע מדע in the Targum. Now the
importance of this statement by Milton is not so much in
its clear indication of his ability to use the Targums, for his
knowledge of them is well authenticated on other grounds.
But, his citation of a Targum reading in connection with
the other elements he has cited, the Hebrew text, the marginal *qere*, and rabbinical commentaries, all these taken
together make certain the form of Biblical text he was here
using. There is no other Biblical text except the rabbinical, which assembles all of these elements at one time.
And they constitute all the elements assembled in such a
text. Further discussion of this will be found in the next
chapter, but it is important to notice here that Milton has
mentioned every one of the different elements found in the
material presented by a rabbinical Bible. He has mentioned and in some way used each one of them in this brief
passage concerning the frankness of speech of Scripture.

The 'insuls rule' from the Talmud which Milton mentioned, 'that all words which in the Law are writ obscenely, must be chang'd to more civill words,' was not,
however, in all probability taken by him directly from the
Talmud itself. This principle of softening the vigor of the
text by substituting in the margin words which are less
offensive is and has long been one of the best known principles of the Massorites and of the קרי in general. Milton
would have found it stated twice in the Introduction to
Buxtorf's *Rabbinical Bible*, using the same word in the
same passages from Deuteronomy and the Prophets as he
cited in the passage we have quoted above. The Introduction Buxtorf printed was a revision of that written by
Jacob ben Chajim ibn Adonijah for Bomberg. This Intro-

duction especially discussed matters connected with the nature of the masorah and the *qere*. The rule concerning indelicate expressions and their *qere* is first expressed as follows:

וליתא לדבריו דהא בהדיא גרסינן סוף פרק הקורא את המגילה עומד תנו רבנן כל
המקראות הכתובין בתורה לגנאי קורין אותן לשבח כגון ישגלנה ישכבנה . . .

This statement is not correct, since we are distinctly told in the Talmud: 'Our sages submit, All the verses wherein are written indecent expressions, decent expressions are read in their stead, e.g. שכב instead of שגל' (Deuteronomy 28:30; Isaiah 13:16; Jeremiah 3:2; Zechariah 14:2)

Ibn Adonijah states the same rule again later in his Introduction, in nearly the same form, and using the same word שגל with its *qere* שכב. His second statement reads:

יקשה בעיני דבגמרא בחדיא גרסינן בפרק הקורא את המגלה עומד תנו רבנן כל
המקראות הכתובים בתורה לגנאי קורין אותן לשבח כגון ישגלנה ישכבנה

We are distinctly told in the Talmud, 'The sages say that all passages which are written in the law in indelicate expressions are rendered decent by the *qere*, as, for instance, ישכבנה instead of ישגלה.'[1]

It is important, it seems to me, to notice Milton's citation of this Talmudic rule, using the same forms found in the Introduction by Jacob in Buxtorf's Bible, because this fact

---

[1]Both of these translations are taken from C. D. Ginsburg's edition of *Jacob ben Chajim ibn Adonijah's Introduction to the Rabbinic Bible, Hebrew and English* (London, 1867), pp. 51 and 63 respectively. I am inclined to think that Milton's objection to the rule, 'Which is more than any Rabbin can prove,' is based primarily upon Jacob's argument that when the Talmud and Massorites differ, he sides with the Massorites and assumes that the Talmud is wrong. cf. Ginsburg, p. 42,

וגם נעיר על ההפרש ש"ש בין נמרא דילן ובין בעלי המסורת בכמה דוכתי ובכולהו נקה בהון קהוותן וגייתי פכהון
מה דנמירנא

'I shall, secondly, notice the differences between our Talmud and the Massorites which exist in many places, and everywhere side with the latter, and state what we have learned from them.' This, Jacob quite obviously does in a large number of instances, objecting to many Talmudic principles concerning the *qere*.

adds its evidence to Milton's having used that work. The use of שול as an example of the rule by both Milton and Jacob leads inevitably to the conclusion that Milton took the rule from this source rather than another. Thus the citation by Milton of this rule becomes part of our chain of evidence that he was using Buxtorf's Bible.

There are, moreover, other passages in Milton's prose which are of importance in their indication of his use of a rabbinical Bible. One of these contains a direct mention of rabbinical commentaries and shows how they have been used. This passage occurs in the *Doctrine and Discipline of Divorce*. I have previously called attention both to it and to its implications, although chiefly to indicate his use of the Hebrew text.[1] But in order to assemble here the most important evidences of Milton's use of the rabbis, that is, his own references to them, I repeat the discussion of the reference in the *Divorce* tract.

In 1643, Milton was wrestling with the reasons which in Scripture made divorce permissible. In turning to the text of Holy Writ for support of his arguments, he encountered in Judges a passage in which there was recorded a domestic situation very similar to his own after his wife had left him to return to her father's house. This passage in Judges concerns a woman who had also left her husband, and returned to her father's house. The Authorized Version reads as if she had been carnally unfaithful to her husband; but Milton argued that there are various meanings for the word *adultery*, and that it need not mean precisely the carnal act. He apparently wished to make the point that it could mean *waywardness*, which may or may not throw some light upon his own domestic difficulties. In order to clear the woman of the charge of carnal unfaithfulness to her husband and thus support his own argu-

[1]Fletcher, *Milton's Semitic Studies*, pp. 73-78.

ment that divorce should be granted for other causes, Milton appealed to various interpretations of the passage in Judges. We are not interested here in his argument, ingenious as that was and highly suggestive in the light it throws on his own situation at or near the time at which he was writing. The important feature of his discussion here is the list of commentators on the passage that he drew up for the support of his case. I quote that portion of his complete statement of his support which is of greatest interest to us here:

He (Grotius) shews also that fornication is tak'n in Scripture for such a continual headstrong behaviour, as tends to plain contempt of the husband: and proves it out of Judges 19:2, where the Levites wife is said to have plaid the whoore against him; which Josephus and the Septuagint, with the Chaldean, interpret onely of stubbornesse and rebellion against her husband: and to this I adde that Kimchi and the two other Rabbies who glosse the text, are in the same opinion. Ben Gerson reasons, that had it bin whooredome, a Jew and a Levite would have disdain'd to fetch her again. And this I shall contribute, that had it beene whoordome, she would have chosen any other place to run to, then to her father's house, it being so infamous for an Hebrew woman to play the harlot, and so opprobrious to the parents.[1]

Milton has here cited so many different readings of the Biblical passage in question, together with so many commentators, that the whole is one of the most important and informative statements in his works concerning his use of various forms of Scripture. He has stated that Josephus, the Septuagint, and the Chaldean agree in making of the offence only a stubbornness and departure. We are not interested here in what Josephus or the Septuagint have done with the subject. But the remainder of Milton's citations greatly concern us. Let us begin with the Hebrew

[1]Mitford, vol. IV:111.

itself and discuss the various elements that have gone into Milton's whole statement.

The Hebrew for the verse in Judges he has cited reads:

ותזנה עליו פילגשו ותלך מאתו אל בית אביה אל בית לחם יהודה ותהי שם ימים
ארבעה חדשים: ויקם אישה וילך אחריה לדבר על לבה להשיבו

And his concubine played the harlot against him, and went away from him unto her father's house to Bethlehem-judah, and was there the space of four months. And her husband arose, and went after her, to speak kindly unto her, to bring her again.
—(American Revised Version) Judges 19:2, 3.

This is the Biblical passage that Milton determined to use for his own purposes in his discussion of the reasons for divorce. He turned first to the Chaldean, which he said interpreted the woman's action as being due, not to actual adultery, but to stubbornness and rebellion against her husband. Let us look at the Chaldean:

ובסרת עלוהי לחינתיה ואולת מלותיה לבית אבוהא לבית לחם דבית יהודה והות
תמן יומין ארבעא ירחין: וקם בעלה ואול בתרהא למלל על לבה לאתבותה

And his concubine despised him, and went away from him to her father's house in Bethlehem Judah, and was there the space of four months. And he rose up, and went after her to speak to her heart, and to bring her back.

As Milton said, this is a different reason for her leaving him.

Then Milton turned to the commentaries of three rabbis. The citation of these rabbis, together with the reference to the Chaldean makes certain the text Milton had before him. Only in a rabbinical Bible could he have found the Hebrew text, the Chaldean, and commenting rabbis. What he said of the comments of the rabbis is informative. He has cited their comment briefly, but it is possible to determine from what he said whether or not he actually read their comments. The rabbis he cited by name are

Kimchi and Ben Gerson; the third is mentioned only by implication. In Buxtorf's Bible, three rabbis comment on this passage in Judges. They are Kimchi, Ben Gerson, and Rashi. Milton stated that Kimchi interprets the misconduct of the concubine as 'stubbornesse and rebellion against her husband.' This is true, Kimchi commenting on the matter in connection with the reading of the Targum, citing other instances of the occurrence of the same verb as used by the Targum. His comment follows:

ותזנה' תרגום ובסרת ותרגום דבר יי' בזה בסר רוצה לו' [מר] בזתה אותו ויצאה
מביתו והלכה לבית אביה או יהיה פירושו זנות כמשמעו כי אשתו היתה אבל בלא
כתובה וקדושין וזנת' מתחתיו'

The Targum here translates like the Targum of (Numbers 15:31) 'he hath despised the word of the Lord' meaning that she despised him, left his house, and returned to the house of her father. Or, its interpretation is harlotry, according to its usual meaning, that she was his wife without a כתובה (marriage contract) and קדושין (marriage sanctification) and she strayed from him.

As Milton pointed out, Kimchi's chief point was that the concubine despised her husband, and not that she was carnally unfaithful to him, her unfaithfulness consisting mainly in leaving him. Milton's interpretation of the word זנות to mean 'a continual headstrong behaviour, as tends to plain contempt,' was obviously suggested by the Targum and Kimchi's comment and interpretation. The word זנה has that meaning in Aramaic. Altogether, Milton's citation of Kimchi's comment here shows careful reading of the rabbi.

One of the 'two other rabbies who glosse the text' is Rashi. Milton stated that he, too, was 'in the same opinion.' Rashi said of the word:

ותזנה עליו פלגשו' זנתה מביתו אל החוץ כל לשון זנות אינו אלא לשון יוצא נפקת
ברא יוצאה מבעלה לאהוב את אחרים

She strayed from his house to the outside world. The phrase זנות means nothing but *going out*, נפקת ברא going away from her husband [presumably] to love others.

Rashi, actually, is 'in the same opinion' solely because he said nothing that directly contradicted what Kimchi had said.

Milton then turned to the third rabbi who commented on the passage, mentioned his name, and summarized his commentary. This third rabbi is Ben Gerson. Milton said that Ben Gerson pointed out that the concubine was not guilty of actual fornication, but that her adulterous act consisted in leaving her husband. The reason that this should be taken as the meaning of her unfaithfulness is that had she been actually carnally unfaithful, she would not have been allowed to return to the house of her father, nor would her husband, a Jew and a Levite, have gone after her to bring her back. I repeat here Ben Gerson's comment, with translation:

וספר עוד כי בימים ההם שלא היה מלך בישראל שיוכיח החוטאים היה איש לוי גר
בירכתי אפרים ולקח לו אשה פלגש מבית לחם יהודה ונתה עליו פלגשו ר"ל שנטתה
ממנו ושבה אל בית אביה לברוח ממנו וזה היה הזנות הזה כי הנטייה איך שתהיה
תקרא זנות אמר זנותיין ותירוש יקח לב והוכרחנו לפרש הענין בזה האופן שאם ונתה
עליו לשכב עם זולת אישה היתה אסור' לבעלה ולא היה ראוי שישוב לבקשה עוד
אבל ענין זנותה ביאר במה שאמר ותלך מאתו אל בית אביה שעמדה שם זמן ארוך
כמו שביאר שעמדה שם שנה וארבעה חדשים וזה ממה שהודה שאין רצונה לשוב אליו
עוד והנה רבותינו ז"ל פירשו זה הזנות לענין קרוב למה שפירשנו וכשראה זה אישה
הלך אחריה לדבר על לבה להשיבה כי ידמה שסרה ממנו על דבר הקטטות שהקניטה
בביתו ולזה הוצרך לפיסה ובזה האופן הלך להשיבה

And the book adds that in those days, when there was no king in Israel, the challenger of transgressors, there was man, a Levite, a sojourner, who lived on the outlying slopes of Ephraim. And this man took a wife unto himself, a concubine from Beth-Lehem Judah. And she ונתה עליו, that is to say, she turned from him and went away to the house of her father. And as for this הזנות, it means that she turned away from him. זנות may be called wine and *must*, which take away the understanding, and the word זנות makes it difficult to understand the occurrence. For if she had actually committed adultery against him, it has not been sufficiently pointed out that he went to seek her again in spite of the matter of the so-called 'adultery,' which is thereby explained. It is said that she went from him to the house of her father and remained there for a long time. And this is further explained as having been for a period of four months. This shows that she had no inclination to return to him, but that he had many. Our rabbis of blessed memory explain that when her husband saw this, he went after her to speak to her heart and to bring her back again, after he had become pacified, for she had vexed him in his house, and because of this, he caused her to hide her face. And this is the explanation of why he went to bring her back.

It will be noted how closely Milton followed the reasoning found in Ben Gerson's commentary. The summary which Milton gave of it contained the very point of Ben Gerson's comment which makes that comment stand out as different from the comments of the other two rabbis. He appears to have been more impressed by the commentary of Ben Gerson than by the commentaries of the other two rabbis. But Milton's account of the comments of all three has now been found to have been faithful to what their comments actually said.

It is clear, therefore, that Milton's whole survey of the passage in Judges including his discussion of the reading of the Targum and of the comments of the rabbis, was, as Keightley pointed out without fully understanding or describing it, based directly upon treatment of the passage in a rabbinical Bible.

I wish next to call attention to one other passage in Milton's works as indicating also his use of the rabbis. In the tract, *Of Prelatical Episcopacy*, there suddenly appears without warning the following peculiar statement, *let him feare lest he and his Baal be turn'd into Bosheth.*

What did he mean by *Baal* being turned into *Bosheth*? I call attention to this statement, not only in order to explain it, for its meaning is of only secondary interest here, but because of the information it affords of Milton's use of rabbinical commentary to the text of the Old Testament. The explanation is to be found only by means of the Hebrew text itself. Any modern lexicon explains that the changing of *Baal* into *Bosheth* is a scribal peculiarity, occurring in the Hebrew text. It was done to indicate that the *Baal*, or *god of the land* who opposed Yahweh and his worship, was made to read *Bosheth*, or *shame*. That is, scribes copying the Torah substituted the word *shame* for the word that meant *god of idolatry*. But in Milton's day, no lexicon explained this, though for his usage in the passage quoted, he would not have needed a lexicon to have understood the substitution and what it meant. The rabbinical commentaries to the passages in Scripture where the change has been made would have been sufficient. From this comment alone, Milton would have been supplied with ample explanation of what the changing of *Baal* into *Bosheth* meant and represented. Without actual quotation of any of the rabbinical comment that explains this point, I would here merely call attention to the comments of the rabbis in Buxtorf's Bible to the following Biblical passages: the twenty-first verse of the eleventh chapter of second Samuel, and the eighth verse of the second chapter of the same book; the thirty-third verse of the eighth chapter of first Chronicles; the twenty-fourth verse of the third chapter of Jeremiah, and the thirteenth verse of the eleventh chapter; and the tenth verse of the ninth chapter of Hosea.

Returning for a moment to Milton's discussion of the rabbis in the *Doctrine and Discipline of Divorce*, I wish here chiefly to point out that it affords more proof, when coupled with the *Baal* and *Bosheth* passage, that he could and did read the *literae rabbinicae*. Specifically, the *Divorce* passage confirms his knowledge of two of the rabbis, and adds a third. Rashi, Kimchi, and Ben Gerson comment upon the text of Judges. In driving home his point, Milton mentioned Kimchi, and specifically cited the commentary of Ben Gerson. This passage, therefore, functions very much like the passage from the *Apology*. It affords further evidence of Milton's direct use of rabbinical commentary on Scripture some ten years before his blindness.

These two passages, the one from the *Apology* and the other from the *Doctrine and Discipline of Divorce*, bear the main burden of the proof that Milton could and did directly employ rabbinical commentaries. These passages have each been fully examined. Let us now summarize the results of such examination.

We have found that in these two passages Milton made use of the Hebrew text, the Targumim, the masorah or marginal readings of the Hebrew text, and the rabbinical commentary to the texts he cited. Moreover, in both passages, he indicated that these were all assembled at once before him. The importance of this is enhanced, because they could all occur together in only one form of the text, that found in a rabbinical Bible. He spoke in detail of certain textual variants and comments by rabbis upon these variants and upon the text itself. Milton's statements about these various points have been found to agree with the facts when subjected to the test of checking them with an actual rabbinical text.

There is in Milton's use of all this apparatus of a rabbinical Bible, much that is remarkable. Of course, the Hebrew text itself would have offered him no difficulties, nor would the Targums have been unknown to him. But it is remarkable to find him making such ready use of the masorah. Any tyro at reading the Old Testament in the original knows, of course, what כתיב and קרי in a general way mean. Such a reader can even follow them on occasion in Kittel's or some other modern edition in which they are provided for in such a way that whoever knows the Hebrew letters can recognize the occurrence of marginal variants. But in a work like Buxtorf's, or in any other rabbinical Bible that was in print in 1640, the masorah, read intelligently, offer difficulties no half-way Hebraist could have overcome. Both the marginal variants and the commentaries appear in a rabbinical Bible in a semi-cursive script, which differs considerably from the square characters that had early become standardized for the printing of scriptural Hebrew. In Buxtorf, as in most, if not all early rabbinical Bibles, the *literae rabbinicae* were uniformly the Italic rather than either the German or the Spanish form. As all the early printed rabbinical Bibles were printed in Italy, and Buxtorf's near Italy, the Italian form of the letters is to be expected.

Milton's statements in the *Apology* and the *Divorce* tract also afford us a list of the rabbis he read in order to cite their comments. All the Biblical passages Milton mentioned are commented upon by Rashi. Ibn Ezra comments upon two of them; and Ben Gerson and Kimchi also appear and are specifically mentioned by name. Although his own references to their comments are the clearest indications that he used them, there remains one other point of contact between Milton and the rabbis. His attention would have been called to their commentaries by the occurrence of references to them in the notes of Tremellius's translation of the Old Testament. Tremellius's notes are of two kinds, textual and exegetical. In the exegetical notes there often occur references to the commentaries of the

rabbis. In his notes on Genesis, Tremellius twice referred
to the commentary of Rashi on the same Biblical book.[1]
Both references are to interpretations by the rabbi of the
passages in question. Tremellius also referred often to
Ibn Ezra, the notes to Genesis containing a number of
references to the interpretations of this rabbi.[2] The references to the commentary of Kimchi are also frequent, the
notes to the book of Genesis containing several.[3] I have
specifically cited here in my notes only a very few of
the total number of references to the commentaries of the
rabbis which occur in Tremellius's notes. As a matter of
fact, such references occur throughout the notes to the
text of Tremellius's Old Testament. The fact that they are
found therein is of no direct significance in connecting
Milton with the rabbis. But these references to the rabbis,
found in Tremellius's notes, constitute an indirect connection of Milton with rabbinical commentary, because they
occur in the notes to the Old Testament text Milton most
used, and refer directly, when they do refer, to the rabbis.
When considered alone, they are valueless as evidence of
Milton's knowledge and use of the rabbis. But combined
with his own references to rabbinical commentaries they
are of some importance as an indication of how the rabbis

[1]In his note to Gen. 10:2, Tremellius referred to Rashi as *Jarchi*, and again in
the note to Gen. 30:37 as *R. Solomo*, both of these names being frequently applied
to Rashi, whose name is explained *infra*.

[2]In the notes to Genesis, Tremellius referred to the commentary of Ibn Ezra on
Genesis no less than five times. The first reference to the rabbi is in the note to
Gen. 1:26, in which the rabbi is called *Abben Hezra*. The same name is used again
in the note to Gen. 4:26 and in 9:21. The note to Gen. 19:11 reads *A. Hezra*, and
to 24:2 *Ibben Hezra*; but all of these are clearly recognizable references to *Ibn Ezra*,
whose name, even today, is found spelled in a variety of ways.

[3]The first is in the note to Gen. 25:17, the second in the note to 37:25, and the
third attached to 37:34. All three of these notes refer to Kimchi as *R.D.K.*, the
same form in which his name is used in rabbinical literature.

would inevitably have been called to his attention by his reading of Tremellius.[1]

We now have before us the more important references to the rabbis in Milton's works. These have been individually examined, and in this examination, several significant points have appeared. We have seen that Milton definitely cited rabbinical commentaries to Scripture, and furthermore, he so referred to them that it has been possible to determine the form in which he knew such commentaries. This was found to have been a rabbinical Bible, or a Jewish Bible in which are to be found the text of the Hebrew, the Aramaic paraphrase of this, the marginal variants and other apparatus, and the commentaries of various rabbis. Not only has it been found possible to determine the form of the text Milton was citing, but also to settle on the edition he used. This was, beyond any reasonable doubt, the Buxtorf edition, as, for the Biblical passages he cited in connection with particular rabbis, the rabbis cited are as they occur in that edition.

The chief importance of thus connecting Milton with such a work is the enormous amount of rabbinical material thereby opened to him. The rabbinical commentaries found in a rabbinical Bible constitute almost a whole literature in themselves. We shall now turn to a more detailed account of the commentaries found in the Buxtorf Bible, and of other rabbinical works to which Milton had access.

---

[1]For Milton's use of Tremellius's notes, cf. *Use of the Bible in Milton's Prose*, pp. 59-63 and *passim*.

CHAPTER II

THE RABBINICAL MATERIALS MILTON CITED OR USED

For obvious reasons, in reconstructing Milton's rabbinical studies or readings, the first works to investigate and the first works on which he necessarily drew are the Hebrew and rabbinical lexicons and grammars of his day. Milton's own lifetime lies almost wholly between that earlier period of Oriental studies when a fascinated interest in the Oriental languages was often the only justification for studying them, and the later period when the study of these languages became systematized. The study of the Oriental languages by Christians during the Middle Ages and even later was, at best, of but little consequence. As Soury stated the situation over a half century ago, it is not difficult to understand the reasons that made this condition inevitable.

In the Middle Ages, as in antiquity, knowledge of Hebrew remained in the exclusive possession of the Jews. Everywhere and always when a Christian wished to learn Hebrew, he was compelled to commence by becoming a disciple of the Rabbis. The same was true even of Greek, and especially of Arabic and other Oriental languages. By long frequentation with a Jew, a Greek, or an Arab, one was able to acquire a certain acquaintance with their respective languages, but before adventuring on the translation of a text, the Christian always was compelled to have it explained to him by someone to whom the tongue was native. Herein lies one of the general laws which emerge from the comparative history of the propagation of human doctrines through the medium of languages. Thus Jerome translated the Hebrew books of the Old Testament. Thus Peter the Venerable, Abbot of Cluny, made his translation of the Koran. Thus Boccaccio and Petrarch read Homer. Of the four conditions necessary to learn a language—to speak it, write it, or to know it, and one other with which it has an essential connection, namely, to have lived a sufficiently long time with those who speak it,—the scholars of the Middle Ages were able to partake only of the last.[1]

The complete change in the study of the Oriental languages which lies between the condition described by Soury and the modern study of the same languages, was taking place just before, during, and just after Milton's lifetime. His own linguistic studies lie wholly in that period of transition from the unsystematic to the completely systematic studies, which, by the end of the seventeenth century, had almost wholly remedied the chaotic condition of the study of Oriental languages obtaining even as late as at the beginning of the century.

The results of this systematization of the study of the Oriental languages had begun to appear a century before Milton's time. In the latter half of the sixteenth century had appeared the first of the great Oriental lexicographical and grammatical works, which were to continue to appear for more than two centuries. Among these were several lexicons and grammars of the Semitic languages which almost immediately became famous and influential all over Europe. Only a few of the more important of these need be mentioned here, specifically those which may be directly or indirectly connected with Milton, or are at least known to have been in England in his time.

One of the earliest and consequently one of the best known of the lexicons was that of Sanctus Pagninus, *Thesaurus Linguae Sanctae*, which first appeared at Leyden in 1529.[2] This work, with a short introduction by the

---

[1]J. Soury, *Des Etudes hébraïques et exégétiques au moyen âge chez les chrétiens d'Occident* (Paris, 1867), p. 14.

[2]I have used the אצר/ אוצר לשון הקדש/ *Hoc est,*/ *EPITOME*/ *THESAVRI*/ *LINGUAE SANCTAE,*/ *AVCTORE SANTE*/ *PAGNINO LVCENSI.*/ Tertia editio./ (design)/ ANTVERPIAE,/ Ex officina Christophori Plantini,/ Architypographi Regij./ M. D. LXXVIII./

author and a list of defective verbs preceding the text, is
made up of four hundred forty-seven pages devoted to the
definitions of Hebrew words from the Old Testament.
These are followed by *Appendix omnium vocum Chaldaicarum, quae passim in Biblis inveniuntur.* For the most
part, the definitions are very brief, but many of them cite
the Biblical passage in which the word occurs, and many
give the meaning provided by the medieval rabbis. The
rabbis most frequently cited are *R. Sal.* (Rashi); *R. Dau.*
(David Kimchi); and *R. Abr.* (Ibn Ezra). These abbreviations for the names of these rabbis are explained in the
printer's foreword to the reader.

Another widely circulated sixteenth century Hebrew
lexicon was that published at Wittenberg in 1568. Its
editor was Johann Avenarius. His lexicon was a full folio,
with a single column using the full width of the immense
pages. Avenarius's citations of passages in which occurred
the words being defined were confined almost entirely to
Scripture. He did, however, occasionally cite rabbinical
passages, drawing chiefly upon Kimchi's works.[1]

Still another early lexicon, published shortly after Milton was born, was Schindler's.[2] This was a much more

---

[1] ספר השרשים/ *HOC EST,/ LIBER RADICVM SEV/ LEXICON EBRAICVM,
IN QVO/ OMNIVM VOCABVLORVM BIBLICORVM PROPRIAE/ ac certae
redduntur significationes, cum vera & dilucida multorum/ locorum scripturae sacrae
explicatione./ Adiecta est plerisq: Radicibus Symphoniacarum/ linguarum deri-
uatio./ AUTORE/ M. JOHANNE AVENARIO/ EGRANO./ PSALMO*
[design] *XXV./* כי קויתיך [design] חם ויֹשר יצרוני./ *Cum Gratis & Priuilegio./
VVITEBERGAE/ EXCVDEBAT IOHANNES CRATO./ ANNO/ M. D.
LXVIII./*

[2] *Lexicon Pentaglotton, Hebraicum, Chaldaicum, Syriacum, Talmudico-Rabbin-
icum, et Arabicum.* In qvo omnes voces Hebraeae, Chaldaeae, Syrae, Rabbinicae,
et Arabicae, adjectis hincinde Persicis, Aethiopicis et Turcicis, ordine Alphabetico,
sub suis singulae Radicibus digeste continentur: Earumque Significationes, Usus
ac Elegentiae, ex SS. Hebraeis Biblis; horum Chaldaicis Paraphrasibus; Testa-
mento N. Syriaco; utroque Babylonico et Hierosolymitano Talmudo, Midraschim,
Rabbinorum Commentatoribus, Theologis et Philosophis; Arabica V. et N. Instru-
menti Translatione, Alkorano, Avicenna, &c. ut et Graeca LXX. Interpretum,

pretentious work than that of Pagninus, or even that of Avenarius. It was published in folio, two columns to a page, and its entries under single roots often run through two or three pages. The list of authorities cited includes most of the chief medieval rabbis, various other rabbinical works, Greek and Latin writers of classical antiquity or later times, and many Christian Orientalists of note. Schindler's work marks an important step forward in Christian exploration of the entire field of Jewish literature, and it is a compendious mine of rabbinical information and citation.

Shortly before the appearance of Schindler's *Lexicon*, Buxtorf published his first Hebrew-Latin lexicon.[1] This was a much larger work than the Hebrew lexicon of Pagninus, and ran to nine hundred sixty single-column pages without the index. It was, of course, much smaller than Schindler's work, as its scope was limited to the vocabulary of the Old Testament. But it was a most ambitious undertaking. It contains many citations of the medieval rabbis, Rashi, the Kimchis, and Ibn Ezra being especially prominent. Many passages in which occur the word being defined are cited, and in many ways this lexicon is much

---

et omnibus Latinis Bibliorum versionibus, docte, ample, ac dilucide proponuntur & explicantur. Variorum item interpretvm difficiles, ac discrepantes sententiae conferuntur, et examinantur. Collectum, et concinnatum a Clarissimo et doctissimo viro, Dn. Valentino Schindlero Œderano, Linguarum Orientalium in celeberrimis Witembergensi et Helmstadiensi Academiis, quondam Professore. Opus novum, nunc post Authoris obitum, ex ipso Authographo fildelissime descriptum, et in locis dubiis cum Bibliis Regiis collatum, communique Reipubl. Christianae bono in lucem editum. Cum triplici Indice: 1. Abbreviaturarum Hebraearum copiosissimo. 2. Nominum propriorum hoc LEXICO citatorum. 3. Omnium vocum Latinarum, quibus dicta Idiomata explicantur, locupletissimo. Cum privilegiis S. Caes. Majest. et Regiae Galliarum. Cura et Auspiciis RULANDIORUM. HANOVIAE, Typis Joannis Jacobi Hennei. M D CXII.

I quote the entire title-page here in order to give a better idea of the enormous amount of material contained in this work.

[1] Johannis Buxtorf I. *Epitome Radicum Hebraicarum et Chaldaicarum*, Basel, 1607.

like a modern work. It became perhaps the most popular and best known of all Christian lexicons of the Hebrew tongue. It has been reprinted many, many times, not only during its compiler's lifetime and immediately after his death, but throughout the succeeding centuries, the nineteenth century seeing published a number of revised, re-edited, and translated editions of it.

The author and editor of this work, John Buxtorf I, mentioned several times by Milton, must be accorded more than passing attention here, not only because he was one of the greatest Christian Hebraists of his day, but because a number of his works in the field of Semitic and rabbinical studies are of so great an importance in connection with Milton. Buxtorf was born at Kamen in Westphalia on December 25, 1564. The original form of the name was *Bockstrop* or *Boxtrop*, from which was derived the family crest bearing the figure of a goat. After the death of his father, who was minister of Kamen, Buxtorf studied at Marburg and the newly founded university of Herborn. At Herborn he met the two recently appointed professors of theology, C. Olevian (1536-1587) and J. P. Piscator (1546-1625). Much later than this residence at Herborn, Buxtorf aided Piscator in the latter's Latin translation of the Old Testament published at Herborn in 1602-1603. From Herborn, Buxtorf went to Heidelberg, and thence to Basel, attracted by the reputation of Grynaeus and Hospinian. After a short residence at Basel, he went to Zurich, where he studied under the famous Bullinger. But he did not long remain there, passing on to Geneva, where he studied under Calvin. Some time after this, he again went to Basel, and Grynaeus, his former teacher, was desirous that the services of so promising a scholar should be secured for the University. For this reason, Grynaeus procured for Buxtorf a situation as tutor in the

family of Leo Curio, son of Coelius Secundus Curio, who
was so well known for his sufferings on account of the
Reformed faith. Also due to the efforts of Grynaeus,
Buxtorf undertook the duties connected with the Hebrew
chair in the University. So well did he perform them, and
so much ability did he display, that at the end of two
years he was unanimously appointed to the vacant office in
1591. He remained in Basel from this time until his death
in 1629, devoting himself with remarkable fervor and
equally remarkable results to the study of Hebrew and
rabbinical literature. He associated a great deal with
learned Jews, and received them into his house that he
might discuss his difficulties with them. He in turn was
frequently consulted by Jews themselves on matters connected with their ceremonial laws. He seems eminently
to have deserved the title which was conferred upon him
of 'Master of the Rabbis.' So great was his partiality for
the society of Jews that it brought him, on one occasion,
into trouble with the authorities of the city, the laws
against the Jews being very strict. Nevertheless, on the
whole, his relations with the city of Basel were friendly.
He remained firmly attached to the University that first
recognized his merits, declining two invitations, from Leyden and Saumur respectively. His correspondence with
the most distinguished scholars of the day was very extensive, and his reputation was spread abroad over all of
Europe. He left works on all phases of Jewish culture and
learning, and connected with Jewish Biblical learning.
He died at the end of a life devoted to Semitic and rabbinical learning, and with his name well known for his scholarly activity in all fields of Jewish lore.

Ten years after Buxtorf's death, there appeared the
work on which he had labored for the last thirty years of
his life. This was the great rabbinical lexicon, which, even

today, must be mentioned in any list of the great lexicons
of rabbinical literature. The work first appeared in 1639,
being completed and edited by the son, John Buxtorf II.[1]
It was an even larger work than Schindler's, drawing on a
much greater range of Jewish literature, and citing a much
larger number of rabbinical works. The entries of the
double-column pages are sometimes the length of short
treatises. These entries are filled with citations of rabbinical and Biblical passages in which occur the words being
defined. Many such citations may appear in connection
with a single word. The work, therefore, contains an
enormous amount of rabbinical lore, and a person reading
it even casually is certain sooner or later to encounter
many curious or unusual bits of information culled from
the rabbis. Buxtorf drew on almost every phase of Jewish
literature for his definitions and illustrations, or the occurrences of either. Much of this literature was, of course,
the older literature of the Targums and Midraschim; but
the medieval rabbis also came in for their full share of

[1]Johannis Buxtorfii P./ LEXICON/ CHALDAICUM, TALMUDICUM/ ET
RABBINICUM,/ In quo/ OMNES VOCES CHALDAICAE, TALMUDICAE
ET RABBINICAE,/ quotquot in universis Vet. Test. Paraphrasibus Chaldaicis;
in utroq; Talmud, Ba-/bylonico et Hierosolymitano, in vulgaribus et secretioribus
Hebraeorum Scri-/ptoribus, Commentatoribus, Philosophis, Theologis, Cabalistis
et Ju-/reconsultis extant, fideliter explicantur,/ Et copia ac delectu exemplorum
Targumicorum, Talmudicorum et Rabbi-/nicorum, eleganter declarantur;/
Passim etiam, suis locis, Hebraeorum et Chaldaeorum Provèrbia, Apophtheg-
mata,/ Sententiae, Ritus, aliaque ad Sacram hanc Philologiam pertinentia, ex
pro-/priis ipsorum libris producuntur, et explanantur;/ Quamplurima denique
Vet. et Nov. Test. loca ex Antiquitate et Historia/ Hebraica nove exponuntur et
illustrantur;/ Ut non solum vulgaris LEXICI, sed amplissimi et instructissimi
THESAURI/ PHILOLOGICI loco esse possit;/ OPUS XXX. ANNORUM,/
Nunc demum, post PATRIS obitum, ex ipsius Autographo fideliter descriptum,
in/ ordinem aequabilem digestum, et multis propriis observationibus passim
lo-/cupletatum, Reipublicaeque Christianae bono in lucem editum/ a/ JOHANNE
BUXTORFIO FILIO,/ Ling. Heb. in Acad. Bas. Prof. ord./ Cum Indice vocum
Latinarum, et Locorum N.T. illustratorum./ Cum Privilegio./ BASILEAE,/
Sumptibus et typis Ludovici Konig, M.DC.XXXX./ (There are two title-pages,
the first carrying the date M.DC.XXXIX.)

citation, both as authorities and as disseminators of older materials, which have since disappeared. Buxtorf's work immediately made available to the scholar who could read Latin, even though his knowledge of Hebrew and the rabbinical literature was small, an enormous amount of well-digested and authentic material drawn from the rabbis. Perhaps no other work, written before or since, has done so much to provide the Christian rabbinical scholar with the proper guidance and material as did this lexicon for the time in which it appeared. Virtually every rabbinical student among Christians since Buxtorf's day has been indebted sooner or later to this great work.[1] This lexicon was also of the greatest importance as an aid to the understanding of textual problems of the New Testament. The critical study of the text of the New Testament, in a most modern manner, was under way by the middle of the seventeenth century. The work done by such seventeenth century scholars as John Lightfoot was, indeed, in many respects so in advance of the generality of scholars of his time that his full importance as a New Testament scholar is only now being appreciated.

The other common tools of the Semitic and rabbinical student, grammars, special lexicons, and so forth, while of great importance as aids to the study of rabbinical literature, can be only noted here. Many of the greatest Hebrew grammarians among Christians have drawn much of their material from the grammars of the late sixteenth and early seventeenth centuries. Many Hebrew grammars appeared, for nearly every student of the subject during the sixteenth century felt the need, as did Bellarmine later, of writing his own grammar. Each of the lexicographers

---

[1] For an excellent tribute to the worth and value of Buxtorf's *Lexicon Chaldaicum*, cf. G. F. Moore's article, 'Christian Writers on Judaism,' *Harvard Theological Review*, vol. xiv (1921), p. 217.

mentioned above produced a grammar or two, Buxtorf producing a Chaldaic grammar in addition to his Hebrew.

All of these lexicons and grammars are important for the student of Milton's Hebrew and rabbinical equipment. They must be constantly employed in connection with him, as they constitute a definite source of supply for the strictly contemporary learning in the materials which they contain.

Turning now to a totally different type of rabbinical work and to which we found Milton actually referring, let us examine more fully the rabbinical Bible he was using. It is a little difficult to describe such a Bible to anyone who has not actually used one. It may appear even more difficult to be certain of which particular edition of such a Bible Milton actually used. But in both cases the difficulties are much more apparent than real. So far as the actual edition of the rabbinical Bible Milton used is concerned, a brief survey of the various editions printed before his blindness of such a Bible soon discloses the narrow range of possibility.

The term *rabbinical Bible* is employed as a descriptive English equivalent for the Bible called מקראות גדולות, the name given to the Hebrew Bible when printed or copied out, as it was originally, with the three Aramaic Targums, marginal variants and other masorah, and rabbinical commentaries. Such a Bible was first printed at Venice by Daniel Bomberg (d.1549) and hence is usually known as the *Bomberg Bible*. Bomberg himself was a Christian printer and publisher of Hebrew works, who was born at Antwerp. He learned the art of printing and of typefounding from his father, Cornelius. About 1515 Daniel went to Venice, and there, from 1517 until his death in 1549, he printed many editions of Hebrew works, including the *editio princeps* of the rabbinical Bible. This latter work appeared in 1517-1518. It was edited by Felix Pratensis, a convert to Judaism. It contained the Pentateuch with the Onkelos Targum and Rashi's commentary; the Former and the Later Prophets, with Targum Jonathan and Kimchi's commentary, with the anti-Christian portions omitted; the Psalms with Targum and Kimchi's commentary; Proverbs with the commentary known as Kawwe-Naki; Job, with the commentaries of Nachmanides and Abraham Farrisol; the Five Scrolls (Ketuvim) with Levi ben Gerson's commentary; Ezra and Chronicles with the commentary of Rashi and also that of Simon ha-Darshan. In addition, this edition contained also the Jerusalem Targum to the Pentateuch; the Targum Shani to Esther; the variants of Ben Asher and Ben Naphtali; the thirteen Articles of Faith by Maimonides; and the six hundred thirteen precepts according to Aaron Jacob Hasan. This edition was not, however, pleasing to the Jews generally, for its editor was a convert.[1] It was soon apparent, however, that such a Bible served a great need, for Christians as well as Jews.

Bomberg therefore printed his second rabbinical Bible in 1525, also at Venice. This second Bomberg rabbinical Bible was edited by Jacob ben Chajim of Tunis, under the title שער יהוה הקדש. This work, although Bomberg's second edition of the rabbinical Bible, is usually taken by Jews as the *editio princeps* rather than the edition edited by Pratensis. This text, more than any other, has influenced all subsequent rabbinical Bibles. In this Bible, as in the best manuscripts, the *masorah magna*, or more important textual notes, are printed above and below the two columns of text; and the *masorah parva*, or lesser marginal notes to the text, together with the *qere*, appear between the two col-

---

[1] Cf. Elias Levita's severe criticism in his *Masoret ha-Masoret* of the Masoretic notes in Pratensis's Bible.

umns. The contents of this edition are: an introduction
to the *masorah* by the editor; Ibn Ezra's Introduction to
the Pentateuch; Moses ha-Nakdan's Treatise on Accents;
the Pentateuch with Targum and the commentaries of
Rashi and Ibn Ezra; the Former Prophets with the Targum of the so-called Jonathan ben Uziel and the commentaries of Rashi, David Kimchi, and Ben Gerson (Ralbag); The Later Prophets with the Targum, and the commentaries of Rashi and Ibn Ezra except for the books of
Jeremiah and Ezekiel, for which books the commentary of
David Kimchi was substituted for that of Ibn Ezra;
Psalms, with commentaries of Rashi and Ibn Ezra; Proverbs, with Ibn Ezra [Moses Kimchi] and Ralbag; Job,
with Ibn Ezra and Ralbag; Daniel, with Ibn Ezra and
Saadia; Ezra, with Ibn Ezra, Moses Kimchi, and Rashi;
Chronicles, with pseudo-Rashi; and the Five Scrolls with
Rashi and Ibn Ezra.

But, like modern critical editions, this work was not
entirely satisfactory. It was impossible to include all the
critical and exegetical apparatus that had been written by
the Jews; but if any of it was omitted, it was certain to be
missed. The result of this dissatisfaction was the publication of the third Bomberg rabbinical Bible, published
also at Venice, in 1546-1548. This was edited by Cornelius Adelkind, and was practically a reprint of the second.
Ibn Ezra on Isaiah was omitted, but Jacob ben Asher
(בעל הטורים) on the Pentateuch was added, as was Isaiah di
Trani on Judges and Samuel. Parts also of the *masorah*
were dropped.

These were restored in the fourth rabbinical Bible, which
otherwise has little to distinguish it from the first three.
An equally undistinguished fifth Bible appeared,[1] and

---

[1] A copy of this Bible has been used to check all passages taken from Buxtorf's
Bible. Cf. *infra.*

then in 1618-1619 Buxtorf's two volumes appeared at Basel.

The Buxtorf rabbinical Bible is a reprint of the third Bomberg. To it in 1620, Buxtorf added the *Tiberias, sive Commentarius Masorethicus Triplex, Historicus, Didacticus, Criticus.* I have never seen copies of the Buxtorf rabbinical Bible without the *Tiberias*, but such exist.

These constituted the available rabbinical Bibles of Milton's day, the next edition that materially changed the text or the accompanying material appearing in the early eighteenth century. Very little uncertainty is therefore possible as to which edition Milton used. The number of editions available is too small to make it a very difficult problem. The Buxtorf edition fits Milton's references to rabbinical apparatus, and there is no particular reason why this Bible, perhaps the best known among Christians throughout Europe of all the six editions up to Milton's time, should not have been used by him.

As already suggested, unless one has actually worked with a rabbinical Bible, it is difficult to know much about one from what has been said thus far, and equally difficult to gain an adequate idea of such a Bible from a mere verbal description. For this reason, and for others that will soon be apparent, the accompanying delineation of a typical page from the Buxtorf Bible of 1618-1619 may prove helpful. The various texts on the page are designated by the Roman letters superimposed upon them.

'a' is the pointed Hebrew text, in this particular instance, the text of the thirteenth chapter of Exodus. There is nothing particularly unusual about this Hebrew text in Buxtorf's Bible, except that, as this is a Jewish Bible, the *qere* is indicated.

'b' is a column of variants, which have accumulated from an early date. This column includes *masorah parva,*

or lesser textual notes, and the *qere*. These are the קרי
already discussed (properly transliterated *qere*, but in Milton's time, and, indeed, until very recently, spelled and
pronounced *keri*). The meaning of this word, as previously stated, is *to be read*, since, according to the opinion of
the rabbis, the word in the margin is to be preferred in oral
reading to the כתיב (ketiv) or *what is written* in the text.
On this account, the vowels of the marginal reading (*qere*)
are placed under the consonants of the text, and in order
to understand both readings properly, the vowels in the
text must be applied to the marginal reading, while for the
reading of the text (the *ketiv*) its own vowels are to be used.
In Buxtorf's text, a small circle over the word in the text
always refers to the marginal reading in 'b' which is
sometimes a *qere* and sometimes one of the *masorah parva*.[1]

The next labelled column, 'c,' is the text of the Aramaic
paraphrase of the Hebrew text. In Buxtorf's Bible, this is
also a pointed text. It is not necessary to discuss the
Aramaic paraphrases here. Briefly, there are several different Aramaic paraphrases extant, not all of them sur-
viving for the same portions of Scripture. None of them
survive for the whole of the Old Testament. But for those
portions of Scripture for which they do survive, they form
the most important variations from the Hebrew text which
we possess. Written down early in the Christian era, they
often provide a reading, in Aramaic to be sure, which
greatly aids in the understanding of faulty, defective readings in the Hebrew text itself. Milton has often cited
these paraphrases or Targums, as they are called. They
have been known to students of the Bible since the earliest
Christian times, but they are not easy to read. A good

---

[1]For further discussion of the difference between *ketiv* and *qere*, cf. Kautzsch,
Gramm. des Bibli. Aram., p. 81, note. See also, Ginsburg, *Intro. to the Heb. Bible*,
pp. 183 ff.

FIGURE I. (Exodus XIII - XIV)
A Page from the Buxtorf Bible

Hebrew student finds that he needs special study in order to use them regularly. In rabbinical Bibles, one of the Targums is usually printed in a column parallel, as here, to the text it paraphrases, with the others, if they exist, for the same Hebrew text elsewhere.

Immediately above and below these two Hebrew and Aramaic columns of text, are to be found collections of Hebrew square characters. These seem to be limits above and below the two columns of text. In reality, they are the *masorah magna*, indicated here by the letter 'd.' These notes embody the traditional rules for spelling, punctuation, and pointing of the text. They also cite other usages of the same words, the number of times a word occurs in Scripture, and various other details connected with the text. Much of this *masorah* is very ancient, but just how ancient, we do not know.[1]

Outside of and sometimes completely surrounding these columns of text and textual notes are columns of printing in characters unlike the square characters of the text itself. These characters, the *literae rabbinicae*, were adapted directly from the manuscripts written by the rabbis before the invention of printing. Three different forms of these cursive letters are commonly recognized by printers. These are the German, the Italian, and the Spanish. The letter-form used by Buxtorf for the commentaries was the Italian. All the commentaries accompanying his particular text were printed in this character. On the page before us three different commentaries appear, the work of three different rabbis.

On the page before us, 'e' marks the commentary of בעל הטורים (*Baal ha-Turim*) the name given to *Jacob ben Asher*. This rabbi wrote two commentaries on the Penta-

---

[1] It is difficult adequately to describe the *masorah magna*. For a complete and highly detailed treatment of it, see Ginsburg, *op. cit.*, pp. 287-468.

teuch. Buxtorf used part of the one first printed at
Constantinople in 1500.[1]

The column marked 'f' is the commentary of אבן עורא
Ibn Ezra. His full name was Abraham ben Meir Ibn Ezra.
He was born in 1092-1093, and died in 1167. His commentaries on Scripture are among the best known of all
rabbinical commentaries, his importance among the Jews
as a Biblical commentator having been surpassed by only
one other rabbi, Rashi. Ibn Ezra's commentary on the
Pentateuch has called forth a host of super-commentaries,
and has perhaps done more than any other work to estab-
lish and insure his reputation. This commentary survives
in many manuscripts and in early printed editions. It was
first printed at Naples in 1488. The commentary on
Exodus found in the printed editions of the Pentateuch
commentary, a specimen of which is now before us, was
originally a separate work. It has been so reprinted,
though very infrequently. A shorter commentary on
Exodus, more like his commentaries on the remaining
books of the Pentateuch, was first printed at Prague in
1840.[2]

---

[1]Jacob ben Asher was born, presumably near the end of the 12th century, and
died at Toledo, Spain, sometime before 1340. He was one of the most active of
rabbinical scholars, and his name became known throughout the entire Jewish
world by virtue of his *Turim* or abridgement of his father's compendium of the
Talmud. The commentary on the Pentateuch, of which part is printed in Buxtorf's Bible, consists only of *gematria* (cryptographs, which, instead of the intended
word, give its numerical value, or a cipher produced by the permutations of letters);
notarikon (a system of short-hand consisting either in abbreviations of words, or in
writing only one letter of each word, sometimes to make a new word); and masoretic calculations. His other commentary on the Pentateuch was not printed,
apparently, until the 19th century.

[2]In an acrostic verse, Ibn Ezra named Toledo as his place of birth, but at another
time he named Cordova. His father's name was Meir, and his family was probably
a branch of the Ibn Ezra family to which the poet, Moses Ibn Ezra (1070-1139)
belonged. His life falls naturally into two unequal parts, due to the fact that some
time before 1140 he left Spain for the remainder of his life. In the first and longer

Ibn Ezra explained his method of exegesis in the introduction to his Pentateuch commentary by characterizing and criticizing the various methods employed in previous commentaries. He knew nothing of the principle of multiple meanings for Scriptural words, and we find an echo of this in Milton.[1] He connected his philosophical speculations with various portions of his Biblical exegesis, and

division of his life, that before 1140, he won a name for himself in his native land. During this period, his creative faculties were chiefly occupied with the writing of poetry, and the greater number of his religious and other poems were probably produced during this period of his lifetime. But the writings appearing during the second period of his life amply indicate that he had also pursued serious studies in all branches of knowledge during that part of his life spent in Spain. Also, he made personal friends of the most prominent Jewish scholars and writers of Spain during this period. In the second period, after leaving Spain alone and bound by no family ties, he wandered in an unsettled fashion over most of Europe. However, he occasionally ceased his wanderings to reside for a time in various places, and often spent several years in each. The year 1140 is usually cited as the definite date of beginning for the second period of his life because in that year he is known to have composed several works at Rome. This date was furnished by Ibn Ezra himself in some of his other works. At least some of his travels, notably those in north Africa and Egypt concerning which there is definite information, were presumably made between the time he left Spain and his arrival in Rome. A whole series of works connected with Biblical exegesis was the result of his stay in Italy. After leaving Italy, he made a stay of several years in northern France. Here he completed several more of his exegetical works and began a new commentary on the Pentateuch. In 1158 he was in London, where he wrote his religio-philosophical work entitled *Yesod Mora*, and also his famous letter on the Sabbath. It is not difficult to understand Ibn Ezra's supreme position and popularity among Biblical commentators. When he left his native Spain, he left as a mature man who had acquired at first hand the whole culture and learning of Spanish Judaism in its period of finest development. For all other European cultures, the Biblical lore to be found in the countries influenced by Mohammedan civilization, which had developed in such fulness shortly before Ibn Ezra's time, was a closed book. Because of the language in which this lore was written, it was confined to those circles in which Arabic was spoken. Ibn Ezra was the first scholar to disseminate this culture on a large scale in the Christian countries of Europe. With his knowledge of Arabic culture in its contacts with Judaism, he left Spain and wandered for over thirty years throughout Europe. The chief products of his many-sided genius were his exegetical works. These commentaries, though written far from Spain, were the most important product, in the field of Biblical exegesis, of the golden age of Spanish Judaism.

[1] *de doctrina*, p. 346, sensus cujusque scripturae unicus est.

endeavored always to defend the text against everything
that might injure its integrity. But nevertheless he is
regarded, since Spinoza wrote his *Tractatus Theologico-
Politicus*, as the precursor of the modern literary criticism
of the Pentateuch. In general his commentaries aimed at
establishing the simple sense of the text on a solid grammatical basis.[1]

Returning now to the picture of the text, the column
labelled 'g' is the commentary of the greatest of all medieval commentators, רשׁי *Rashi*. His full name was Solomon
bar (ben) Isaac, and the name *Rashi* was formed, as was
so often the case with the popular names of rabbis, from
the initials of his title and of his names.[2] The *editio prin-*

---

[1] Again this principle of Biblical exegesis finds an echo in Milton, *ibid*. 'Ratio
recte interpretandi scripturas utilius quidem a theologis traditur, quam diligen-
tius aut fidelius observatur; linguarum peritia; fontium inspectio; scopi animad-
versio; locutionis propriae et figuratae distinctio; causarum, circumstantiarum,
antecedentium, consequentium consideratio; locorum cum aliis locis comparatio;
fidei quoque analogia ubique spectanda est; syntaxeos denique haud rare anomalia
non omittenda: exempli gratia, ubi relativum non ad proximum antecedens, sed
ad principalius, quamvis remotius, referendum est;'

[2] Rashi was born at Troyes in or about 1040, and died there in 1105. Because of
his fame, many legends have clustered about his name and his life. The name *Yarchi*
or *Jarchi*, often applied to him as early as the sixteenth century, originated in the
confusion of him with another rabbi of Lunel, and a similar error caused the town
of Lunel to be regarded as Rashi's birthplace. But actually he was born at
Troyes. Tradition has been responsible for many mythical journeys through
Europe, Asia, and Africa. These may have resulted from accounts of the actual
travels of Ibn Ezra, for it is certain that Rashi's travels were not extensive. However, he did apparently leave Troyes when he was about twenty-five years old.
His return to that city marked the beginning of the activity that made the rabbinical schools of Champagne and northern France at first rival and then surpass
those of the Rhenish provinces. Rashi undoubtedly acted as rabbi in his native
city, but his principal income was derived from his vineyards and the manufacture
of wine. About 1070 he founded a school that attracted many disciples and pupils.
This school became even more famous and important after the death of his own
teachers. One of his daughters marrying one of his most famous pupils, his family
became largely responsible for the propagation of rabbinical learning throughout
France. Rashi's training and his learning found their most complete expression in
his commentaries, possibly begun while he was still in Lorraine. His last years

ceps of Rashi on the entire Old Testament was the Bomberg Bible of 1525, in which, however, the text only of Proverbs, Job, and Daniel was used. All of his Biblical commentaries are to be found in Buxtorf's Bible.

Within the commentaries of these two great rabbis, Ibn Ezra and Rashi, is contained an enormous amount of material, exegetical, explanatory, and otherwise useful to a reader of the Bible. Access to these commentaries was afforded Milton by their presence in Buxtorf's rabbinical Bible. But these commentaries are not all the rabbinical material to be found therein, and which such a Bible made

were greatly saddened by the massacres of Jews which took place at the beginning of the Crusades (1095-1096) in which he lost relatives and friends, but was himself spared.

His commentary on the Pentateuch was first printed without the scriptural text at Reggio in 1475, and is the first dated Hebrew book in print. Five years later it was printed in square characters. Its first appearance with the text was at Bologne in 1482, the commentary being printed in the margins. A great many editions of the Pentateuch have been published with Rashi's Commentary only. At different times, other parts of the Old Testament appeared with his various commentaries. Probably no other commentaries have received the attention of translators and editors that Rashi's have received, and certainly no others have been made the subject of so many super-commentaries. His attainments as a commentator appear the more remarkabe when it is remembered that he confined himself almost entirely to Jewish fields of learning. In spite of legendary statements to the contrary, he knew no other languages than Hebrew, Aramaic, and French. He knew nothing of secular science, but in Biblical and rabbinical literature, his learning was extensive and reliable. His numerous quotations show that he was familiar with almost all the Hebrew and Aramaic works of his predecessors. His fame rests almost wholly upon his commentaries to the Bible and to the Talmud. Except for a few books of the former, and a few treatises in the latter, his commentaries cover the whole of both Bible and Talmud. They are not, however, consecutive commentaries, but detached glosses on difficult terms or phrases. Their primary characteristic and their primary aims were clarity. Rashi's explanations always seemed adequate, long after his own age.

The two principal sources from which he derived his exegesis were the Talmudic-midrashic literature, and the hermeneutic processes it employed. Unfortunately, he attributed too great an importance to the second of these, often at the expense of the first, although he intended only to explain the simple, obvious meaning of the text before him. Also, his lack of scientific or rigorous method has, unfortunately prevented him from occupying the rank in the realms of Biblical exegesis merited by his other qualities.

available to Milton. In the Buxtorf Bible, a number of other commentaries by important rabbis are to be found, though these are not represented on the page we have been describing.

Connected with the Former Prophets and certain other books of the Old Testament, Buxtorf printed commentaries labelled רד״ק *RaDaK*. These are the commentaries of rabbi David Kimchi, called in French, *Maistre Petit*.[1] In a general way, this rabbi in his commentaries adhered to the literal meaning of Scripture, and his exegesis is based on grammatical principles and rationality. In the introduction to his commentary on the Prophets, he emphasized the duty of explaining the Bible always from a religious standpoint. His commentary on the Psalms which Buxtorf did not print is especially noted for its polemics

[1]David Kimchi was born in Narbonne, the son of Joseph Kimchi, who has been called 'the first successful transplanter of Judaeo-Arabic science to the soil of Christian Europe.' Joseph had been forced to leave his home in southern Spain because of religious persecution. He settled in Narbonne, Provence, and probably spent the remainder of his life there. Joseph himself was the author of many exegetical works, only a few of which have survived. He died when David was still a child. David was the youngest of Joseph's children, and after the latter's death, the oldest brother, Moses, undertook the rearing of the child. Moses, too, wrote many commentaries, and there have been preserved those on Proverbs, Ezra, and Nehemiah, which are printed in Buxtorf's and other rabbinical Bibles as the work of Ibn Ezra. Moses's grammar, *Mahalak*, became important during the sixteenth century as it was the shortest and most useful textbook for the study of Hebrew by Gentiles. It was edited many times, and was translated into Latin by Sebastian Münster. Elias Levita wrote annotations to it.

David Kimchi appears to have been reared and educated entirely by his brother, Moses. David was a scholar throughout his entire lifetime, supporting himself very early in life by instructing the young Jews of Narbonne in the Talmud. His early training was of such a nature that he became exceedingly well acquainted with the whole range of Hebrew and Jewish literature. His most important work, in some ways, was his *Miklol*, written originally in two parts. The first part was a grammar, and the second a dictionary. David wrote commentaries on Genesis, the Prophets, Psalms, and Chronicles. Some scholars ascribe to him also commentaries on the remaining books of the Old Testament. He wrote a philosophical explanation of Creation, based on the first chapter of Genesis, and another on Ezekiel's vision, based on the opening chapters of Ezekiel. Only the latter is contained in Buxtorf.

against Christianity. Throughout the later Middle Ages, David's commentaries were held in the highest respect among Christians as well as Jews, and numerous fragments of them appeared in Latin translation. The influence of these commentaries was especially noticeable in the European vernacular translations of the Old Testament that accompanied the rise of Protestantism. With various minor omissions, all of David's commentaries, except those on the Psalms and Chronicles, have been printed in all editions of the rabbinical Bible since 1516.

Another rabbi much of whose commentary was printed by Buxtorf but none of which appears on the page being described here was רלבג *RaLBaG*. His full name was Rabbi Levi ben Gerson, and he is variously called by the Greek form of the name, Gersonides, the French, Leon de Bagnols, and the Latin, Magister Leo Hebraeus. Levi was born in Bagnols in 1288, and died there in 1344.[1] He was guided in his commentaries by principles laid down by Maimonides, adopting the method of presenting the literal meaning of a text, then summing up the philosophical ideas and moral maxims contained in each Biblical section. He interpreted the Wisdom literature of the Old Testa-

---

[1]Levi was undoubtedly related to the famous Nachmanides. Very little is known of his life beyond the fact that he lived in Orange, Avignon, and in a town called in Hebrew עיר האזוב *city of Hyssop*. In spite of the ban put by the Jews on the teaching of philosophy, Levi was very early initiated into all its branches. His works are saturated with philosophy, and probably chiefly because of that fact, he never held a rabbinical office. He supported himself, apparently, entirely by the practice of medicine. His works show a wide acquaintance with Biblical and Talmudical literature, and a very high order of linguistic attainment. In his works he made use of Hebrew, Aramaic, and Arabic, calling Latin the language of the Christians. His greatest work, the *Wars of God*, was highly philosophical in nature, drawing heavily upon Aristotle's philosophical works. Levi appears to have known Aristotle's works almost wholly through Maimonides and Averroes. The conclusions at which he arrived in his philosophy and its speculations were introduced into his Biblical commentaries on every possible occasion, and he tried his best to reconcile his speculations with the text of Scripture.

ment almost wholly in a philosophical manner. To Levi,
Jerusalem symbolized man, who, like that city, was selected for the service of God. In opposition to the exegetes
of his time, Levi did not, however, allegorize the historical
and legislative portions of Scripture. He endeavored, on
the other hand, to give a natural explanation, which usually became metaphysical, to the various miracles in the
narrative. His theories, some of which influenced Spinoza,
especially the latter's treatment of miracle, met with general opposition among the Jews of his day. His ideas were
attacked on the ground that they were unorthodox, and
some zealous rabbis even went so far as to forbid the study
of his commentaries because of these charges. But by
Buxtorf's time, much of the orthodox distrust of Levi's
works had passed away.

Another rabbi whose commentary appears in Buxtorf's Bible was *Saadiah (Gaon)* סעדיה גאון. Not much is known of this
rabbi, aside from the extent and nature of his commentaries, in so far as these survive. The commentary to Daniel
which passes under his name is printed in Buxtorf's Bible.[1]

[1]Saadiah's native country and period cannot be precisely determined. The commentary to Daniel, usually ascribed to him, most probably belonged to another
Saadiah. In this commentary, if it was his, he displayed a profound knowledge of
Talmud and Targum. The latter was often quoted and explained. Apparently
he was acquainted with the works of earlier commentators, to whom he referred
under the general terms פתרים *interpreters* and אנשי לבב *men of understanding*.
Only once (in the commentary on Daniel 6:15) however, did he actually quote
another rabbi by name, Mattithiah Gaon. He very often based his interpretations
on the interchange of letters of the same class, as א and ע, ל and ר; and also on
the interchange of letters occurring near each other in various alphabetical com-
binations, as א and ב in the expression אב, or א and ל in אלבם. As in the
Talmudic method of interpretation, Saadiah often explained foreign nouns as well
as Hebrew proper names by resolving them into the syllables of which they were
constructed. His commentary on Daniel 6:19 and Ezra 1:9 shows that he knew Arabic. Possibly it was his native tongue, as he is supposed by some scholars to have
lived in north Africa. It is not known, however, where he lived or when. Some
scholars believe that he wrote about the beginning of the twelfth century, perhaps
in France or Italy. But others believe that he wrote much earlier than this, and
that his familiarity with Arabic indicates that he could not have lived in Europe.

Buxtorf printed some of the commentary of one other rabbi, Isaiah (ben Elijah) di Trani (the Younger). His name is usually given as ריא"ז (*Rabbi Isaiah Aharon of blessed memory*); or as ריב"א (*Rabbi Isaiah ben Elijah*). He wrote commentaries on the book of Joshua, (first printed at Leipzig in 1721); Judges and Samuel, (both of which are usually found in rabbinical Bibles and are in Buxtorf); and Kings. Only fragments of the latter survive, and have been printed only in the more inclusive rabbinical Bibles, and are in Buxtorf. His commentaries are confined to simple, concise, and rational exegesis. His chief importance as a commentator lies in the fact that his were the first commentaries to be issued in Italy which were free from allegorical interpretation of the text. He lived during the thirteenth and fourteenth centuries.

The chief reason for this brief account of the nature and contents of Buxtorf's *Biblia Hebraica* being included here is to afford the reader a better idea of the enormous amount of rabbinical material to be found therein. Between the covers of this one book, Milton came in contact with a whole world of rabbinical literature, all centering, as Jewish literature has always centered, in the text of Scripture. The work of the commenting rabbis occupies several thousand pages. Rashi's commentaries alone make a volume of hundreds of pages. Ibn Ezra's commentaries, as found in Buxtorf, bulk less, perhaps, than Rashi's, but still they represent the equivalent of a heavy volume or two. Ben Gerson's commentaries also run to many pages, and the commentaries of David Kimchi are even larger. The lesser rabbis occupy much less space; but altogether, in Buxtorf's rabbinical Bible is found sufficient material to constitute a complete library of Jewish Biblical commentaries.

The history of the use of Buxtorf's Bible in England is

not well known. Its editor, Buxtorf, had, by the time of the appearance of the Bible in 1618, acquired a reputation by his works in the field of Jewish studies that made a work like his rabbinical Bible almost immediately famous. Indeed, the work was eagerly awaited by scholars all over Europe. For this reason alone, the Bible must have been known in England soon after its appearance. There is at least one important bit of evidence that the Bible was well known in England before Milton went to Cambridge, and this evidence is somewhat connected with Milton, though only indirectly.[1]

In 1623, two years before Milton left his home in London to take residence at the University, there appeared in London a book that is very valuable for the information it gives us about Hebrew and rabbinical works known in England at that time.[2] This was a book written by John

[1]Perhaps the best known seventeenth century citation in England of Buxtorf's Bible is to be found in John Selden's *De Dis Syris* in the following passage: 'Sed locupletes heic autores nobis sunt Onkelos et alter ille, quisquis fuerit paraphrastes Chaldaeus sub Jonathanis nomine tritus, Salomon Jarchi, Rabbinorum alii, qui Mosem eo loci de novorum numinum initiis intelligunt. Et praeponderant heic, meo quidem judicio, Editiones Bombergiana, Gariana, Buxtorfiana, Complutensi et Antverpiensi, quibus apud Onkelum legunt *tunc incepisse homines &.*' The first edition of Selden's work appeared in 1617; the passage just quoted does not appear in it, but does appear in the second and editions subsequent to 1628. Cf. the standard edition of Selden's Works, the 3 volume *opera* of 1726, vol. II, col. 227. I wish to point out Selden's mention of Buxtorf *after* Weemes had already mentioned the Bible, for Selden's work is so well-known in general and so little known in detail that it might easily be concluded from the mention of Buxtorf in most accessible editions of the *De Dis Syris* that Weemes was four or five years later. But the absence of the whole passage in the first edition makes this impossible.

[2]THE/ CHRISTIAN/ Synagogue./ Wherein is contayned the diverse Reading, the/ right Poynting, Translation, and collation of scripture with scripture./ With the customes of the Hebrewes and Proselytes, and of all/ those Nations, with whom they were conversant./ Digested into three bookes./ The First, shewing the meanes both inward and outward, to attaine to the knowledge /of the sense of the whole Scripture./ The Second, unfolding the true sense of the Scripture it selfe, as also teaching the/ right way of gathering doctrines from any text of Scripture./ The Third, teaching the true manner of Confirmation, Illustration, and Applica-/ tion of Doctrines, rightly gathered from the true sense of Scripture./

Wemys or Weemse, entitled *The Christian Synagogue*. The book is a curious guidepost on the trail of the study of Hebrew in England. The work is divided, by pagination, into two parts, the first very much longer than the second. Considerable use is made in the first part of Hebrew characters. In this part of the book, these are uniformly crude characters, apparently hand-cut in wood, by an inexpert and extremely uncertain hand. These appear both in the text itself and in the margins especially provided and ruled off for notes. These Hebrew characters are not the earliest to appear in London printing, but they are of a period when Hebrew characters greatly taxed a London printer's resources. The vowel-points are even more crude than the letters, if this were possible. In the second part of the book, however, the Hebrew type employed is no longer so crude as that of the first part of the book. It is a Continental type, probably German, regularly cut and entirely uniform throughout the second division of the book. This type is unpointed, and not much of it occurs, there being considerable transliterated Hebrew in this division.

However, the importance to us of this book does not consist in its printing of Hebrew characters, interesting as that may be. It is rather in the contents and their references to Hebrew and rabbinical works that we are primarily interested here. Each page of the book has its two side margins ruled off from the text, and in these margins appear references to and citations of various works. These marginal references and citations form a sort of epitome of

Serving generally for a helpe to the vnderstanding, of all; that desire to/know and obey the will of God in holy Writ: But more specially for all young students in Divinitie, that they may more easily vnderstand/ the Languages of Canaan, and Greece, and make a profitable vse of them/ in Preaching./ By IOHN WEEMSE of Lathoquar, in Scotland,/ Preacher of Christs Gospell,/ Math. 25. 29./ [two lines of Greek quotation]/ Revel. 1. 3./ Blessed is he who readeth, &c./ LONDON./ Printed by I.D. for Iohn Bellamie, and are to be sold at his Shop,/ at the two Grey-hounds in Corne-hill, neare the Royall Exchange. 1623./

information regarding the state of Hebrew and rabbinical learning and its dissemination in England at about the time Milton was entering the University.

The author of this work, John Weemse, Weemes, or perhaps most commonly Wemyss, is of unexpected importance to the Milton student. Born about 1579, the only son of John Weemse of Lathockar in Fife, he was educated at St. Andrew's, where he graduated M.A. in 1600. So far as is known, he acquired his education wholly in Scotland at that University. Having been appointed minister of Hutton in 1608, he became somewhat prominent by various connections with the politico-religious quarrels of the time, and was finally charged to appear before the court of high commission to answer charges of irregularities in carrying out the form of ritual prescribed by the five articles of Perth. He and his fellows were dismissed with a reprimand, and after this warning, Weemse devoted himself exclusively to study. The book in which we are interested, *The Christian Synagogue*, appeared in 1623 as the direct result of this study, and went rapidly into several editions.

It is interesting to note that Weemse was at St. Andrew's, acquiring considerable knowledge of Hebrew and rabbinical literature only a few years before Thomas Young, Milton's tutor, was in residence there. The fact that Young unquestionably had much to do with Milton's Semitic interests and studies makes all information concerning Young's own training in, and knowledge of, Hebrew important. Young was born in 1587 or 1588. He matriculated at St. Andrew's in 1602, shortly after Weemse had proceeded M. A. there. Young's graduation to M.A. was in 1606. Thus, Weemse's familiarity with Hebrew and rabbinical literature, acquired, we may be sure, at St. Andrew's, becomes an indication of the nature and amount of such knowledge Young would have been able to acquire at the same University. Weemse's book, *The Christian Synagogue*, is, therefore, not only an epitome and repository of rabbinical and Hebrew knowledge generally accessible in England at the time of its appearance, but it also forms a basis for information concerning the general Semitic training available to Thomas Young at St. Andrew's.

Weemse's knowledge of Hebrew seems to have been considerable. Especially notable is his apparent familiarity with the rabbinical writings. The foreword to his book states that he was 'well qualified in all good learning.' Nevertheless, it is a little startling to find him mentioning a Christian divine, Perkins, and then following that mention with the expression ז״ל, a formula used by the rabbis when they refer to a venerated rabbi. We might well expect a reasonable number of references to the rabbis, however, for the author tells the reader that he 'besides the most approved of the Greeke and Latine writers, hath well read with deliberation also, the ancient customes of the Iewes, in their owne Rabbines, and hath mentioned so many of them, as gives no small light for the understanding of the text, and likewise hath had conference upon the same things with the most approved Schollers of the Kingdome.' This promise of drawing on rabbinical learning is amply fulfilled. Weemse cited a large number of rabbinical works whose presence in England at this date, 1623, is thereby assured. He mentioned several lexicographers, most of whom are of importance in connection with Milton and who have already been discussed in that connection. Thus, Weemse cited repeatedly the lexicon of Avenarius,[1] and also the 'Chaldee' lexicon edited by Sebastian Münster which included many Aramaic words, that the lex-

---

[1] p. 204; Avenarius's lexicon has been discussed earlier in this chapter.

icon of Avenarius did not include or otherwise take into account.[1]   In addition to these lexicons, that of Elias Levita is also frequently mentioned.[2]   Levita's work was very popular, and I assume that the edition of Levita's work to which Weemse referred was that published by Fagius in 1541.[3]   Weemse also referred to Schindler's *Pentaglotton*, and in the case of this work, the edition is unmistakable.[4]   This is the only seventeenth century lexicon that Weemse cited.   He also referred to both of Buxtorf's grammars, the Hebrew and the Aramaic.

From the point of view of the present study, however, the most important references Weemse made are to Buxtorf's Bible.   He referred to its *masorah*, and to the *Tiberias*, both unmistakable references to the Buxtorf Bible. This is the earliest reference I know of to that Bible in England.   Coming as it does from a Scotchman educated at St. Andrew's, it greatly strengthens the supposition that the Hebrew Bible sent by Thomas Young to the youthful Milton, mentioned in the *Familiar Epistle* of March 25, 1625, was a copy of the Buxtorf Bible.   Weemse also mentioned the following rabbis, whose commentaries appear in Buxtorf: Ibn Ezra, Gersom (Ben Gerson), Rabbi David Kimchi, Rabbi Salomon (Rashi), and also the three Targums, Jonathan, Onkelos, and Uziell.   In addition to these, he also mentioned Maimonides.

This is a large body of rabbinical and Hebraic material

---

[1]P. 205. This is Sebastian Münster, *Dictionarium Chaldaicum*. Basel, 1527.

[2]Pp. 35, 119, 130, 187, 195.

[3]OPVSCVLVM RE-/CENS HEBRAICVM A DOCTISSI-/MO HEBRAEO ELIIA LEVITA GERMANO GRAMMA-/tico elaboratum, cui titulum fecit תשבי id est, Thisbites,/ in quo 712. uocum, que sunt partim Hebraice, Chaldaiae,/ Arabice, Grecae & Latinae, queque in Dictionarijs non facile/ inueniuntur: & a Rabbinis tamen Hebreorum, in scri-/ptis suis passim usurpantur: origo, etymon, et/uerus usus docte ostenditur & explicatur,/ per PAULUM FAGIUM, in gratiam/ studiosorum linguae San-/ctae latinitate do-/natum./ Rationem Tituli inuenies in Praefatione authoris./ Impressum ISNAE in Algauia, Anno/ M.D.XXXXI./

[4]Pp. 4, 26, 71, 75, 143. Schindler's lexicon was first published in 1612.

which Weemse presents us. The chief importance of his references to such works is that they afford the best possible evidence that such works were being used in England during the first quarter of the seventeenth century. Weemse quoted nearly every rabbinical reference he used. That is, by 1623, considerable quantities of rabbinical writings were sufficiently available for the purposes of copious quotation, although for many of the rabbis so quoted and for some of the other works drawn on, there were no translations in print so early as this.

Besides the Hebrew and Aramaic lexicons and grammars, and Buxtorf's rabbinical Bible that have been discussed and described at some length in this chapter, there are other rabbinical works and materials that may be suggested in connection with Milton. Many of these are mentioned by Weemse, and thus known to have been available in England by the beginning of Milton's career at the University. I shall mention a few of these here only as possibilities so far as Milton is concerned, and shall not at this time examine them in that connection, or as sources for him. I mention them here as materials suggested for investigation rather than as those which my work is now about to employ.

Thus, another group of rabbinical literature was available to Milton of the same nature as the Buxtorf Bible. This group was made up of separate editions of the various books of the Old Testament, usually with the text of the original with Latin translation and with the best known rabbinical commentaries upon the particular book selected, with a translation of this commentary or with the original and translation. Such works for selected books of the Old Testament were very popular products of some of the presses of the sixteenth century. The amount of commentary thus translated was not large, but such works

called attention to rabbinical commentaries in general.
Milton has mentioned a number of those printer-editors,
who produced such works, conspicuously among them,
Schickard, Fagius, and Buxtorf. The works these editors
produced were of a wide variety, but most of them were
within the field of Hebrew studies, and, together with
Bomberg and other Italian printers, they were largely
responsible for the dissemination among sixteenth and
seventeenth century Christians of suitable text-materials
for the study of the Semitic Biblical tongues. Their importance in making available rabbinical glosses on Scripture, whether in the original or translation, was very great.

I have elsewhere called attention to Paul Fagius, whose
work Milton knew very well.[1] It is unnecessary here to
review his life, but several of his works are of importance
in connection with Milton's rabbinical readings. Fagius
published an edition of Levita's *Thisbites*, a kind of dictionary, already mentioned, with Latin translation; a
Latin version of the *Pirke Aboth;* many scriptural commentaries with liberal portions, in Latin translation, from
the rabbis; a Latin translation of Kimchi's commentary

---

[1] A complete list of Fagius's works may be found in Cooper's *Athenae Cantabri-
gienses*, (Cambridge, 1858, 3 vols.), vol. I pp. 96 f., 538, and vol. III pp. 85. The
more important for our purposes here are

*Sententiae vere elegantes, piae, mireque, cum ad linguam discendam tum animum
pietate excolendum utiles, veterum sapientum Hebraeorum, quas* פרקי אבות *id est
Capitula, aut si mavis, Apophtegmata Patrum nominant: in Latinum versae,
scholiisq. illustratae.* Isne, 1541.

Opusculum Hebraicum Thisbites inscriptum ab Elia Levita. Isne, 1541.

*Versio Lat. Praefationis Hebraicae Eliae Levitae Germani in Lexicon suum
Chaldaicum.* Isne, 1541.

Exegesis sive expositio dictionum Hebraicarum literalis in quatuor capita Geneseos.
Isne, 1542.

Precationes Hebraicae ex libello Hebraico excerptae, cui nomen, Liber Fidei, Heb.
et Lat. Isne, 1542.

*Targum, hoc est, Paraphrasis Onkeli Chaldaica in Sacra Biblia, ex Chaldaeo in
Latinum fidelissime versa.* Strasburg, 1546.

*Commentarium Hebraicum R. David Kimchi in 10 primos Psalmos Davidicos cum
versione Latina,* n. d.

on the first ten Psalms; a translation of the Onkelos Targum, with additional rabbinical commentaries; and many expository works drawing heavily on the rabbis. These works of Fagius are all rare, and difficult, but not impossible, to secure. Each needs to be examined in connection with Milton. Fagius's works are especially important for the light they throw upon the range of Milton's readings in the available rabbinical literature of the time.

Milton has also mentioned another editor of Jewish works under the name, difficult to identify, of *Sichardus*. This was, as an entry in the *Commonplace Book* makes certain, William Schickard (1592-1635) of Tübingen. Like Fagius, he was responsible for the publication of a number of Jewish and rabbinical works done into Latin. In addition to these, Schickard published a number of treatises on various Jewish or Biblical subjects, and it was to one of these, the *Jus regium hebraeorum*, that Milton referred in the *pro populo defensio*.[1] This work was a perfect mine of information drawn from the rabbis concerning the Hebrew and Jewish kings. Schickard wrote several other works that drew much from the rabbis, but which need not be considered here. He is, however, an important writer to connect with Milton, especially as an indication of Milton's acquaintance with the work of some of the best Continental Semitic scholars of the time.

The other works of the elder Buxtorf, already mentioned in connection with the *Biblia Rabbinica*, should also be mentioned here, for this great Swiss editor and author of works by and about the Jews, prepared many such works

[1] The first edition of this book appeared at Strasburg in 1625. I have before me an edition of 1674, published at Leipzig with a title-page reading as follows: Wilhelmi Schickardi/ Hebr. Ling. in Academia Tubingensi/ quodam Professoris,/ מִשְׁפַּט הַמֶּלֶךְ/ JUS REGIUM/ HEBRAEORUM,/ E tenebris Rabbinicis erutum, &/ luci donatum./ Cum/ ANIMADVERSIONIBUS & NOTIS/ JO. BENEDICTI CARPZOVI,/ Hebr. Ling. in Academia Lipsiensi/ Professoris./ Lipsiae,/ M. DC. LXXIV.

for publication. Many of these works can definitely be connected with Milton, directly or by implication.

In addition to such works as those just mentioned, there is a large number of other Jewish works, in print long before Milton's time and with which he may have been familiar, that need to be considered in connection with him. Much has been said recently of his connection with and use of the *Zohar*. There is no need to consider here his connection with this work, except to point out that the *Zohar* belongs with a whole library of Jewish works in print and accessible to the seventeenth century scholar who could read them. The chief difficulty in considering such works in connection with Milton is to make a definite connection between him and them. A large number of such works, all of which contain material which would have been of great interest to him in connection with *Paradise Lost*, might be cited. And he *may* have read any or all of them. But the burden of proof for such reading rests squarely upon the investigator who suggests such connection. It would be fruitless here even to suggest or mention the titles of such Jewish works. A much greater knowledge of Milton's rabbinical readings is needed before a definitive statement can be made about what he knew and what he did not know in the whole realm of rabbinical literature. But it will never be possible, I am sure, merely on the basis of his ability to read rabbinical Hebrew, to assume that he therefore read any rabbinical work in which occurs an idea or a statement similar to one he has somewhere used.

My work from this point on will consist almost wholly of the investigation of his use of rabbinical commentary on Scripture. This investigation will proceed entirely on the firm basis of definite connection of such material with Milton. In order to keep within reasonable bounds, even such works as those just mentioned, works by Fagius,

Schickard, and Buxtorf, other than the *Biblia Rabbinica*, will be excluded from consideration. This will be done solely in order to keep the present work pointed directly at a single goal, and to allow it to be as exhaustive as possible with respect to the material it presents. To permit discussion of Milton's use of Jewish works other than Biblical commentaries to intrude here, would make this study assume too great a bulk.

But undoubtedly each of the editors and authors mentioned produced works that should be examined in connection with Milton. Then, and not until then, many Jewish works may perhaps be definitely connected with him that now are unknown or uncertain in that connection. The possibilities of the subject are ultimately perhaps very great; but at first, only careful examination of works actually known to have been used by Milton will suffice. The examination of these may or may not indicate the use by him of other works, not at present known to have been used by him; that is, the examination itself must determine this point.

We have now in this chapter investigated certain Hebrew and rabbinical lexicons, and the nature of the Buxtorf Bible in order to provide a more adequate idea of the range of the rabbinical material to be found therein. We have found that some of the lexicons contain material of the kind that would have been most interesting to Milton for his purposes in *Paradise Lost*. We have also found that this Buxtorf's Bible contains a wealth of commentary material, all of which would have been accessible to Milton in this one Bible. We have examined this commentary, noted its authors and the characteristics of their work. This rabbinical Bible, on the testimony of Weemse, is known to have been in England at least by 1623, or shortly before Milton went to Cambridge. His use of it, based on its nature and his own rabbinical citations, is uncertain solely because if he has cited an earlier edition of the rabbinical Bible it would be impossible from his citations to distinguish it from the Buxtorf edition. Because Buxtorf's other books, as he was a Gentile scholar, were so well known throughout Europe, the uncertainty connected with Milton's use of this edition of the rabbinical Bible is so minimized that I am ready to say that he almost certainly used it.

CHAPTER III

RABBINICAL COMMENTARIES ON CREATION

Turning our attention to the possible passages in the rabbis from which Milton might have drawn ideas or other material, apparently, as we face the immense quantity of rabbinical commentary in Buxtorf, the only remaining question before us is where to begin. As the commentaries themselves begin with Genesis, and as the opening chapters of Genesis deal with Creation, one naturally thinks at once of the attention Milton in *Paradise Lost* devoted to his attempt to depict the whole process of Creation. And no fitter beginning of an attempt to evaluate Milton's indebtedness to the rabbis could suggest itself than examining the influence of the rabbinical commentaries attached to the Biblical story of Creation upon Milton's account of the beginning of all things.

In his whole treatment of Creation, Milton has very strictly observed the limitations imposed by the account contained in the first and second chapters of Genesis. He has, however, taken frequent advantage of such ambiguities and actual discrepancies as occur in the two distinctly different accounts in those first two chapters. Thus, he took advantage of the ambiguity of the first chapter as to the precise nature of the cosmos therein created, and depicted two distinct phases of Creation in *Paradise Lost*.

If we agree to set aside for the moment the account of the Temptation and the Fall of Man, the most tremendous event set forth in *Paradise Lost* is the Creation of the Visible Universe. Like other events of importance in the poem, the approach to the full account of Creation is carefully arranged, and the actual account itself comes as an anticipated climax. The reader is fully prepared for it, and the account proceeds much more effectively because of this preparation. But the certainty of securing such an anticipated result is the certainty of genius. Thus, the events related in connection with the Warfare in Heaven and the Fall of the Rebel Angels form a background and preparation for the grandeur of the process of Creation.

The atmosphere of awesome sublimity that the genius of Milton succeeded in securing throughout his account of the Act of Creation is also due partly to the indirect directness with which he presented it. The first account of Creation in the poem is a greatly abbreviated anticipation of the second, a forerunner of the stupendous treatment of it that is to come. The first account appears at the end of Book III, when Uriel, the Guardian Angel of the Sun, briefly sketches for Satan's benefit the Creation of the Universe. The presentation is indirect, because set forth in the speech of the Angel. It is also direct, because it represents the account of an eyewitness, and it anticipates the full-length account that follows it some books later. Only a supernatural Being could have done justice to the subject. Only through Uriel, Angel of the Sun, and later through Raphael, God's messenger to Adam, could any account of Creation have been presented. The first, the account by Uriel, prepares for the more detailed relation by Raphael to Adam. Of the aesthetic aspects of this second and complete account of Creation, the possibilities for explanations and appreciations are limitless. But let us look at its whole structure for a moment.

The events related by Raphael in connection with Creation fall quite obviously into two distinct categories. One set of events of which he speaks is clearly concerned with the account of the Creation of the whole Visible Universe. Another set is concerned equally clearly with an account of the Creation of this Earth and its manifold forms of life. For these two distinctly different aspects of Creation, Milton, perforce, drew on different sources. These sources were primarily Biblical; but the two aspects of Creation which are so clearly discernible in Raphael's account were drawn from different parts of the Bible.

But let us look for a moment at the first part of Raphael's account that concerned the Creation of the Cosmos, the whole Universe of which this Earth is but an infinitesimal part.

Milton's general conception of the Creation of the Cosmos is one that had long been known to European thought. He conceived of the act of Creation as an *ordering* of the elements, already existent in Chaos, not the *creating* of those elements themselves. In *Paradise Lost*, he had much to say about the existence prior to Creation of the elements from which the Universe, the Cosmos, or, at least as part of the poem implies, the whole Ptolemaic System, was made. And in the *de doctrina*, he elaborately refuted the idea of *creatio ex nihilo*, becoming as scholastic in his argument as any scholastic he or any other humanist ever condemned.

Now I would by no means suggest that Milton first encountered in rabbinical commentaries to Scripture the idea of Creation as an ordering of already existent but utterly chaotic elements. The indestructibility of matter was taught by the ancient Greeks, by the Ionian school, by Plato, by Aristotle, and by many of the medieval philosophers. But by these thinkers, and, indeed, by Milton, the eternity of matter was asserted or assumed merely to aid them in their explanations of the origins of the Universe. This theory was readily assimilated by the rabbis. It was, obviously, not difficult for medieval Jewish philosophers to reconcile such a theory with Scripture, and the possibilities permitted by the use of figurative expressions

in connection with it opened to them a wide field of speculation.

It is, therefore, not at all surprising to find in Ibn Ezra's
commentary to the first chapter of Genesis that the nature
of Creation is discussed from precisely the same point of
view from which Milton has discussed it, both in *Paradise
Lost* and in the *de doctrina*.   Moreover, it is especially
interesting to find that Ibn Ezra had, several centuries
before the poet, resorted to exactly the same argument
later used by Milton in trying to show that the Hebrew
verb ברא *he created* did not mean to 'cause to come into
existence out of nothing.'   Milton has said of this verb:

Materia autem prima quae fuerit, varie disputatur.   Moderni
plerique volunt ex nihilo emerisse omnia; unde et ipsorum credo
sententia orta est.   Primum autem constat, neque Hebraeo verbo
ברא, neque Graeco κτίζειν, neque Latino *creare*, idem quod ex
nihilo facere significari: immo vero unumquodque horum idem
quod ex materia facere passim significat.   Gen. 1:21, 27.   *creavit
Deus—quae abunde progenuerunt aquae, marem et foeminam creavit
eos.*   Isa. 54:16.   *creavi fabrum, creavi interfectorem.*   Qui dicit ergo,
creare est ex nihilo producere, neque exemplo probat principium
quod aiunt dialectici.   Nam et scripturae quae afferuntur loca
receptam hanc sententiam nullo modo confirmant, sed contrarium
potius innuunt, nempe non ex nihilo facta esse omnia.   2 Cor. 4:6.
Deus qui dixit ut e tenebris lux splendesceret.   At has tenebras nequa-
quam fuisse nihil patet ex Isa. 45:7.   *me Jehovam &c. formantem
lucem et creantem tenebras.*   Si tenebrae sunt nihil, Deus certe cre-
ando tenebras creavit nihil, id est, creavit et non creavit, quae con-
tradicentia sunt.[1]

Ibn Ezra's discussion of the nature of Creation, employing
the same explanation of the verb ברא *he created* used by
Milton, with precisely the same reference to the creation
of darkness and what was meant by the use of that phrase
in the seventh verse of the forty-fifth chapter of Isaiah,

[1]*de doctrina*, p. 128.

is to be found in the rabbi's commentary to the first chapter of Genesis. He there said:

ברא' רובי המפרשים אמרו שהבריאה להוציא יש מאין וכן אם בריאה יברא ה' והנה שכחו ויברא אל' את התנינים ושלש בפסוק אחד ויברא אל' את האדם וברא חשך שהוא הפך האור שהוא יש ווה דקדוק המלה ברא לשני טעמים זה האחד והשני לא ברה אתם לחם ווה השני אל"ף תחת ה"א... וטעמו לגוור ולשום גבול נגור והמשכיל יבין

Most of the commentators said that ברא meant to 'produce something out of nothing,' (as in Numbers 16:30); but they forget (Gen. 1:21 and 27 where it is distinctly stated that the act expressed by the verb ברא was a formation from water and earth respectively), or (Isaiah 45:7) where darkness is the object of the verb ברא; darkness is nothing but the absence of light. The following is the explanation of the verb ברא, (which has two meanings. One is as it is used here, and the other as in 2 Sam. 12:17 where ברא means ברה *to eat . . .*) It also means *to cut, to decree,* to set a limit by cutting off a portion, and the wise will understand it.

In his commentary to the first chapter of Ecclesiastes, the rabbi further explained his conception of Creation as an arrangement of pre-existent elements. There he said:

כל נמצא תחת השמש מורכב מארבעה מוסדים מהם יצאו ואליהם ישובו והם האש והרוח הנה... והמים והארץ וגו'... ואחר שהודיע הארבעה השרשים שהם עומדים על מתכונתם ואם תקרה להם תנועה בסוף ישובו כשהיו וגו'

Everything under the sun is composed of four elements, from which they (everything) came forth, unto which they (everything) return, namely, fire, air, water, and earth . . . And after having shown that the four elements are stationary (immutable and immovable), and that in case of being set in motion they return to where they have been before . . .

Milton's conception of the nature of Creation is very similar to this. In *Paradise Lost*, he has treated with considerable detail the whole idea of how Creation proceeded, and has especially emphasized the pre-existence of the elements. Between Heaven and Hell, as he depicted them in the poem, lies 'a dark, illimitable ocean, without bound, without dimension.' Milton's first description of this Chaos is as it appeared to Satan, Sin, and Death after Sin had unlocked and opened the doors of Hell. The fiendish trio gazed forth, and

> Before thir eyes in sudden view appear
> The secrets of the hoarie deep, a dark
> Illimitable Ocean without bound,
> Without dimension, where length, breadth, and highth,
> And time and place are lost; where eldest Night
> And *Chaos*, Ancestors of Nature, hold
> Eternal *Anarchie*, amidst the noise
> Of endless Warrs, and by confusion stand.
> For hot, cold, moist, and dry, four Champions fierce
> Strive here for Maisterie, and to Battel bring
> Thir embryon Atoms; they around the flag
> Of each his Faction . . .
> . . . To whom these most adhere,
> He rules a moment; *Chaos* Umpire sits,
> And by decision more imbroiles the fray
> By which he Reigns: next him high Arbiter
> *Chance* governs all. Into this wilde Abyss,
> The Womb of nature and perhaps her Grave,
> Of neither Sea, nor Shore, nor Air, nor Fire,
> But all these in thir pregnant causes mixt
> Confus'dly, and which thus must ever fight,
> Unless th' Almighty Maker them ordain
> His dark materials to create more Worlds,
> —Book II:890-916.[1]

Satan begins his journey through this fearful scene, and eventually meets Chaos personified, the 'umpire' of the wild turmoil throughout his realm. Chaos tells him that all that has been created so far has been wrested from his domain:

> 'I upon my Frontieres here
> Keep residence; if all I can will serve,
> That little which is left so to defend,

[1]Throughout, my quotations from *Paradise Lost* are taken from the second edition of 1674 [B.M. 1076. f. 20].

Encroacht on still through our intestine broiles
Weakning the Scepter of old *Night:* first Hell
Your dungeon stretching far and wide beneath;
Now lately Heaven and Earth, another World
Hung ore my Realm, link'd in a golden Chain
To that side Heav'n from whence your Legions fell:'
—*ibid.* 998-1006.

Satan then continues on his way through the terrible
wilderness of Chaos,

Into the wilde expanse, and through the shock
Of fighting Elements, on all sides round
Environ'd,   —*ibid.* 1014-1016.

Later, reaching the Sun, Satan hears of the Creation from
Uriel, who describes the effect of it upon the disorder of
Chaos,

'I saw when at his Word the formless Mass,
This worlds material mould, came to a heap:
Confusion heard his voice, and wilde uproar
Stood rul'd, stood vast infinitude confined;
Till at his second bidding darkness fled,
Light shon, and order from disorder sprung:
Swift to thir several Quarters hasted then
The cumbrous Elements, Earth, Flood, Aire, Fire,'
—Book III:708-715.

The same sight which greeted Satan from the mouth of
Hell had previously confronted Christ and his cohorts
when they set out upon their mission of Creation, as
Raphael described this to Adam later in the poem:

'On heav'nly ground they stood, and from the shore
They view'd the vast immeasurable Abyss
Outrageous as a Sea, dark, wasteful, wilde,
Up from the bottom turn'd by furious windes
And surging waves, as Mountains to assault
Heav'ns highth, and with the Center mix the Pole.'
—Book VII:210-215.

I wish here merely to point out the similarity between the elaborated conception of Creation as Milton has poetically embroidered it in the poem, and the basic conception of Creation set forth in the commentary of Ibn Ezra. To say that Milton secured his whole idea of Creation from Ibn Ezra would be going too far, I think. But it is worthy of note that in his denial of the theory of *creatio ex nihilo*, in his conception of the existence of the elements before Creation, and in the selection of the four elements, earth, air, fire, and water, Milton has employed precisely the same basic ideas of Creation as those set forth by Ibn Ezra. It is remarkable that he is in complete agreement with the rabbi on all of them. There is a strong suggestion that Milton drew on or at least was familiar with the rabbi's discussion of Creation in Milton's use of the identical argument over the meaning of the Hebrew word ברא *he created* on which the rabbi also based his chief refutation of the *creatio ex nihilo* theory.[1]

I have, however, discussed the similarity between the ideas of Milton and of Ibn Ezra on the nature of Creation

---

[1] I am well aware of the extreme improbability of the *fact* of Ibn Ezra's denial of the theory of *creatio ex nihilo* which is so attractive to the orthodox Jew. But the question here is, What did seventeenth century Gentile scholarship believe that Ibn Ezra taught? It seems clear to me that Gentiles generally, and many Jews have held that in the recension from which I have quoted, Ibn Ezra did deny the theory of *creatio ex nihilo*. Even Friedländer's elaborate explanation of what Ibn Ezra actually meant in this passage (cf. his *Essays on the Writings of Ibn Ezra*, London, 1877, pp. 4 ff.) points out the frequent misunderstanding of this passage. Other recensions of Ibn Ezra's commentary are necessary to understand what he really meant, and while they make it clear that God originally created from nothing, it is extremely doubtful that Milton knew these recensions. I should venture so far as to say that he certainly did not know them, although this is only an opinion. This point is of great importance in clarifying the whole question of Milton's rabbinical readings. Can we infer that he knew rabbinical works that are known to exist, but which cannot be in any way connected with him? Certainly we should scarcely think of assuming his knowledge of English or Latin works that are in no way connected with him except through possible parallels. Why should we be any more ready to admit his use of works requiring much more explanation of the bare possibility of his having used them?

chiefly in order to get before us here some basic aspects of
the process of Creation as set forth in *Paradise Lost*. For
the fundamental process of Creation as set forth therein,
Milton did not depend entirely upon the material found in
the opening chapters of Genesis. We can be certain of the
other portions of Scripture that he used in his account of
Creation, for he himself listed in the *de doctrina* those
Biblical passages concerned with Creation. He pointed
out that Creation was dealt with in the Old Testament in
other places than in the first and second chapters of Genesis. He said, 'Mundi ejusque singularum partium creatio
narratur Gen. 1. Describitur Job .26:7. &c et 38. et passim
in psalmis et prophetis. Psal. 33:6, 9. et 104:5. Prov. 8:26
&c. Amos. 4:13.'[1] These scriptural passages sometimes
describe the Creation of the Visible Universe and sometimes the Creation of this Earth. This, too, was Milton's
method of dealing with Creation in *Paradise Lost*. That
is, it is possible to examine separately his accounts of the
Creation of the Visible Universe and of the Creation of
this Earth and its forms of life. We shall now turn to the
examination of the first of these, or to the Creation of the
Visible Universe.

Milton's principal account of the Creation of the Universe is contained in Book VII of *Paradise Lost*. After
Raphael had recounted to Adam the story of the Revolt of
Satan and the resulting Warfare in Heaven, followed by
the Fall of the Rebel Angels, Adam asked him to tell of
Creation. Book VII opens with an invocation of a muse
extremely difficult fully to identify. But she is clearly
the Spirit of Creation:

> Descend from Heav'n *Urania*, by that name
> If rightly thou art call'd, whose Voice divine
> Following, above th' *Olympian* hill I soare,

[1] *de doctrina*, p. 134.

> Above the flight of *Pegasean* wing.
> The meaning, not the Name I call: for thou
> Nor of the Muses nine, nor on the top
> Of old *Olympus* dwell'st, but Heav'nlie-borne,
> Before the Hills appeerd, or Fountain flow'd,
> Thou with Eternal Wisdom didst converse,
> Wisdom thy Sister, and with her didst play
> In presence of th' Almightie Father, pleas'd
> With thy Celestial Song.
>
> —Book VII: 1-12.

Then follows the express statement that the poet now intends to turn to the 'half' that yet 'remaines unsung,' (line 21) of

> how this World
> Of Heav'n and Earth conspicuous first began,
> When, and whereof created,
> —*ibid*. 62-64.

The poetic task here projected is the explanation of the original and nature of the contents of that

> narrower bound
> Within the visible Diurnal Spheare;
> —*ibid*. 21-22.

The poet is about to concern himself with Creation, its origin and nature, with the laying out and establishment of the Universe.

Raphael begins his Angelic account of all this by pointing out that after the complete rout of the Rebel Angels and their Fall, God received his Son returned in triumph. He then informed the Son that He was about to create 'another world,' and furthermore that the Son himself will be the Agent by means of which this Creation will be accomplished.

Then begins the relation, in strict accordance with the treatment in the *de doctrina*, of the Act of Creation of the

Visible Universe.   This account of Creation is a little more indirect than that in Book III, but is of the same general nature, and is again direct discourse.[1]   The Act itself is then described:

> 'Mean while the Son
> On his great Expedition now appeer'd,
> Girt with Omnipotence, with Radiance crown'd
> Of Majestie Divine, Sapience and Love
> Immense, and all his Father in him shon.
> About his Chariot numberless were pour'd
> Cherub and Seraph, Potentates and Thrones,
> And Vertues, winged Spirits, and Chariots wing'd,
> From the Armoury of God, where stand of old
> Myriads between two brazen Mountains lodg'd
> Against a solemn day, harnest at hand,
> Celestial Equipage; and now came forth
> Spontaneous, for within them Spirit livd,
> Attendant on thir Lord: Heav'n op'nd wide
> Her ever during Gates, Harmonious sound
> On golden Hinges moving, to let forth
> The King of Glorie in his powerful Word
> And Spirit coming to create new Worlds.
> On heav'nly ground they stood, and from the shore
> They view'd the vast immeasurable Abyss
> Outrageous as a Sea, dark, wasteful, wilde,
> Up from the bottom turn'd by furious windes
> And surging waves, as Mountains to assault
> Heav'ns highth, and with the Center mix the Pole.
> "Silence, ye troubl'd waves, and, thou Deep, peace,"
> Said then th' Omnific Word, "your discord end:"
>   Nor staid, but on the Wings of Cherubim
> Uplifted, in Paternal Glorie rode
> Far into *Chaos*, and the World unborn;
> For *Chaos* heard his voice: him all his Traine
> Follow'd in bright procession to behold
> Creation, and the wonders of his might.

[1]Raphael, who tells Adam of Creation, was himself absent while it took place, see Bk. VIII:228 ff.

Then staid the fervid Wheeles, and in his hand
He took the golden Compasses, prepar'd
In Gods Eternal store, to circumscribe
This Universe, and all created things:
One foot he center'd, and the other turn'd
Round through the vast profunditie obscure,
And said, "thus farr extend, thus farr thy bounds,
This be thy just Circumference, O World."
Thus God the Heav'n created, thus the Earth,
Matter unform'd and void: Darkness profound
Cover'd th' Abyss: but on the watrie calme
His brooding wings the Spirit of God outspred,
And vital vertue infus'd, and vital warmth
Throughout the fluid Mass, but downward purg'd
The black tartareous cold Infernal dregs
Adverse to life: then founded, then conglob'd
Like things to like, the rest to several place
Disparted, and between spun out the Air,
And Earth self ballanc't on her Center hung.'
                              —Book VII:192-242.

The Universe has now been created; the remainder of the process is only concerned with details.

Milton's basic sources for this account of Creation have often been noted. The account of the ride into Chaos and the subsequent circumscribing of that portion of it which was to become the Visible Universe are clearly from some other part of the Old Testament than Genesis. And the account of the action of the Spirit of God in spreading its mighty wings over the Abyss is just as clearly a poetic rendering of the idea contained in the second verse of the first chapter of Genesis.

Most commentators have noted that lines one hundred ninety-two to two hundred thirty-one are based upon material found in the eighth chapter of Proverbs. Milton has, moreover, suggested the same Biblical passage earlier in Book VII in the address to the Muse of lines one to twelve.

As has been often noted, these lines also indicate clearly enough that Milton had Proverbs in mind:

> Heav'nlie borne,
> Before the Hills appeerd or Fountain flow'd,
> Thou with Eternal wisdom didst converse,
> Wisdom thy Sister, and with her didst play
> In presence of th' Almightie Father, pleas'd
> With thy Celestial Song.
> —VII:7-12.

This, too, is unmistakably from the eighth chapter of Proverbs, not from Genesis. Both invocation and the first part of Milton's account of Creation, then, rest squarely upon the material found in this chapter of Proverbs. The passage held for Milton a curious fascination. He had devoted considerable attention to it as early as the decade of the 1640's, and had used the same idea in the *Tetrachordon*.[1] The passage is likewise one of the most prominent among those he mentioned as of greatest importance among the Biblical accounts of Creation. The Biblical reading is as follows:

> Jehovah possessed me in the beginning of his way,
> Before his works of old.
> I was set up from everlasting, from the beginning,
> Before the earth was.
> When there were no depths, I was brought forth;
> When there were no fountains abounding with water.
> Before the mountains were settled,
> Before the hills I was brought forth;
> While as yet he had not made the earth, nor the fields,
> Nor the beginning of the dust of the world.
> When he established the heavens, I was there:
> When he set a circle upon the face of the deep,
> When he made firm the skies above,
> When the fountains of the deep became strong,

[1] Vol. IV:155.

> When he gave to the sea its bound,
> That the waters should not transgress his commandment,
> When he marked out the foundations of the earth,
> Then I was by him, as a master workman;
> And I was daily his delight,
> Rejoicing always before him,
>   —(American Revised Version) Proverbs 8:22-30.

Milton's interest in the process of Creation undoubtedly led him to resort to this account in Proverbs for much of the basic material in his principal account of the Creation of the Visible Universe. The most superficial comparison of Milton's account, already quoted, and this account in Proverbs reveals the close connection between the two. Milton's task as a poet has been to weave into his poem the basic elements encountered in Proverbs, and he has quite obviously done this.

But the similarity between the two passages is not complete, nor are they absolutely identical in so far as their materials are concerned. The differences which exist between the two accounts consist, however, very largely of differences of detail. Milton has apparently used the material that the Proverbs passage afforded him and then has drawn on his imagination or on some other source for embellishment of that material. His changes are, however, all rather minute, and because of this, he presumably had some reason for making them. Were they more basic than they are, we might suspect him of having primarily used his imagination to have effected them. But because of their very slight and yet noticeable nature, it is worth while to ask, or at least to look for, reasons for the changes.

One of the most obvious sources of the changes Milton has made from the Biblical text is the rabbinical commentary to the Proverbs text in Buxtorf's Bible. Because of Milton's often manifested interest in these verses, it would have been natural for him to have read the rabbinical commentaries accompanying the text in his Buxtorf Bible. These may at least be examined for discussions of the text which might have suggested such changes as appear in Milton's verse. If they possess any peculiar treatments of detail which are to be found also in Milton's treatment, certainly his use of such commentaries on this passage in Proverbs will almost inevitably be established.

Let us, therefore, turn to the commentaries found in Buxtorf on Proverbs and see what they have to offer on the passage in question. There are three different commentaries, each of which has something to say about the verses in which we are interested. One of these commentaries is that of Ben Gerson, the rabbi mentioned by Milton in the *Doctrine and Discipline of Divorce*, another is Ibn Ezra's, the rabbi so often cited in Tremellius's notes, and the third belongs to Rashi. All three commentaries on this passage are interesting and of considerable value to the Milton student. Because these are the original and identical texts that would have been read by Milton, I present the Hebrew itself, to which I append a literal translation.

The first commentary to be presented will be that by Ben Gerson. This rabbi's comments follow:

יי' קני ראשית דרכו קדם מפעליו מאו בבריאת העולם רוצה לומר שבראשית הדברים
שקנה או ועשה קנה הדבר אשר היה חדושו בבינה ותבונת השם ית' בו והם הגרמים
השמימיים אבל תדע' כי הש"י לא חסר להיות עמו זאת התבונה והחכמה אשר נברא
בה העולם כמו שבארנו בהם מספר מלחמות יי' ושם התרנו הספקות הנופלות בוא
והנה מעת היות הזמן קני קדם מפעליו קדם מפעליו האחרים: מעולם נסכתי מראש' מעת היות
עולם נתנה לי הגבורה והשררה והגדולה' מקדמי ארץ בראשית מה שנברא בארץ:
באין תהומות חוללתי' קודם היות התהומות נבראתי כי השמים קודמים במעלה
ובמציאות על התהומות קודם שיהיו שם מעינות ונהרות רבות מהמים: בטרם' שהטבעו
ההרים על מכונם ולפני שימצאו גבעות חוללתי: עד לא עשה' הש"י ארץ וחוצות

הנכבד שבעפרות תבל והגבוה מהם והוא מקום הנגלה מן הארץ ובו ג"כ ארץ וחוצות
והנה כפל העניּן במלות שונות: בהכינו בעת שהכין השם ית' השמים להיות במספר
ובתכונו ובמרחק ובגודל שהם בו והכוכבים אשר בהם כדי שייאות להמצא מהם אלו
התנועות אשר בו העולם השפל שם הייתי כי בתבונה כונן הש"י השמים כמו שקדם
כאשר חקק הש"י מחוגה על פני תהום שהוא כדור הארץ כמו שביארנו בפרשת בראשית
והוא כמו מרכז לגרם השמיּמיי ולפי המחוג' ההיא המציא השמים סביבה במשכו רגלי
המחוגה ההיא זה מזה בגלגל גלגל: באמצו שחקים ממעל' כאשר אמץ שחקים ממעל
ונתן להם חוזק וקיום עד שהם חזקים כראי מוצק וזה היה אפשר כאשר רצה הש"י
שיקבל איכות דומה ומתיחסם לקושי כאמרם לחים היו השמים ביום ראשון בשני
נקרשו' בעזוו עינו' תהום ר"ל כאשר נתן הש"י עוז וקושי למה שהיה מהחומר הראשון
אצל עינות תהו' והוא כדור הארץ כי זה כולו נעשה בתבונה וזה כי לולי עוז הארץ
וקיומה לא היה בכאן דרך לתנוע' הגלגלים: בשומו לים חקו' כאשר שם השם ית'
לים חוקו שם הייתי וזה היה כשגזר שיקוו המים מתחת השמים אל מקום אחד ותראה
היבשה' ומים לא יעברו פיו בדרך שישאר זה המקום שרצה שיהיה נגלה תמיד כאשר
חקק מוסדי ארץ והוא החלק הנגלה מהארץ שהוא היסוד למה שיתהוה בה מהצמחים
והב"ח: ואהיה' אצל השם ית' אמון ומגדל ומנהיג הדברים המיוחסים לבינה ובזה אהיה
לו שעשועים יום יום כי תמיד הש"י מתענג ומשתעשע בהשיגו עצמו אשר בזה תושג
לו זאת התבונה ובכל עת משמחת אני לפניו והוא עצמותו והשגתו ובמה שאפשר
בדברים העלולים מהתבונה אשר אצל הש"י:

Ben Gerson on Proverbs 8:22-30

22. *God possessed me in the beginning of his way, before his works
of old*—in the creation of the world. Meaning to say that in
the beginning of the things which he created then and made,
he possessed the word (Wisdom), which was its peculiarity.
The Wisdom and understanding of the Holy One blessed be
He were in it. And they (Wisdom and Understanding) were
the strength of the heavens. Indeed, you must remember that
God did not fail to have with him this Wisdom and this Understanding, by means of which the world was created, as we have
set forth. . . . . . Up to the time that was the time (of creation) he possessed me before his other works.

23. *From eternity I was set up, from the beginning*. From eternity,
strength, and authority, and greatness were given to me.
before the earth was—in the beginning of whatever was created
in the earth.

24. *When there were no depths, I was brought forth.* Before there were depths, I was created; just as the heavens were older in degree and in existence than the depths so before there were fountains and streams flowing with water.

25. *When not yet*—the mountains were settled in their arrangement, and before the hills were derived, I was brought forth.

26. *While not yet had he made*—God, the earth or the abounding fields, as the dust of the world and the high place. This was the hidden principle disclosed in the earth, and in it also [were] the earth and the fields. And this is a repetition of the sense in different words.

27. *When he prepared*—at the time the Holy One blessed be He prepared the heavens to be, in number, in arrangement, in extent, and in greatness, all of which are in them. And now it was fitting to derive from the morning stars, which were in them (the Heavens) the movements which were to be in the lower world. I was there, for God established the heavens according to plan, as of old when he drew a circle with a compass upon the faces of the abyss, which (the circle) became the sphere of the earth. This is explained in the first portion of Genesis. And this was as if there were a pivotal point for dividing the heavens by means of the compass. This (the marking off of the heavens) came about as [the compass] turned around.

28. *When he made firm the skies above*—referring to the earth with the skies above. And he gave them (the skies) support and existence so that they became as a thing well established. And this was possible (done) since God desired that it (they) receive the quality of its (their) form. And they were solidly joined in stiffness, as it is said (Palestinian Talmud) 'moist were the heavens on the first day; on the second they became solid.' *When the fountains of the abyss became strong.* This means when God gave strength and stiffness to what had been primeval matter near the fountains of the abyss. And this (the sky) became the sphere of the earth. This was all made according to plan, and it was done so for if not, there would have been no way for the movements of the spheres to have taken place.

29. *When he set for the sea its bound.* As when the Holy One blessed be He set to the sea its limit, I was there. And this was as

when he ordained, when he gathered the waters under heaven
to one place. And the dry land was seen, for the waters did not
run over their limits as they had done before. This (Wisdom)
was what was continually uncovered when he decreed the establishment of the earth. And this (Wisdom) was the revealed
gift of the earth, the basis of what was taking place in it in the
way of growths and forms of life.

30. *And I was*—near the Holy One blessed be He, strong and great
and a leader. The words are connected with Wisdom. And in
this I was daily to him a delight, for always God enjoys and
takes delight in realizing himself. This consists in whatever
may be realized by him, which is understanding.
and I always rejoicing before him. And this is his very being
and fulfilment. This applies also to the matters concerned
with Understanding, which is near God.

Before discussing the commentary of Ben Gerson, the commentaries of Ibn Ezra and Rashi should be included here.
That of Ibn Ezra on the same passage follows:

יי' קנני ראשית' זה גם מדברי החכמ' קננו מלשון קונה שמי' ראשית דרכו כלו' ראשי'
כוונתו בבריאה כמו כי הוא ראשית דרכי אל' קדם מפעליו מאז כמו כי הוא ראשית
דרכי אל קדם כמו ראשית והטעם קדימה לעולם קדימת חיוב לא קדימת זמן כי הזמן
מכלל הנבראים כאמרו יי' בחכמה יסד ארץ: מעולם דרך המקרא לסמוך הקדומים
למלת עולם כמו מעולם אל גוי מעולם הוא כלומר קדמון נסכתי נבחרתי כמו נסיכי
סיחון מקדמי ארץ מקדמוני ארץ: באין' חוללתי' עניני עושתי וטעמו ענין התחלה
וקרוב מלשון ואל ישרה תחוללכם: באין' נכבדי מים' טעמו ובאין נכבדי מים והוא
ענין כבדות ורבוי וממנו התכבד כילק התכבד כארבה: בטרם הרים הטבעו' כמו
על מה אדניה הטבעו ושניהם עקרם מלשון טבעו בים סוף והטעם על יסודותם הטבועים
בעמקי המים: עד לא עשה ארץ וחוצות תרגום בטרם עשה כמו אני יי' עשיתי ארץ
וחוצות הם השווקים והטעם על הקרקעית הראויה ליישוב' וראש כטעם קדם וכן
מעולם נסכתי מראש' עפרות תבל כאילו אמר וקודם עפרות תבל הוא היישוב והוא
כסל ענין במלות שונות: בהכינו שמים שם אני' בי"ת בהכינו בחוקו בשומו בעוזו באמצו
כלם נשיאי זמן והכוונה אני הייתי מצואה או לא קדמוני בבריאה וטעם בהכינו כטעם
כונן שמים ובמאמר יהי רקיע' בחוקו חוג בעת שחקק הגלגל על פני תהום שהוא המרכו
וחוג כמו וחוג שמים יתהלך ונקרא הכלי העשוי לעשות בו רושם העגולות מחוגה על
שם החוג הנרשם בו ומלת בחוקו דינו להיות דגוש כי שרשו חקק חקק מן וחקות עליה או

יהיו שני שרשי' בענין אחד חקק וחוק ומזה השרש מי יתן בספר ויוחקו: באמצו שחקו'
ממעל' הוא לשון אומץ וחוזק וטעמו כטעם בהכינו' בעזוז לשון עוז הוא לשון כח וחוזק
והוא מקור ובא שלם והושאל התוקף והחוזק למים כמו ובמי' עוים נתיבה וכן הושאל
לו גם העצמה באומרו את מי הנהר העצומים: בשומו לים וגו' כאמ' אשר שמתי חול
גבול לים חק עולם ולא יעברנהו:

IBN EZRA ON PROVERBS 8:22-29

22. *the Lord possessed me in the beginning.* This also is spoken of
Wisdom (החכמה). *possessed me* (קנני) this verb occurs also in
the phrase קונה שמי' (*possessor of heaven,* Gen. 14:19)
beginning of his way (ראשית דרכו) that is, his first intention of
Creation as in the expression הוא ראשית דרכי אל (*He is the chief
of the ways of God,* Job 40:19). *before his works of old* (מפעליו מא)
קדם) קדם *before* means ראשית *beginning.* קדם *before* always
means *first in importance,* not first in point of time. For time
was among those things which were created, as it is said *In
wisdom the Lord established the earth* (Proverbs 3:19).

23. *from eternity* (מעולם). It is the custom of the text to attach
prefixes to the word עולם *eternity* as in this case מעולם *from
eternity.* That is, from the very first. נסכתי *I was set up,* that
is, נבחרתי *I was chosen,* as נסיכי סיחון *the chosen ones of Sihon,*
(Joshua 13:21).
or ever the earth was, as if it had said מקדמוני ארץ *before the earth
was.*

24. *I was brought forth.* The meaning here is that *I was born,* according to the sense of the expression התחלה *birth,* like the expression ואל שרה תחוללכם *and to Sarah that bare you,* (Isaiah 51:2).
heavy with water. The meaning is not heavy (in weight) but
abundant in the sense of numerous as in *make thyself many as
the locust,* התכבד כילק התכבדי כארבה (Nahum 3:15).

25. *before the mountains were settled,* like על מה אדניה הטבעו *whereupon
were the foundations thereof fastened?* (Job. 38:6.) The roots
of both are the same as that in the expression טבעו בים סוף *are
sunk in the Red Sea.* And the meaning is, 'on the bases that
are sunk in the depths of the sea.'

26. *When he had not yet made the earth or the fields.* This means, as
the Targum reads בטרם *before* he made. Thus *I the Lord I made
the earth and the fields.* . . . . . .

27. *When he prepared the heavens I was there.* The בי"ת (the preposition) in בהכינו *when he prepared* as in בחוקו *when he set* etc.

refers to a definite time. That is, I was in existence at Creation, even before it. בהכינו *when he prepared*, the meaning of the root כון *when he prepared*, or *when he made* is used in connection with the establishing of the heavens. And by command was the רקיע *expanse*.

When he set a circle. At the time when he enscribed the circle or sphere (הגלגל) on the faces of the deep, there was a center. And there was the circle such as וחוג שמים יתהלך *and the vault of the heaven he walketh* (Job 22:14). And the tool or device that made the mark of the drawing on it was called מחוגה *compass* on account of the circle which is traced with it. And the word בחוקו *when he set* ought really to have a dagesh, for its root is חקק as in the phrase וחקות עליה *portray upon it* (Ezekiel 4:1). Or it is possible that in this case there are two roots with the same meaning, חקק and חוק.

28. *When he established the sky above.* This is the same as the expression בהכינו *he established*, and בעזוז *he strengthened*. This is כח *strength* and חוזק *power*. And this רקיע *expanse* is the fountain [of the waters above]. And when this was complete and endowed with strength, then he strengthened the waters, as ובמי' עזים נתיבה *a path in the mighty waters*, (Isaiah 43:16).

29. *When he gave to the sea its bound.* As it is said

שמתי חול גבול לים חק עולם ולא יעברנהו

who have placed the sand for the boundary by a perpetual decree that it cannot pass (Jeremiah 5:22).

The commentary of one other rabbi, Rashi, appears on this Creation passage in Proverbs. Rashi's comment is more succinct than that of the other two rabbis, but otherwise is about the same in its general import. His comment was:

יי' קנני' קודם בריאתי של עולם: נסכתי מראש' לשון נסיכי בני אדם: חוללתי''

נבראתי: בטרם הרים הטבעו' בתוך המים: ארץ וחוצות' ארץ ישראל ישאר ארצו'

וראש עפרות תבל' אדם הראשון: בחקי חוג על פני תהום כשרקע חוג הארץ על

המים: חוק גבול בל יעבור: חוג' לשון הקף' כמו ובמחוגה יתארהו קונפא"ש בלע"ז:

בעזוז' כשהגביר עינות תהום' בחקי מוסדי ארץ בחקותו מלשון חקו' כמו על כפים

חקותיך וכן ומחק הארץ: דבר אחר גזר על ים סוף כשבראו על מנת להקרע לפני

משה: אמון' גדילה אצלו לשון האמונים עלי תולע: יום יום' אלפים שנה:

RASHI'S COMMENTARY ON PROVERBS 8:22-30

22. *the beginning of his way*, before the beginning of the world.

23. *I was set up from everlasting.* The expression is the same as נסיכי אדם *the great ones of man* (Micah 5:4).

24. *I was created*, I was brought forth.

25. *Before the mountains were settled*, in the midst of the waters.

26. *the earth and the fields*, meaning the land of Israel and the other lands.
    the beginning of the dust of the world, refers to the first Adam, man.

27. *when he stretched a circle on the faces of the deep.* As when he stretched the *circle or sphere* חוג of the earth on the waters, a great limit that could not be over-run.
    חוג *circle*, the meaning is הקף *circumference*, or *what is marked out*, as in ובמחוגה יתארהו *and marked out with a compass* (Isaiah 44:13). קינפא"ש בלע"ז *conps, compass* in the foreign tongue (Provençal).

28. *became strong*, as when he strengthened the fountains of the deep.

29. *when he marked out the foundations of the earth*, from the expression חקו *to cut*, as על כפים הקתיך *I have graven thee on the palms of the hands* (Isaiah 49:16). And so with the earth. Another meaning is *cut off*, as *and he cut off the Red Sea*, (*divided the Red Sea in sunder*, Psalms 136:13).

30. *master workman* (אמון) I was a great one near him. The expression is taken from האמונים עלי תולע *those brought up on scarlet* (Lamentations 4:5).
    daily (יום יום) means *two thousand*.

We now have before us the text of the commentaries on the passage in Proverbs to which Milton devoted so much attention in connection with his account of Creation. The three rabbis whose comment has just been presented have about the same matters to explain, but they employ different means for doing so. The next chapter will be devoted to a comparison of these commentaries with Milton's account in *Paradise Lost* of the Creation of the Visible Universe.

CHAPTER IV

THE CREATION OF THE VISIBLE UNIVERSE IN
PARADISE LOST

In Milton's account of Creation, contained in Book VII of *Paradise Lost*, one of the most obvious and noteworthy deviations from the text of the eighth chapter of Proverbs is in his use of *compasses* as the name of what the Creator laid upon the face of the deep instead of the *circle* mentioned in the twenty-seventh verse. So far as I know, this deviation has never been adequately explained by any commentator.

The poet described the actual process of blocking out the confines of the Visible Universe in the following lines, spoken of the Son, after he had been carried in the paternal chariot 'far into Chaos and the World unborn'

> 'in his hand
> He took the golden Compasses, . . .
> . . . to circumscribe
> This Universe, and all created things:
> One foot he center'd, and the other turn'd
> Round through the vast profunditie obscure,'
> —Book VII:224-229.

The employment of the word *compasses* for the name of the instrument which marked out the confines of the Visible Universe leads to a curious dilemma. The word has supposedly come from the reading in the Authorized Version for the verse in Proverbs, 'when he set a compass upon the face of the deep,' with the marginal note reading, 'or *a circle*.' Milton's commentators have almost wholly called attention to the reading of the Authorized Version as the source of Milton's usage, and have been content with having done so.[1] To accept this explanation of the use of the word *compasses*, while quite justifiable so far as the basic idea of Milton's lines and of the Biblical passage is concerned, lays the poet open to the grave charge of having either misunderstood or mistranslated the Hebrew original in which the word is clearly חוג *circle*. At first glance, it would appear that Milton has, without reference to the Hebrew original of the passage, followed the reading of the Authorized Version. The question might even be raised as to whether or not he knew the original, or, knowing it, why did he ignore it? As I have already stated, no commentator is of much assistance in understanding what has happened here, and, as there is the possibility of charging Milton with a lack of knowledge with the Hebrew, the point becomes one which it is necessary for us to investigate.

Certainly the Hebrew word in the original is actually *circle*. The reading of the Authorized Version has been corrected in the Revised, and apparently for the most part, Milton's usage has been looked upon as too close a following of the Authorized Version, or as an error of poetic licence. In other words, it has never been satisfactorily explained, for neither was, I think, the case.

It appears plain that the use of the word *compasses* could have been no error on the poet's part based on the reading of the Authorized Version, for even that Version printed *circle* in the margin. Moreover, none of the other

---

[1]The two most exhaustive commentators, Todd, (*The Poetical Works of John Milton*, London, 1809, vol. III, p. 368) and Verity (*Paradise Lost*, Cambridge, 1910, p. 537) both point to the verse in Proverbs in their notes and add but little to this. Todd called attention to "Dionys. *Perieg.* ad finem:" and quotes two lines which contain the same idea. Verity called attention to Dante's *Paradiso*, XIX:40-42. But neither commentator supplies any information as to why Milton deviated from the Hebrew word. Masson (*The Poetical Works*, London, 1896, vol. III, p. 368) has the bare mention of Proverbs 8:27. Addison's much earlier note is interesting, but irrelevant.

Biblical Versions to which Milton had ready access afford any warrant for his use of the word *compasses*.[1] It is also unreasonable to suppose that he deliberately employed the word and idea without some authority for having done so. Equally improbable is it that he erred in the use of it, or accepted it from the Authorized Version without being aware of the meaning or usage in the original. We have found him with too ready access to the Hebrew for all parts of the Old Testament to suppose that here he was unaware of the change he was making. But the idea of the use of the compasses in the laying out of Creation was not new with Milton. It had been spread throughout European literature by Dante's use of the figure in the *Paradiso*.[2] The idea is certainly more poetic than that of the circle, because it permits the employment of the compasses by the hand of the Creator in the description of the process of Creation. But even with Dante as an example, it is extremely doubtful if Milton would have so far deviated from the Hebrew text as to have made the change from circle (חוג) to compasses (מחוגה) had he not had more direct and more authoritative warrant for it than mere literary usage.

Such direct and authoritative usage he found ready at hand in the commentaries of the rabbis on the Proverbs passage in Buxtorf. All three of the commenting rabbis, Ben Gerson, Ibn Ezra, and Rashi, were struck by the idea of the *circle* (חוג) and felt that it called for an explanation.

---

[1] None of the following Biblical editions or versions in some manner connected with Milton would have supplied the *compass* idea: Pagnini, *Biblia Hebraica*, Antwerp, 1584, and later with Vatablus's notes (I have used the relatively late edition of Paris, 1745). Junius-Tremellius, 1580, 1596, 1617, 1630, 1633, 1651 (the last three are various editions of the second). None of the versions (Vulgate, LXX, Targum, Syriac, Arabic, or interlinear Hebrew, all with Latin translations and original texts) to be found in Walton's *Biblia Sacra Polyglotta*, London, 1654 *ss.*).

[2] As cited *supra* by Verity, XIX:40-42.

Each explained it in terms of the compass (מחוגה). The poet's description of the compasses and their use is perhaps nearest to that of Ben Gerson, but all three rabbis yield important and authoritative information concerning the compasses.

Milton described the Son as taking the 'golden compasses' and then

> 'One foot he center'd, and the other turn'd
> Round through the vast profunditie obscure,'
> —Book VII:228-229.

In doing so, Milton followed Ben Gerson's commentary very closely. Ben Gerson said:

והוא כמו מרכו לגרם השמימיי ולפי המחוג' ההיא המציא השמים סביבה במשכו רגלי
המחוגה ההיא זה מזה בגלגל גלנל

And this was as if there were a pivotal point for dividing the heavens by means of a Compass. This was how he established the heavens (the confines of the Universe): he drew around a leg of the compass, and [the marking off of the heavens] came about as the compass turned around.

This commentary by Ben Gerson not only supplied the idea of the compasses, but it also supplied the whole figure of their employment which Milton used. The imaginative insight of Ben Gerson's conception of the process became woven into Milton's poetical treatment of the same process with only the slightest of changes. It will be noted that Ben Gerson in this short passage has used the word מחוגה *compass* two distinct times. He was explaining the laying out of the Universe and the *setting of a circle* (בחוקו חוג על פני תהום) upon the chaos of the abyss (תוהם). But he described the operation as one which was performed by means of *compasses*, or as a process rather than as a result. Milton has followed him precisely in this.

The second rabbi whose commentary is to be examined on this Biblical passage is Ibn Ezra. His comment is very much like that of Ben Gerson in its basic nature, in fact, it would be difficult to determine to which of the two Milton owed most for his use of the idea of the compass. But Ibn Ezra is perhaps less informative concerning the process of the use of the instrument. Ibn Ezra said of the Biblical phrase *when he set a circle:*

בחוקו חוג בעת שחקק הגלגל על פני תהום שהוא המרכז וחוג כמו וחוג שמים יתהלך

ונקרא הכלי העשוי לעשות בו רושם העגולו' מחוגה על שם החוג הנרשם בו

At the time when he set a circle on the faces of the abyss, which was done as if there were a center. And this circle is the same as that in the phrase *and the vault of the heavens he walketh* (Job 22:14). And the instrument which is used to trace circles with is called a *compass* (מחוגה) on account of the *circle* (חוג) which is traced with it.

In this commentary, there is, perhaps, less elaboration of the process by means of which the circumscribing of the Universe was accomplished than in Ben Gerson. But the employment of the *compass* is as clearly noticeable as in the other rabbi. Ibn Ezra's explanation of the meaning of the word מחוגה *compass* is peculiar to himself, as is much of his commentary. But he is none the less explicit in connecting it with his explanation of the phrase בחוקו חוג *when he set a circle.*

The third rabbi to comment on this verse is Rashi. His comment is shorter than the other two, but his mention of the *compass* even more certain, as he actually provides the French form of the word from which our English word *compass* was derived. Rashi said

חוג' לשון הקף כמו ובמחוגה יתארהו קינפא"ש בלע"ז:

circle. The meaning is הקף *circumference,* or *what is marked out,* as in ובמחוגה יתארהו *and marked out with a compass* (Isaiah 44:13). קינפא"ש בלע"ז *conps* compass *in the foreign tongue.*

It is curious to find Rashi actually using the Provençal form which has come to be the English word for the name of the instrument that marks out a circle. However, while Rashi's comment again calls attention to the compass idea, it adds nothing to what the other two rabbis have contributed except the connection of חוג *circle* with הקף *circumference* in the act of Creation. The idea contained in הקף *circumference* finds an echo, perhaps, in the words which Milton makes the decree of the founding of the Universe. These are spoken by the Son of God after having turned the compasses:

' "This be thy just Circumference, O World." '

Taken together, the commentaries of these three rabbis form an authentic basis for Milton's usage in the matter of the compasses. They provide him with ample reasons for having made the change from *circle* to *compasses*, and, being direct commentaries on Scripture, they carry the necessary authority to have warranted the change being made.

Consequently, instead of Milton's use of the compass idea indicating that he had made a mistake in his understanding of the Hebrew original, or that he had too closely followed the text of the Authorized Version, and without warrant had made use of the compasses, it appears that exactly the reverse is true. In order to have used the compass, he went considerably beyond the original text itself to the commentaries of the rabbis in Buxtorf's Bible, and there secured discussions of the Biblical verse which provided him with the whole idea he has used in *Paradise Lost*.

Perhaps the true reason for Milton's change from *circle* to *compasses* lay not so much in his assiduous reading of the commentaries of the rabbis upon this particular passage in the eighth chapter of Proverbs as it did in his awareness of the same factors that caused the learned translators of the Authorized Version to make the same change. It was undoubtedly the rabbinical treatment of the word *circle* which led to its appearing as *compass* in the Proverbs text of the Authorized Version. For in their commentaries, the rabbis regularly explained the word חוג *circle*, wherever it occurred in the Old Testament, in terms of מחוגה *compass*. The word חוג *circle* is relatively rare in the Old Testament. But for each passage in which it occurs, the rabbis have discussed it in connection with and in terms of מחוגה *compass*, the instrument that marks out the חוג *circle*. It was this practice of the rabbis which so greatly influenced the translators of the Authorized Version to make the change in their textual reading from *circle* to *compasses*. They retained the word *circle* in the margin, but the text read *compass*. Milton was led to do the same thing for precisely the same reasons, that is, the fact that in those rabbinical commentaries to Biblical passages containing the word חוג *circle*, the rabbis have in each case explained the word by reference to מחוגה *compass*. This is so striking, and so constant, that the fact could scarcely have failed to have engaged Milton's attention in connection with his own use of the circle-compass idea in his treatment of the Act of Creation. In order to show how regularly the rabbis treat the word חוג *circle* in this manner, I include here their commentary, as it appears in Buxtorf, on the occurrences of the word in the Hebrew text.

The word חוג *circle* occurs as a noun in but two other places in the Hebrew of the Old Testament besides the passage in Proverbs. It also occurs once in the form of a verb, or in a verb-form, assumed to be a *qal* perfect, but no other verb-forms being found, this is perhaps conjectural. The first of the nominal forms occurs in the fourteenth verse of the twenty-second chapter of Job, *and he walketh in the circuit of heaven*, where the Revised Version

has translated the Hebrew word חוג *circle* as *circuit*. In
Buxtorf's Bible, both Rashi and Ibn Ezra, the two rabbis
whose commentary on Job Buxtorf printed, have felt it
necessary to explain the word חוג *circle*. Ibn Ezra said
of it,

וחוג שמים' על חוג שמסיה יתהלך ולא ידע מה יעשה למטה בארץ

and the circle of the heavens. He walks on the circle of the heavens,
but it is not known what he does in the earth below.

This is not particularly enlightening in connection with the
word חוג *circle*; but Rashi is more informative. He said,

וחוג שמים יתהלך' ולא ידע את אשר בארץ: חוג' עוגל מחונה שמים כמו ובמחוגה
יתארכו קומפ"ש בלע"ז:

and the circle of the heavens, but it is not known what [he does] in
the earth.

חוג *circle* is עוגל *something round*. The compass of the heavens,
as in ובמחוגה יתארכו *marked out with a compass* (Isaiah 44:13). This
is קומפ"ש בלע"ז *comps* compass *in the foreign tongue*.

As in his commentary to Proverbs, Rashi again makes
synonymous, or nearly so, the two words חוג *circle* and
מחוגה *compass*, the two being so inevitably connected with
each other that the rabbi almost equates them.

The other nominal usage of חוג *circle* occurs in the
twenty-second verse of the fortieth chapter of Isaiah,
he sitteth upon the circle of the earth. Buxtorf has printed
the commentaries of two rabbis, Rashi and David Kimchi,
upon Isaiah. Rashi explained this occurrence of חוג *circle*
about as he explained the one in Job:

חוג' לשון מחונה עוגל קומפ"ש בלע"ז:

circle, what is turned out by the compass, this is the קומפ"ש בלע"ז
comps—compass—in the foreign tongue.

Kimchi presents a little more complete discussion of the
text:

היושב' כאלו אמר על השמים כי הם חוג הארץ כמו שיעשה אדם במחונה העולה
כי למחונה יש שתי אצבעות האחת יעמוד ובשנית יקיף העגולה והנה הנקודה בתוך
העולה והארץ כמו הנקודה כי היא התחתון שבעגולה והשמים סביב הארץ כמו העולה

sitteth, as if it said 'on the heavens,' for these are the circle of the
earth. So when a man makes a circle with a compass, for there are
two legs to the compass, one standing still and the second going
round the circle. And there is a point in the midst of the circle.
And the earth is as the point, for this is beneath the arc of the circle,
or below it, and the heavens surround the earth as a circle.

The figure of God having turned out the limits of the Universe with a compass is here found complete, even the operation of the compass and the resulting circle being mi-
nutely described, with the earth as the center of the circle
and the arch of the heavens above it. Kimchi means that
God sits in heaven, as the heavens are this arch above
the earth.

The occurrence of חוג as a verb is in the tenth verse of
the twenty-sixth chapter of Job, and here the form cannot
be, or is not usually translated as a verb, *he hath described a
boundary upon the face of the waters*. But in the Hebrew,
the word is actually a verb. In Buxtorf, Rashi and Ralbag
comment on it. Ralbag said of it,

חג' הגביל וייחסו למחונה לפי שהמחונה מגבלת תכליות השטה העול המתחדש בסבתה:

חג the circle, and it is traced out with a compass. The compass
marks the limit of the extent of the circle, which is the extent of
the arrangement [of the universe].

Rashi has about the same remarks to make of the word
here that he has made of it in its other occurrences, again
explaining its meaning in Provençal,

חוג' בלע"ז קומפ"ש לשון ובמחונה יתארהו סיבבם בחול' להיות לו חול חוק גבול
עולם לא יעבור הים אותו חוג' עד שיכלה אור וחשך

קומפ"ש בלע'ז in the foreign tongue, *comps*, compass, from the expression ובמחונה יתארהו *and mark out with a compass* (Isaiah 44:13).
This means to turn round in a circle to be to it the circle of limitations,

the great sphere of the world that the sea might not pass over the mark of the circle while the light and the darkness were being finished.

These are the rabbinical comments upon all those passages in the Old Testament in which the word חוג *circle* occurs. Thus, it may be seen that the whole idea of the use of compass in the process of Creation originated with the rabbis. The process in Proverbs which the Hebrew text literally stated was *laying a circle upon the face of the deep* becomes a process of marking out with compasses. Whether we seek the origin of the basis for the change for the Authorized Version or for Milton, in both cases we find that the authority for each was the rabbis. Just why the translators of the Authorized Version were so greatly influenced by rabbinical opinion as to use the word *compass* in the text itself, cannot, perhaps, be determined. But for Milton, the poetic possibilities were sufficient to induce him to use the idea, and the result in the poem is wholly effective and pleasing.

But there are other portions of the commentary to the passage in Proverbs that Milton has used.

MILTON'S MUSE AND BEN GERSON'S UNDERSTANDING

It has been often noted that Milton, in his invocations to his Muse, has connected that Muse in some mysterious fashion with Creation. It is a little difficult to understand why he has done this, and it is even more perplexing to realize that in doing so, he has provided us with *two* spirits both of whom were present with the Son of God during the process of Creation. It has not only been difficult, therefore, to understand why he connected his Muse with Creation, but still more difficult to understand just what he meant when he further insisted that this Muse was one of two Spirits present with the 'Omnific Word' at Creation.

There are certain aspects of that Muse, Urania, 'by that name if rightly thou art called,' which are somewhat clarified by what Ben Gerson has had to say of תבונה *Understanding*. Milton's Muse may be difficult to identify, but the Spirit invoked at the beginning of Book VII is quite clearly the Spirit of Understanding, conceived in the same sense as by Ben Gerson.

Milton addressed this Spirit in the opening lines of the book:

> Descend from Heav'n *Urania*, by that name
> If rightly thou art call'd, whose Voice divine
> Following, above th' *Olympian* Hill I soare,
> Above the flight of *Pegasean* wing.
> The meaning, not the Name, I call: for thou
> Nor of the Muses nine, nor on the top
> Of old *Olympus* dwell'st; but Heav'nlie borne,
> Before the Hills appeerd, or Fountain flow'd,
> Thou with Eternal wisdom didst converse,
> Wisdom thy Sister, and with her didst play
> In presence of th' Almightie Father, pleas'd
> With thy Celestial Song.
>
> —Book VII:1-12.

Here is a Spirit invoked who, like Wisdom 'before the hills appeerd or fountain flow'd,' was in existence before and present at Creation, much of the invocation of her being taken directly from the text of Proverbs. But the Muse was present at Creation *with* Wisdom, and the two 'sisters' performed, according to Milton, as in the Biblical text Wisdom alone was said to have performed. It will be recalled, perhaps, that there is nothing in the Biblical passage which in any way suggests the presence of *two* Spirits at Creation with the Son of God, or, in the Old Testament, God himself. In the eighth chapter of Proverbs, and especially in verses twenty-two to thirty quoted earlier, Wisdom makes vibrant the lyrical, singing passage concerning Creation. The Speaker here is presumably a feminine personification of the idea of Wisdom, the abstract quality. Certainly throughout the chapter, and especially again in these verses, she makes no reference whatever to a companion or sister Spirit having been present with her during the accomplishment of the events described. According to the text of Proverbs, Wisdom appears to have been alone with God at Creation. The text of Scripture, therefore, could not have suggested to Milton the strange idea of having two, apparently equal Spirits present with the Son on his mission of Creation.

But the commentary of Ben Gerson supplies such a conception of two such accompanying Spirits as Milton presented in his invocation of his Muse. The Biblical text supplies an account of the whole process of Creation in the words of Wisdom, a Spirit who was present when the events of Creation took place. The rabbi, in his commentary to these verses, has, in his treatment of the Spirit of Wisdom, anticipated Milton's two accompanying Spirits, one of whom was Wisdom. Ben Gerson stated that God had with him at Creation not only Wisdom (חכמה) but also Understanding (תבונה). He was very explicit on this matter, taking pains to point out the presence of both of these Spirits at Creation as follows:

אבל תדע' כי הש"י לא חסר להיות עמו זאת התבונה והחכמה אשר נברא בה העולם

Indeed, you must remember that God did not fail to have with him (at Creation) Understanding and Wisdom by means of which the world was made or created.

To Ben Gerson, Understanding (תבונה) was very like Wisdom (חכמה); but they were not identical. Like Wisdom (חכמה) Understanding (תבונה) was 'nearby God' (אצל הש"י). She (and in Ben Gerson's Hebrew as in Milton's English, the gender is feminine) was present with Wisdom at Creation. I have pointed out elsewhere that Milton thought of the Holy Spirit as manifesting itself in various forms, and he was undoubtedly employing two different aspects of the same Holy Spirit in his invocation.[1] Although this Spirit was, in comparison with the Father or the Son, a minor element in his theology,[2] Milton has made some very definite statements concerning it. He said that one of its forms was as *lucem veritatis*,[3] and apparently another was as the Muse invoked at the opening of Book VII.[4]

In the invocation to Book VII with its treatment of the Muse invoked as an aspect of the Holy Spirit, there is a strong suggestion of the influence of Ben Gerson's commentary. For Ben Gerson mentioned, not one, but two very similar Spirits who accompanied and were present with God at Creation. The idea of two such Spirits present at Creation is clearly used by Milton in the lines

'The King of Glorie in his powerful Word
And Spirit coming to create new Worlds.'
—Book VII:208-209.

That is, the 'King of Glory' was accompanied by two Spirits at and during Creation.

Moreover, Milton's conception of his Muse here makes of her a sort of 'goddess'[5] of the ability to understand the difficult material he is about to discuss. This, intentionally or otherwise, is a poetic conception of Ben Gerson's Understanding (תבונה). The use of this conception, together with the introduction of two Spirits into the Creation process,

---

[1]Fletcher, *Milton's Semitic Studies.*
[2]Denis Saurat, *Milton: Man and Thinker* (New York, 1925), pp. 134-135.
[3]*de doctrina*, p. 111.
[4]*Ibid.*, pp. 120-121. Milton stated that the Holy Spirit may be invoked 'Sed invocatur Spiritus. . . Si unquam Spiritus esset invocandus, tunc certe potissimum, cum a nobis petitur; jubemur tamen non se a seipso, sed a Patre tantum petere.'
[5]He calls her 'goddess' in VII:24.

constitute the major changes Milton made from the Proverbs text. One authority for both of these changes and the
ideas underlying them was Ben Gerson's commentary on
Proverbs, to which Milton had access in Buxtorf.

The evidence that Milton actually read Ben Gerson's
commentary on this particular passage is cumulative. I
have pointed out so far the poet's use of three distinct
elements found in Ben Gerson's commentary and not
found in the scriptural passage itself nor in Christian commentaries upon it. Another fact which points toward
Milton's use of this rabbinical material here is the extreme
care with which he read these particular verses themselves.
The best evidence of this care is his use of the word *play*
in the lines

> and with her didst *play*
> In presence of th' Almightie Father,
> —Book VII:10-11.

Verity has commented upon the use of this word, pointing
out the change from the word *rejoice* used in both the
Authorized and Revised Versions, and further suggesting
the possibility of the word *play* having come from the
Vulgate *ludens*.[1] But Milton apparently never intentionally employed the Vulgate, and he did not employ it here.[2]
On the contrary, all that he has done here is to translate
the Hebrew with more care than had his English Version.
The Hebrew reads מְשַׂחֶקֶת. This is a *piel* participle with
feminine ending of the verb שׂחק, and clearly means *playing*
or *sporting*, only by oblique implication securing the much
softened meaning given to it by the Authorized and retained by the Revised Version.[3] The fascination which

---

[1] A. W. Verity, *op. cit.*, p. 530.
[2] Cf. *Use of the Bible*, pp. 67 ff.
[3] Cf. Brown, Driver, and Briggs, *op. cit.*, p. 965b. There was nothing particularly
remarkable about Milton's ability in this instance to supply a better translation of

this passage in Proverbs held for Milton, and the care with which he studied it, so apparent in his use of it, would, therefore, account fully for his meticulous use of the word *play*. It would strongly suggest further that he read the commentary of Ben Gerson, for evidently the two Spirits mentioned by the rabbi appealed sufficiently to Milton's poetic sense, as well as to his conception of the nature of the Holy Spirit, to permit him to have identified his Muse with one of those Spirits.

His invocation now becomes an invocation of the Spirit of God in the form of Understanding, for, as he says, this Spirit was with God when Creation took place. God created the Universe according to Understanding. Milton further suggested, and in this also he followed Ben Gerson, that Understanding and her sister Wisdom were together with the Creator when all that he was about to relate took place. Certainly, for his purposes, he could have invoked no more fitting Muse.

The similarities I have been pointing out between Milton and Ben Gerson each contribute to the chain of evidence connecting poet and rabbi. There are, moreover, other ideas found in both that are noteworthy.

BEN GERSON'S UNDERSTANDING AND HER RELATION TO THE PLAN OF CREATION

Both Milton and Ben Gerson agree that God effected the Creation of the Visible Universe *according to Plan*. I call

the Hebrew word משחקת than that found in the Authorized Version, except that he may have been totally blind when he did it, as would be indicated by line 27. But the lexicons available in his day would have enabled him to have discovered the best translation of the word. Cf. Pagninus, *op. cit.*, p. 409a: 'Ludere. *idem in Piel et Hiphil*, ut Ludo ego? Prouerb. 26:19; &.' Also, Buxtorf, *Lexicon Talmudicum* (Basel, 1639), col. 2370, sub שחק. '*Ab Hebraeo* שחק *Ridere, ample scilic. et pleno ore atque distento*.' The same verb, in the same stem and with the same meaning occurs a number of times elsewhere in the Old Testament, Prov. 26:19; 1 Chron. 15:29; 1 Sam. 18:7; 2 Sam. 6:5; and *passim*. The meaning, *ludere* or *to play*, is perfectly clear in these other passages.

attention to this chiefly because there is no Biblical basis
for it in the Proverbs passage. But both rabbi and poet
point out clearly that Creation was the result of God's
plan. Moreover, there is a distinct similarity between
both conceptions of this planning. To understand and
examine this similarity is not only more clearly to understand Milton's idea, but further to realize how he drew on
rabbinical commentary for elaboration of that idea and
perhaps even inauguration of it.

We have already seen and noted that Milton's conception of two Spirits having been present with God at Creation is also found in Ben Gerson's commentary to the
twenty-seventh verse of the eighth chapter of Proverbs.
The rabbi stated, as already pointed out, that *God did not
fail to have with him at Creation Wisdom* (חכמה) *and Understanding* (תבונה). Now the word *Understanding* (תבונה) means
the whole process of ratiocination. It includes the meaning *planning*. The rabbi in a different portion of his commentary to this passage, used the word תבונה (Understanding) with precisely that meaning: השמים להיות במספר ובתכונה
שהכין השם ית' *God established the Heavens according to plan*.
This is the same Understanding which, half-personified in
the manner of the Proverbs text, he had previously said
was, with Wisdom (חכמה), one of the two *first causes of the
Heavens*. That is, אצל הש"י *near God*, or with him at
Creation.[1]

Ben Gerson's full conception now begins to be clear.
Not only was the personification of the abstraction *Understanding* (תבונה) with God during the process and aiding in
Creation, but, and perhaps this is more important, the
abstraction itself, (תבונה), the *plan* of the whole process of

---

[1] The word חורסים may be translated, as I have translated it, as *strengths*. But it means
more than that. *First cause,* or *Veranlassung, Ursache,* are perhaps better translations. Cf. Jac. Klatzkin, *Thesaurus Philosophicus* (Leipzig, 1928, *ss.*), vol. I, p. 119.

Creation, was present there. *Understanding* (תבונה) was therefore said to have been present at Creation because it was, both in the abstract sense and in the figurative sense, one of the bases on and by which the world was created. Figuratively, Understanding (תבונה) was one of the two Spiritual agencies which were present. Abstractly, and absolutely, God created the world through and according to a *plan*. Ben Gerson's word תבונה means both of these. Thus, in his characteristically philosophic fashion, he has anthropomorphized God, endowed him with reason, and then explained the Creation in terms of the rational process. The result is a most conveniently conventionalized treatment and arrangement of the process of Creation which should have been most welcome and agreeable to any poet laboring with cosmic problems.

Freely paraphrasing Ben Gerson's statement, and leaving entirely out of account for the present the personification of Wisdom in the eighth chapter of Proverbs, the rabbi has said that in the very beginning of things, which God was to create, before he even began to create them, He already possessed Wisdom (חכמה). That is, God possessed the wisdom necessary to create. This was the peculiarity (חדוש) of Wisdom (חכמה), that it was in God's possession when he first began to create, indeed, before he began he possessed it. Likewise, when he began the process of Creation, he possessed both a plan (תבונה Understanding) and the Wisdom (חכמה) required to execute it. Only through and by means of this *plan* and this *wisdom* was Creation accomplished. Both plan and wisdom were necessary in order that God's other works might be created. That is, both plan and wisdom existed first in the mind of God. Then through them, as if they had become detached from his mind and taken on separate existences of their own, was Creation brought about. In this sense, then, they constituted the first causes or bases of Creation.

These rabbinical conceptions of Wisdom and Understanding, as expressed by Ben Gerson, remarkably anticipate Milton's statements about his Muse and the Spirit of God having been present at Creation. We have already seen how Milton expressed this.

He also employed the idea of God's planning before Creation. In *Paradise Lost*, God announces to his Son that he is about to create a Universe. This is expressed as an intention of purpose. The Deity points out that Satan has drawn off a large number of the Angels, although plenty remain to possess the Realm of Heaven and to perform and maintain the Heavenly offices. God then continues:

> ' "But least his (Satan's) heart exalt him in the harme
> Already done, to have dispeopl'd Heav'n
> . . . I can repaire
> That detriment, . . .
> . . . and in a moment will create
> Another World," '
> —Book VII: 150-155.

Later in the poem, Milton again dwells on the planning before Creation:

> 'What he *Almightie* styl'd, six Nights and Days
> Continu'd making, and who knows how long
> Before had bin contriving,'
> —Book IX:137-139.

And again:

> ' . . . What he decreed
> He effected;'
> —*ibid.* 151-152.

Milton also discussed the planning of Creation in the mind of God at some length in the *de doctrina*, in the chapter on Creation.[1]

When God announced the project of Creation to the Son, He further informed him that Creation would be accomplished

> ' "by thee
> This I perform, speak thou, and be it don:" '
> —Book VII:163-164.

But not alone,

> ' "My overshadowing Spirit and might with thee
> I send along," '
> —*ibid*. 165-166.

This is the same pair of Spirits mentioned later in the same Book as having accompanied the Son, as previously quoted in the lines

> 'The King of Glorie, in his powerful Word
> And Spirit coming to create new Worlds.'
> —*ibid*. 208-209.

The Son of God it was who marked out the confines of the Universe, but once it had been marked out, it was the Spirit of God which

> 'on the watrie calme
> His brooding wings the Spirit of God outspred,
> And vital vertue infus'd, and vital warmth
> Throughout the fluid Mass,'
> —*ibid*. 234-237.

---

[1] *de doctrina*, p. 124. 'Secunda species externae efficientiae vulgo dicitur CREATIO. Sed ante mundum conditum quid egerit Deus, insipiens nimis sit qui quaerat; nec qui respondeat multo sapientior: nam quod rationem reddidisse se plerique arbitrantur, cum dicunt eum, 1 Cor. ii. 7. *sapientiam in mysterio latentem ante saecula praefinisse,* elegisse nimirum, reprobasse, aliaque eo spectantia decrevisse, parum profecto hoc esset Deum ab aeterno in iis decernendis totum fuisse occupatum, quae spatio sex dierum perficienda, paucis annorum millibus varie

That is, the plan or intention which first existed in the mind of God as an idea became 'instinct with Spirit.' Having become so, one aspect of God's Spirit, or one of the two Spirits which accompanied the Son upon his Creative mission was actually the plan or intention to create a Universe which had previously and first existed as an idea in the mind of God.

There is no need and less reward for attempting to hold Milton doctrinally to strict account for what he has said here.[1] If it is understood that he first had the Deity plan Creation, and then sent a personification of that plan which was also one aspect of God's Spirit, along with the Son to Creation, Milton's presentation offers no difficulties.

Then, indeed, was Milton's Muse, in turn the same or very nearly the same as the Spirit of God that accompanied the Son at Creation, present 'at the first' as the poet had exclaimed in his invocation of her at the beginning of the poem. And she was also Understanding, or the Spirit of Understanding of all that took place in Creation. This dual nature of Milton's Muse arises from the nature of the two Spirits God sent along with the Son, each an aspect of the Holy Spirit. God's Spirit present at Creation in *Paradise Lost* is an embodiment of the Deity's plan for and of Creation. In essence, it is an aspect of the Spirit of God which has many aspects. Milton's Muse was conceived of in the same manner, and both are aspects, perhaps identical, of Holy Spirit. For Milton evidently conceived of the Spirit present at Creation as having first

gubernanda, tum demum immutabili statu in omne aevum vel ad se recipienda, vel ab se rejicienda erant.'

[1] *de doctrina*, pp. 110-111. Milton says of the Holy Spirit 'nunc Patris potentiam atque virtutem, illum imprimis afflatum divinum omnia creantem ac foventem significari: quomodo locum illum Gen. 1:2. *Spiritus Dei incubabat*, multi intelligunt et antiqui et recentiores.' Sumner, in his notes to the English translation, suggests that Milton has followed the rabbinical interpretation of this verse. This, to Sumner, was heretical. But why accuse a poet of doctrinal heresy?

come into being as the idea or plan of Creation in the mind of God. He also conceived of his Muse in the same manner, and, in so far as each was in essence Holy Spirit, identified them.

Small wonder, therefore, that he appealed to his Muse for aid in describing Creation. For his Muse, as Holy Spirit or one aspect of it, came into being as an idea of Creation in the mind of God before Creation took place. The idea or plan of Creation then assisted in the process of Creation in the elaborate representation Milton felt to be necessary,

'So told as earthly notion can receave.'

—*ibid.* 179.

Milton's conception of the Holy Spirit is in many ways peculiar to him and difficult to understand. But whether it be the Spirit employed in the epic with its veiled, almost mystic implications, or the more prosaic but no less complicated Spirit in the *de doctrina*, the conception somewhat mirrors and reflects the indecision of his age. For Deism had already begun to raise its contentious head, and decision was difficult. In a way, it is impossible to follow Milton logically through the ramifications of his conception of Holy Spirit, for, I believe, that conception was much more a poetic conception than a logical one. But his attitude toward his Muse and her expressed relations to and with the process of Creation provide us with some information not otherwise forthcoming concerning his Holy Spirit. Such a conception as finds a parallel in Ben Gerson's commentary and is connected with the Muse in a way already pointed out, is, it seems to me, eminently in accord with Milton's statement in the *de doctrina* that the *Spiritus Sanctus* was *mundi fundamenta, post Filium, Filioque longe inferiorem.*[1]

[1]*de doctrina*, p. 123.

A RABBINICAL CONCEPTION OF THE RELATION OF WISDOM TO THE WORKING OUT OF CREATION

The manner in which the idea of Creation aided in the working out of Creation itself also finds support and confirmation in Ben Gerson's commentary. In fact, the rabbi aids greatly in the understanding of what Milton was trying to do with his conception of Creation as he worked it out in the poem. Milton had before him the artistic problem of depicting the whole process of Creation in a manner that would provide and, indeed, insure to the fullest extent the most poetic treatment possible. He needed and had evidently thought much of how to secure a way of depicting Creation which would most readily yield a comprehensible poetic account of that Titanic occurrence. He likewise felt the necessity, it is true, of conforming to certain doctrinal standards. But as the chapter on Creation in the *de doctrina* is examined, it is apparent that Milton did not, even there, confine himself to too rigid and systematic a conception of the process involved. In fact, the account of Creation in the prose treatise is a most remarkable counterpart to the account in the poem. The treatise deals almost wholly with broad, general ideas of Creation, supplying very few details, and all but disregarding the temporal element. In the poem, just the opposite is true. The basic principles of Creation are obscure and not at once apparent. Indeed, sometimes they are confused, as is the case with various locations, such as the mouth of Hell. But the poetic account is well supplied and embellished with details. Some of them are a little difficult to understand, but there is a reason for this. Always the difficulty arises, when it does arise, because Milton is much more concerned with a poetic solution to a problem than he was interested in its doctrinal solution. That is, his chief interest lay in a presentation that would adequately express in considerable detail the much more vague and even obscure general idea that lay back of the detail. Thus his problem of presenting Creation in the poem became one of discovering a method of presenting the process of Creation in such a way as would secure artistic adequacy rather than doctrinal truth. In a general way, the broader doctrinal bases of the poem are clear enough; but no amount of explaining can ever quite reconcile all of the ideas and implications that Milton allowed to creep into the poem. Logically, the poem is unconvincing, and must so be held to have been even to its own time, for it was over a century after its publication before many of its basic doctrines were, with the indisputable evidence afforded by the *de doctrina*, fully comprehended. But poetically, the poem has always been and still is one of the most aesthetically convincing works of literary art produced by the western world. The chief reason for this being true is the care with which Milton worked out his various compositional problems. A fine instance of the exercise of such care and the achievement of a convincing result is his solution to the problem of presenting the process, not the Act, of the working out of Creation.

We of today, having virtually discarded all ideas of Creation as a definite act, experience some difficulty, not only in discerning the problem, but more especially the need for and importance of the elaboration that is so prominent in a discussion in which we have at best but little belief. But such was not the case in Milton's day and for his age. A most real problem to him was that of how to represent Creation in a poetic manner. Professor Saurat has called attention to Milton's conception of the actual instantaneousness of Creation, but which, in representation, was necessarily spread out over the time of six days. This was done 'in condescension,' as Bishop Newton said, 'to the capacities of angels, and so narrated by Moses, in condescension to the capacities of men.'[1]   That is, Milton conceived of Creation as having actually occurred instantaneously; but to angels or men, it can only appear as a process.   He stated the case in *Paradise Lost* as follows:

> 'Immediate are the acts of God, more swift
> Than time or motion, but to human ears
> Cannot without process of speech be told,
> So told as earthly notion can receave.'
> —Book VII:176-179.

Consequently, Milton set himself the task in the poem of representing Creation as an instantaneous Act of God which in some comprehensible manner stretched out over the period of six days.   How was this to be presented in order to preserve both its instantaneous and its 'six-day' aspects?   This was his problem.

The poet's solution of this problem is not difficult to follow in the poem.   First, he had the Son mark out with the 'golden compasses' that portion of Chaos which was to be used for the Cosmos.   Then followed the Act of Creation itself. This consisted in bringing to Chaos the presence of the Spirit of God, the Holy Spirit, or the two aspects of that Spirit of God which accompanied the Son at Creation.   This contact of the Spirit of God with Chaos, or the 'watery calm,' provided the basis or principle for everything that was to be.

Milton conceived of the primeval matter, which before was 'unformed and void' as now being brought into contact with the Spirit of God, or with the plan and principle of the Cosmos and all it was to contain:

> 'on the watrie calme
> His brooding wings the Spirit of God outspred,
> And vital vertue infus'd, and vital warmth
> Throughout the fluid Mass,'   —Book VII:234-237.

[1]D. Saurat, *op. cit.*, pp. 115-116.

The beginnings to the solution of Milton's representational problem are now discernible.   Milton thought of the contact of the Spirit of God with the elements of Chaos as an impregnation, an idea he suggested very early in the poem when he said that the Spirit of God:

> Dove-like satst brooding on the vast Abyss
> And mad'st it pregnant:
> —Book I:21-22.

The various aspects of the Universe are then 'born' shortly thereafter, apparently as separate parts of what was in reality a single, instantaneous process.   The results were the successive 'births' on the Six Days of Creation, each following the commands of the Son of God.

The idea of representing the various detailed parts of Creation passing through a process of parturition is repeated in the latter part of the account of Creation as the various created elements of Earth itself appear:

> 'The Earth was form'd, but in the Womb as yet
> Of Waters, Embryon immature involv'd,
> Appeer'd not:'
> —Book VII:276-278.

> 'Fermented the great Mother (the Earth) to conceave,'
> —*ibid.* 281.

> 'Meanwhile the tepid Caves, and Fens and shoares
> Thir Brood as numerous hatch, from the Egg that soon
> Bursting with kindly rupture, forth disclosed
> Thir callow young,'   —*ibid.* 417-420.

> 'The Earth obey'd, and strait
> Op'ning her fertil Woomb, teem'd at a Birth
> Innumerous living Creatures, perfet formes,
> Limb'd and full grown: out of the ground up rose
> As from his Laire the wilde Beast'
> —*ibid.* 453-457.

'The grassie Clods now Calv'd, now half appeer'd
The Tawnie Lion, pawing to get free
His hinder parts,' —*ibid.* 463-465.

'came forth whatever creeps the ground,'
—*ibid.* 475.

Such was Milton's solution to the problem of representing Creation as an instantaneous Act that, nevertheless, was spread out over the time of the Six Days. From whence came the germ of the idea that yielded the solution? What influenced him to select the particular idea that he employed?

It is well known that the discussion of the ways and means of Creation was a favorite during the Renaissance. Every history of the world, in order to be authentic, necessarily began with Creation, dealing with it in any one of a dozen well known ways. Common enough was the idea of Creation that thought of it as a birth-process. A very comprehensive statement of such an idea is to be found in English as early as 1586. It is the statement made concerning Creation by Timothy Bright in his *Treatise of Melancholy*.[1]

Bright stated the idea as follows:

Whereof this Spirit (of God) is made, I take it to bee an effectuall, and pregnant substance, bred in all things, and at what time the Spirit of the Lord did as it were hatch, and breed out all living thinges, out of the Chaos mentioned in Genesis. Which Chaos, as it was the matter of Corporall, and Palpable Substance to all things, so did it also minister this lively Spirit vnto them, diverse and several, according to the diversitie of those seedes, which God indued it withall: to some more pure, to othersome more grosse.

---

[1]Timothy Bright, *A Treatise of Melancholy* (London, 1613), pp. 54-55. (First edition, 1586.) My colleague, Professor T. W. Baldwin, first called this passage in Bright to my attention.

The germ of the idea was, therefore, readily available to Milton as part of the currently received opinion of his day regarding one mode of Creation. But why did Milton select this particular idea for the solution of his problem of representing the Act and Process of Creation in *Paradise Lost*? If Bright's statement, or one similar to it, suggested a solution, nevertheless, neither it nor similar ones are of much assistance in discovering why Milton selected the particular method he used in the poem. He might have chosen any one of a number of other ideas about how Creation took place; but he actually used this one. Can we discover why?

A suggestion for representing Creation as a birth-process, and the Act of Creation as an impregnation-process is to be found in the original Hebrew of the first chapter of Genesis. The participle מרחפת *brooding*, in the statement of the second verse that reads ורוח אלהים מרחפת על פני המים *and the Spirit of Elohim was brooding on the faces of the waters*, is translated *moved* in the clause *moved upon the face of the waters* by both the Authorized and Revised Versions. It has been noted often enough by editors and commentators that Milton in *Paradise Lost* has used the Hebrew meaning rather than the English translation in the line

> 'His brooding wings . . . outspred'
> —Book VII:235.[1]

This, however, was not sufficient for Milton's purposes. He wanted and needed a representation of Creation which would not only contain and take into account the Act itself, but which would also include all the elements of his

---

[1] A. W. Verity, *op. cit.*, p. 370. The scholarship of the time knew the meaning and significance of the word מרחפת, as the *ferebatur* of the Vulgate, and the *incubabat* of the Junius-Tremellius and the Pagnini Latin Bibles would indicate.

complete idea of Creation, which thought of it as not only being instantaneous so far as God was concerned, but which also occupied the time of the Six Days so far as man's comprehension was concerned. The Hebrew of the second verse of the first chapter of Genesis gave him a hint, but more than this was needed for the complete idea he was trying to express than the figure of a bird brooding on a nest. He had used the figure of a brooding bird early in *Paradise Lost*, as we have already seen, in the lines

> Thou (his Muse, the same as in Book VII) from the first
> Wast present, and with mighty wings outspread
> Dove-like satst brooding on the vast Abyss
> And mad'st it pregnant:
> —Book I:19-22.

He was fully aware of the significance of this figure. Even in these lines, the problem of how to represent Creation as the result of one instantaneous Act had been solved, and the reason of and means for such a representation had been discovered.[1] The 'dove-like' brooding represents the very beginning of his solution of the entire problem of expressing his whole idea of Creation, as he thought of it as having taken place, and as he set forth that idea in the *de doctrina*.

In his working out of that solution in the details of the poem, it becomes possible to observe his much-discussed imagination at work. He began with the idea of impregnation of the stuff of Chaos by the Spirit of God. This was the Act of Creation. Then begins the process that results in the appearance of the various parts of the Universe. Brooding over eggs in a nest in order that they may hatch is obviously the figure Milton selected to represent the first step in the process of Creation, or, in his own words,

[1]Verity, *op. cit.*, p. 370.

'on the watrie calme
His brooding wings the Spirit of God outspred,
And vital vertue infus'd, and vital warmth
Throughout the fluid Mass,'

                              —Book VII:234-237.

His representation of the process of Creation is that this
process is the result of the Act of Creation. The Act of
Creation was the impregnation of the stuff of Chaos by the
Spirit of God. The process of Creation, the result of this
Act, was a short period of incubation, the Six Days, and
then successive births of the various parts of the Created
Universe. Not only the Act itself, but also the succeeding
process, the incubation and births, were due to the presence in a portion of Chaos of God's Spirit.

Now Milton has his complete idea of a way to represent
in a figurative manner the Act and the process of Creation
as he had already outlined it. How did he work it out?
It is extremely interesting to follow him from this point.
His idea complete, he tells of the impregnation of the stuff
of the Universe, the elements in Chaos, then of the incubation period, and then of the Six Days, each succeeding
the other and displaying its new wonders according to
command. But when we turn to the poem itself, we discover that the foregoing sentence has compressed hundreds of lines of the poem. That is, the actual performance
was not so simple as that. But following the poem, we can
now almost see Milton at work upon a full-fledged idea.
He knows, and now we know, precisely what he wants to
say, although the complexity of the process of expression is
most remarkable. If one looks at Verity's notes for the
remainder of the treatment in Book VII of the process of
Creation, the character and quantity of suggested sources
for the material Milton is pouring forth are astounding.[1]

[1]Verity, *op. cit.*, p. 529 ff. The notes for Creation occupy about fifteen pages.

This mass of source-material tells an impressive story, the story of how Milton treated an idea, once it was fully formed in his mind.

With an idea full-blown, fully formed and rounded out in his mind, he now embellished it with all the accumulated lore in his retentive memory that in any way could be connected with it. Every author he had ever read and remembered, who touched on Creation, is now raided. The recalled significant passage is seized upon and worked into an immense mosaic, which in this case was the seventh Book of *Paradise Lost*. The end of the process has been noted many times; but I should like to call attention to an unusual opportunity to observe what took place at the beginning of it and to trace Milton's treatment of an idea from its inception to its embodiment in his finished verse. I refer to Ben Gerson's treatment of the whole idea of Creation as a process in the rabbi's commentary to the eighth chapter of Proverbs.

In his remarks on the twenty-ninth verse of that chapter, Ben Gerson touched on the precise relationship of Wisdom (חכמה) to the whole process of Creation of the Visible Universe. The commentary to this verse deals primarily with the explanation of the phrase *when he set for the sea its bound*. In explaining this particular phrase, the rabbi offered an explanation of the result of God's thus shutting off the sea. He went on to speak of what was next revealed by God's limitation of the domain of the waters. Most significant of all, from our standpoint, is his statement to the effect that Wisdom (חכמה), which to Milton was the Spirit of God in one of its aspects, was the basis of all that went on in the process of Creation. Ben Gerson said:

שיהיה נגלה תמיד כאשר חקק מוסדי ארץ והוא החלק הנגלה מהארץ שהוא היסוד
למה שיתהוה בה מהצמחים והב"ח:

This (Wisdom) was what was revealed after he ordained the establishment of the earth. And this was the gift revealed in the earth; this it was (i.e. the presence of God's Spirit, חכמה) which was the basis of all that was happening in it (the earth), in the way of developments and of forms of life.

This passage, while clear enough to one thinking in terms of the idea of Creation as an act of God, is somewhat obscure to our modern minds. But the whole passage is in complete accordance with Ben Gerson's notion of the nature of Creation. This rabbi was essentially Aristotelian in his viewpoint, and this point of view is especially prominent in his treatment of Creation. Milton would have needed no great amount of explanation for the above passage in order to seize upon its significance in connection with his whole problem of representing the process of Creation of the Visible Universe. But for us it may clarify the rabbi's statement to refer to his more complete idea of how Creation actually came about.

Ben Gerson held that the Prime Matter of the Universe, the 'stuff' of Chaos, was originally without perfection or imperfection, perfectly inert and lifeless. It was, in the true Aristotelian sense, without form, indeed, in his commentary to the twenty-eighth verse, the rabbi speaks of Creation as the desire of God that the 'stuff' of Chaos שיקבל איכות דומה *receive the quality of the form* of certain created entities. Creation, as to Aristotle, was the giving of form to the formless 'stuff' and the tumultuous elements of the תהום *abyss*. But he also held that in order for Creation to have been possible, the matter of Chaos was possessed of what Doctor Adlerblum has called 'one redeeming feature, namely the possibility of perfecting itself within a certain degree through the aid of the perfect existence (God or God's Spirit).'[1] God extended this aid

[1] Nima H. Adlerblum, *A Study of Gersonides* (New York, 1926), p. 56.

through his Spirit, and Ben Gerson conceived of this Spirit as having been present at Creation in at least two aspects, one of which was Wisdom (חכמה) and the other as Understanding (תבונה). Through and by means of the presence of these two Spirits, or these two manifestations of the Holy Spirit of God, there was continuously revealed God's 'gift' to Chaos, or to the stuff of Creation. This gift, the presence of Wisdom, was the quality of becoming perfected or receiving the quality of form to a certain degree through the process of Creation. This process consisted of the revelation of the presence of God's Spirit in the Universe. The fact that this Spirit was present, accounted for all that took place at Creation, 'of developments and of forms of life.' The revelation of Wisdom and Understanding or plan in the Universe was the real process of Creation. As these were gradually and continuously revealed, the process of Creation went forward, or as this process went forward, more and more apparent became the presence of God's Spirit in the Universe. The basis of and the reason for what was taking place in Chaos was, in fact, the presence in it of the Spirit of God.

There is one striking similarity between Ben Gerson's treatment of the whole idea of Creation and Milton's treatment of the same idea. Milton's detailed account of the process of Creation in *Paradise Lost* is a poetic treatment in a figurative manner of a process that he fundamentally held to have been a 'mystery.' In the *de doctrina*, the discussion of Creation is entirely confined to the nature of God's relationship to his Created Universe.[1] The elaboration of Milton's definition of Creation is wholly confined in the *de doctrina*, not to a discussion of the ways

---

[1] *de doctrina*, p. 124. Milton's definition of Creation is: *Creatio est qua Deus Pater Verbo et Spiritu suo, hoc est Sua Voluntate, quicquid est Rerum Produxit, ad Patefaciendam Potentiae et Bonitatis Suae Gloriam.*

and means of Creation itself, but how God could have begun the process that resulted in the finished product, the Visible Universe. Of the particularized account contained in the poem, the prose treatise has not one word to say. Only the theory underlying the process is therein set forth. If we look for the logical details of the process, we find them, not in the treatise, but entirely in the poem.

The representation of the process of Creation as having taken place as a process of impregnation and parturition or birth was, therefore, only a figurative description for poetic purposes in the poem. Milton's basic idea of the process of Creation was as an ordering of the elements contained in Chaos by the presence in that Chaos, or by contact with it, of the Spirit of God. The agency which established and maintained this contact with the stuff of the Universe was a manifold Spirit, consisting not only of *Verbo et Spiritu Suo*, but also of God's will, glory, power, and other manifestations of his Spirit. These are in the poem represented by the host of Angelic orders which accompanied the Son on his creative mission. Thus, the theory of Creation that represents Milton's thought on the subject, is to be found set forth unadorned in the *de doctrina*. In *Paradise Lost* are to be found all the embellishments of that theory which his highly poetic nature found attractive and useful.

It is now apparent, therefore, that there is much similarity between Milton's conception of the process and nature of Creation and that set forth by Ben Gerson. The rabbi's representation of a dual-natured, abiding Spirit having been present, in contact with the stuff of Creation by Act of God at the very beginning is very similar to Milton's. Ben Gerson further held that the process of Creation itself was but the working out or revelation of the presence of this Spirit in the Primeval Matter, whence came the various forms that appeared during the Six Days. The revelation of the Spirit, already present in the Universe because put there by the Power, and Will, and Glory of God, is the very core of Milton's idea of Creation. Both poet and rabbi were fundamentally much more concerned with God's relationship to the Universe than they were with precise descriptions of the progress of Creation. In the poem, Milton developed a treatment of the *order* of Creation's progress, but how figurative this parturitive process of Creation actually was to him becomes apparent upon referring to the *de doctrina*, where none of the details of the process are permitted to appear.

MILTON'S CRYSTALLINE SPHERE AND BEN GERSON'S STRUCTURE OF THE HEAVENS

Further in connection with Ben Gerson's commentary of the eighth chapter of Genesis, it is important to note what he has had to say about the formation and structure of the Heavens. In connection with his discussion of the compasses and what they marked out, he has identified the Heavens (שמים) with the limits of the Cosmos. That is, the effect of the turning compasses was the same for both rabbis and poet. For Milton, the compasses marked out *thy just circumference, O world*. This, for the poet, was the Great Crystalline Sphere of the Universe, at once the 'narrower bound' of the 'visible diurnal sphere,' and a sort of insulating division between High Heaven and the World. It also served as a partition 'firm and sure' which cut off the Visible Universe from the buffetings of the winds of Chaos, all the extremes to be found in the realm of Chaos and old Night. Introduced into Milton's cosmic system, this Crystalline is a most curious sphere. Beyond it, apparently, is the *Primum Mobile*, or outermost

shell of all.[1]   But it was apparently the Crystalline Sphere
that served as insulating medium and protection against
the storms of Chaos.

So, in Ben Gerson's commentary, the circle marked out
by the compasses upon the face of the Abyss became a
sphere of waters, a great supporting and stiffening of the
celestial waters.

The nature of this sphere in both writers is so similar
that I here quote both accounts of it.   Milton has said:

> 'and God made
> The Firmament, expanse of liquid, pure,
> Transparent, Elemental Air, diffus'd
> In circuit to the uttermost convex
> Of this great Round: partition firm and sure,
> The Waters underneath from those above
> Dividing: for as Earth, so he the World
> Built on circumfluous Waters calme, in wide
> Crystallin Ocean, and the loud misrule
> Of *Chaos* farr remov'd, least fierce extreames
> Contiguous might distemper the whole frame:
> And Heav'n he nam'd the Firmament:'
>
> —Book VII:263-274.

Ben Gerson had the following comment to make upon the
creation of the firmament:

באמצו שחקים ממעל' כאשר אמץ שחקים ממעל ונתן להם חוזק וקיום'... ומתיחסם
לקושי כאמרם לחים היו השמים ביום ראשון בשני נקדשו' בעווז עינו' תהום ר"ל כאשר
נתן הש"י עוז וקושי למה שהיה מהחומר הראשון אצל עינות תהום והוא כדור הארץ

when he made firm the skies above, referring to the Earth with the
heavens above.   And he gave to the sky support and existence. . . .
And the heavens were solidly joined in stiffness, as it is said, 'moist

---

[1]For a discussion of the nature of Milton's *Primum Mobile* and of the limits of
the Universe, see A. H. Gilbert, 'The Outside Shell of Milton's World,' *Studies
in Philology*, vol. xx (1923), pp. 444 ff.   It must always be remembered that in
Paradise Lost, the word *world* (*this pendent world*) means the Universe, not the
planet on which we live.   Milton usually capitalized the word.

were the heavens on the first day; on the second they became solid.'

when the fountains of the Abyss became strong. This means when God gave strength and stiffness to what had been primeval matter near the fountains of the Abyss. And the Heavens (the firmament השמים) became the great Sphere of the Earth.

Milton's 'expanse of liquid, pure' was made up of the waters, which were stiffened, at the same time forming a firm partition between the Universe and Chaos. His statement describing the extent of this sphere of waters, reaching 'in circuit to the uttermost convex of this great round,' implied the uttermost limits of the Visible Universe, just within the confines of the *Primum Mobile*. Thus, the firmament marked the farthest extent of the Cosmos as Milton thought of it. The idea of the rabbi, so far as the firmament or השמים *expanse* was concerned, is markedly similar, so much so that it is quite apparent that both poet and rabbi were thinking in terms of the same fundamental system. In so far, of course, as they were both dealing with conventional and definitely agreed upon aspects of the Ptolemaic system, there is no need for remarking on the similarity between them.

But the whole point of this discussion of the similarity between certain portions of Ben Gerson's commentary on the eighth chapter of Proverbs and certain ideas Milton has made use of in *Paradise Lost* centers in the fact that wherever else Milton may have encountered such ideas, the rabbis would have determined his use of them.

For, in dealing with Scripture, Milton had a definite scheme for the gradation of authorities. This is so well known that it is necessary here only to refer to it in order to point out why he drew on rabbinical commentaries as sources.[1] The fact that in dealing with the process or idea

[1] Milton's evaluation of scriptural authorities may be noted in a passage in *Eikonoklastes*, vol. III:516, and *passim* in his prose works. In the list of authorities

of Creation he was dealing with scriptural materials, imparted an authority for him to rabbinical commentaries on the text of Scripture which, as in the cases of their actual citations in his prose works, far outweighed in significance the authority as sources of other and more conjectural opinions. Thus, the reason for his selection of the particular presentation of the process of Creation he adopted and of the nature and function of the firmament, was the fact that he found both of these ideas in the most authentic sources possible, next to the text of Scripture itself, in the rabbinical commentaries attached directly to the Hebrew text.

One other interesting idea employed by Milton in his account of Creation finds an explanation in Ben Gerson's commentary. It will perhaps be recalled that Milton ended his account of the Creation of the Visible Universe with the line,

> 'And Earth self balanc't on her Center hung.'
>   —Book VII:242.

The meaning of this line has been variously explained, but none of the explanations, I think, quite fits the case or explains entirely the idea contained therein.[1] Keightley's explanation of the line implied that, as the earth was the center of the Universe, its own center was a sort of hypothetical termination of the golden chain on which the whole Universe was suspended. This was not, I think, precisely what Milton had in mind. In order to understand what Milton meant by the line, it is first necessary

---

as he arranged them in dealing with Judges 19:2, referred to and discussed in the previous chapter, his order of authoritative merit appeared to be, first, the Hebrew text itself; secondly, Josephus; thirdly, the Septuagint; fourthly, the Targums; and fifthly, the rabbinical commentaries adjoining the Hebrew text in a rabbinical Bible.

[1] See Verity, *op. cit.*, p. 538 for discussion of the meaning of this line, together with citation of other commentators.

to notice that in his account of Creation just preceding the line in question, he attempted to crowd together all the salient points concerning Creation that were contained in the chief passages of Scripture treating of Creation. As already mentioned, he himself in the *de doctrina* distinctly cited those passages that he considered the most important in connection with Creation. Among the passages he cited were certain verses in the twenty-sixth chapter of Job. In his description of the earth hanging 'self-balanced' on her center, he employed the idea found in the seventh verse of that chapter of Job, *he stretcheth out the north over empty space, and hangeth the earth upon nothing*. It is certain that it was from this verse that there came Milton's idea of the Universe hanging as 'this pendent World' over the 'nothingness' of the Abyss of Chaos, and from it also, but more indirectly, came his idea of the earth itself hanging 'self-balanced' on its center. The connection of the idea of the earth being hung over 'nothingness' found in the text of Job, and Milton's idea of the same earth being hung self-balanced from her center, is to be found in Ben Gerson's commentary to the text of the passage in Job. The rabbi's explanation is a striking one, involving perhaps both a symbolic and a literal significance. But it explains in a most satisfactory manner the meaning of Milton's line and how the earth hung self-balanced on her own center. The rabbi said:

על בלימה' על מה שאין לו מציאות בעצמותו והוא מרכו הארץ כי עליו נתלית הארץ
כמו שהתבאר בטבעיות

on nothing, that is, on something that has no existence in reality, and this is the center of the earth, from which point the earth is suspended.

Milton's line is now clear. The Biblical text of the verse in Job supplied the idea of the earth having been suspended, and the account and comment of the rabbi completed the idea that the earth had been hung from its own center in a manner that caused it to be self-balanced.

Other very minor points connected with Creation are to be found in the commentaries to those various scriptural passages Milton mentioned as dealing with Creation. But for the most part, they are even more trivial than the one just pointed out. I therefore omit discussion of them here, because, unlike Ben Gerson's commentary of the verse in Job which we have just examined, they supply no new interpretation of Milton's lines.

We are now ready to summarize the first part of our discussion of Milton's indebtedness to and use of rabbinical commentaries for certain of his ideas of Creation or of their elaboration. We have seen that his idea of Creation as an arrangement of pre-existent elements finds support in the commentary of Ibn Ezra to the first chapter of Genesis. This notion of Creation was a very common one, but Ibn Ezra's comment is directly upon the text of the Biblical passage itself, and thus would have possessed great authority for Milton. Moreover, both rabbi and poet in support of their similar refutations of the theory of *creatio ex nihilo* make use of identical material when they point out that the truth of the matter rests in the meaning of the Hebrew word ברא *he created*. It is remarkable that both employed the argument based on the use of the word ברא in the seventh verse of the forty-fifth chapter of Isaiah, and the meaning of the phrase 'create darkness' as the bases for their discussion of the nature of Creation in the first verse of the opening chapter of Genesis. Then, in Milton's presentation in *Paradise Lost* of Creation, Act and Process, certain details of the process, such as the use of the compasses in marking out the confines of the Universe, were almost certainly suggested and positively authenticated by the rabbinical treatment of the word חוג *circle* which occurs in the Proverbs text on which Milton based his primary account of Creation. Especially was he indebted to Ben Gerson's discussion of the whole Proverbs passage. He invoked a Muse very much like Ben Gerson's Spirit of Understanding, and in his idea of the presence of two Spirits at Creation, he was employing an idea found fully elaborated in the commentary of the same rabbi; and a great deal of light is shed on the nature of Milton's Muse by Ben Gerson's treatment of Wisdom and Understanding in his commentary to the same passage. In addition to these points, we have seen how Milton's whole conception of the working out of the process of Creation, especially his poetic treatment of that process, is based on the ideas of the rabbis. Ben Gerson, again, is especially useful for the idea of the birth-like process of Creation. It would, perhaps, be going too far to attribute to the same rabbi the source of Milton's 'crystalline sphere' or insulating shell between the *Primum Mobile* and the rest of the Universe, but certainly the fact that Milton found this sphere mentioned by the rabbis would have been an influence in determining his use of it.

Thus we have seen that many of the details and a few of the basic ideas connected with the process of Creation which Milton selected for presentation in *Paradise Lost* are to be found in rabbinical commentaries to scriptural passages dealing with Creation. Some of the material found therein could scarcely have served as basic source material for Milton, but all of it would have had its influence upon him. Other portions of the commentary give every indication of having been his basic sources for certain phases of Creation which he has presented in *Paradise Lost,* in so far as the Creation of the Visible Universe was concerned.

CHAPTER V

THE CREATION OF THE EARTH AND ITS FORMS OF LIFE IN *PARADISE LOST*

The second phase of Creation as Milton has presented it in *Paradise Lost*, was concerned more especially than the first with the Creation of this Earth, particularly of its various forms of life. As was the case with the first aspect of Creation presented in the poem, this second aspect also exhibits many details unmistakably drawn from rabbinical commentary.

After Raphael had related to Adam the story of the Creation of the Visible Universe by Act and Word of the Son of God in company with God's Spirit, he then described in much greater detail the work of the Six Days that followed the Act of Creation itself. Milton's account of this work, while based directly and very largely upon the text of the first two chapters of Genesis, has nevertheless used a great many of the detailed embellishments on that text found in the rabbinical commentary of Rashi on those two chapters. Rashi commented on the whole Pentateuch, and his commentary was printed by Buxtorf along with that of Ibn Ezra. These two commentaries are not much alike. Each is characteristic of its author, that of Ibn Ezra being much more philosophic, presenting constantly various theories or traces of theories that involve entire philosophical systems. Rashi's commentary, on the other hand, is always more detailed, less imaginative, and never distinctly philosophic. For this reason, the importance to us here of Rashi's commentary on those chapters of Genesis concerned with Creation is chiefly in connection with details of the more specific account, both in the Bible and in

Paradise Lost, of the forms of life that appeared on the Earth.[1]

In this chapter, I shall examine the commentary of Rashi, as found in Buxtorf, on the opening chapters of Genesis. As already suggested, Rashi was chiefly interested in this portion of his commentary in the Creation of the various forms found on this Earth. But his commentary on these chapters was by no means wholly confined to that phase of Creation. I shall, therefore, first discuss those parts of his commentary that deal with the Creation of the Cosmos. As there are not many of these, and as they do not seriously disturb the title of this chapter, I present them here rather than in the preceding chapter where they more logically belong. Presenting them in the present chapter keeps the discussion of Rashi's commentary almost entirely within the same chapter, and this has many advantages. I shall not present here all of the text of Rashi's commentary on the first three chapters of Genesis, as I have done with the commentators' texts on some of the other Old Testament passages dealing with Creation. I refrain from doing so for several reasons. Rashi's commentary on the opening chapters of Genesis is too long to print entirely, for much of it has not at all been used by Milton. Also, Rashi's commentary on the whole Pentateuch is perhaps the best known and certainly the most easily available of all rabbinical commentaries. Excellent editions of the original text of the whole Pentateuch commentary have been prepared, and nearly every modern

---

[1]M. Denis Saurat, in his stimulating book, *Milton: Man and Thinker*, (New York, 1925, p. 255) makes it appear that Rashi was somehow known to Milton through Walton's *Biblia Polyglotta* of 1654 ss. As nearly as I can determine, M. Saurat refers to one of the Targums, which is something quite different from Rashi's commentary. But I am not certain that I understand Professor Saurat's statement or his basis for it. It would be farthest from my desire to do him an injustice; but Walton did not print rabbinical commentaries.

European language has one or more usable translations of at least that portion of the commentary dealing with Creation. There is little in Buxtorf's text of Rashi, at least for these few chapters, that is sufficiently different from other Rashi texts to warrant reproducing the whole text here. Those who are further interested in Milton's use of the commentary on these chapters are referred to any of the standard texts of Rashi, or to Bamberger's German translation of the commentary on the Pentateuch.

I shall therefore print only those extracts from Rashi's commentary on Genesis that I have used in connection with Milton.[1] I have found that Milton used Rashi's commentary to a very great extent. The commentary of the rabbi in many instances supplies us with a better understanding of what Milton was trying to do, not only because of the fuller explanation the rabbi provides, but because we are by it afforded the point of origin for the material Milton was presenting. It is particularly enlightening in many cases for the understanding of what the poet was doing if we can see the actual source of his ideas.

To begin with, Rashi throws important light upon Milton's representation of the *order* in which Creation proceeded and in which its various parts appeared. In Milton's account of Creation, it is very apparent that he made no attempt to tell which of the various parts of Heaven and Earth was first created. When Creation is discussed by Raphael at some length in Book VII, he seems deliberately to refrain from saying which part of the Universe was first created. Thus, his reproduction of the command of Creation is entirely ambiguous concerning the priority of the parts of the Cosmos:

[1]There is an abundance of literature about Rashi, dealing with all phases of his life and work.

' "Silence, ye troubl'd waves, and thou Deep, peace,"

. . . .
   "thus farr extend, thus farr thy bounds,
This be thy just Circumference, O World."
Thus God the Heav'n created, thus the Earth,
Matter unform'd and void:'
            —Book VII:216-233.

Especially do the last two lines of those quoted above entirely confuse the determination of the priority of Heaven or Earth in Creation. These lines imply that there was no priority, for obviously they make no choice.

How then did Milton conceive of the order in which Creation proceeded?

His conception is not particularly complicated, but it is peculiar. All the elements of Heaven and Earth were created all at once, at the time of the Act of Creation, and were then put in their various places as the Works of the Six Days:

'Swift to their several Quarters hasted then
The cumbrous Elements, Earth, Flood, Aire, Fire,'
            —Book III:714-715.

The entire process was performed by the Son of God in company with God's Spirit:

'on the watrie calme
His brooding wings the Spirit of God outspred,
And vital vertue infus'd, and vital warmth
Throughout the fluid Mass, but downward purg'd
The black tartareous cold Infernal dregs,
Adverse to life: then founded, then conglob'd
Like things to like, the rest to several place
Disparted,'
            —Book VII:234-241.

That is, Creation took place as an Act of God which then

proceeded as a development or process, and as such it produced *order* in at least a portion of Chaos,

> 'the rest to several place
> Disparted,'   —*ibid.* 240-241.

Milton recurs to this idea of Creation being an ordering of
the formlessness of Chaos many times.   He spoke of

> The rising world of waters dark and deep,
> Won from the void and formless infinite.
>   —Book III:11-12.

The same idea occurs again, later in the same Book, in
Uriel's brief account of Creation, delivered to Satan:

> '*Confusion* heard his voice, and wilde uproar
> Stood rul'd, stood vast infinitude confin'd;
> Till at his second bidding darkness fled,
> Light shon, and order from disorder sprung:'
>   —*ibid.* 710-713.

This very closely follows the more formal presentation of
the same subject in the *de doctrina*, especially in the development of the idea of the relationship of primeval matter
to the process of Creation.   Matter, according to Milton,
was originally utterly formless, and, like Ben Gerson's
matter, discussed in the previous chapter, neither perfect
nor imperfect, *sed materia non erat in suo genere imperfecta.*
If matter possessed any quality at all, if matter in its
original state could be said to have been either good or evil,
Milton, like Ben Gerson again, decided that it possessed at
least the potentiality for goodness, since it essentially had
proceeded from God, *neque enim materia illa res mala est,
aut vilis existimanda, sed bona, omnisque boni postmodum
producendi seminarum.*   The relation of this primeval matter to Creation was that Creation was the process of giving
form or forms to chaotic and formless matter, *accessione
duntaxat formarum (quae et ipsae materiales quoque sunt)*

facta ornatior. The inert, formless, chaotic condition of matter before the Creation has been mentioned in *Paradise Lost* many times, notably in

'the wide womb of uncreated night,
Devoid of sense and motion?' —Book II:150-151.

This first matter, chaotic and inert, was, through the process of Creation, fashioned into order, *substantia erat, nec aliunde quam ex fonte omnis substantiae derivanda, indigesta modo et incomposita, quam Deus postea digessit et ornavit.*[1]

[1] In the *de doctrina*, the discussion of Creation in connection with primeval matter was very closely reasoned in a most formally logical manner. The excerpts quoted above in my text are all taken from a single paragraph, which, with its introductions, reads as follows: *Hactenus constat Deum Patrem causam esse primam rerum omnium efficientem. . . . Materia autem prima quae fuerit, varie disputatur. . . . Ex materia igitur quacunque mundum fuisse conditum palam est. Actio enim et passio relata cum sint, nullumque agens extra se possit agere, nisi sit quod pati queat, materia nimirum, Deus ex nihilo creare hunc mundum videtur non potuisse non ob virium, aut omnipotentiae defectum, sed quia necesse fuit aliquid jam tum fuisse, quod vim ejus agendi potentissimam patiendo reciperet. Cumque itaque non ex nihilo sed ex materia esse facta haec omnia et scriptura sacra et ratio ipsa suggerat, necesse est materiam vel fuisse semper extra Deum, vel aliquando ex Deo. ut extra Deum semper fuerit materia, quamvis Principium tantummodo passivum sit, a Deo pendeat, eique subserviat, quamvis ut numero; ita et aevi vel sempiterni nulla vis, nulla apud se efficacia sit, tamen ut ab aeterno, in quam, per se materia extiterit intelligi non potest, nec, si ab aeterno non fuit, unde tandem fuerit intellectu est facilius; restat igitur hoc solum, praeunte praesertim scriptura, fuisse omnia ex Deo. . . .* Primum hoc omnibus notissimum est quatuor esse genera causarum, efficientem, materialem, formalem, et finalem. Deus cum prima, absoluta, et sola rerum omnium causa sit, quis dubitet quin omnes causas in se contineat et complectatur? Materialis igitur causa erit aut Deus aut nihil; nihil autem nulla causa est, et tamen formas etiam maxime humanas ex nihilo volunt: materia autem et forma velut causae internae rem ipsam constituunt; adeoque omnia aut duas tantummodo causas habuerint, easque externas, aut Deus perfecta et absoluta rerum causa non fuerit. Deinde omnimodam, multiformem, et inexhaustam virtutem in Deo esse, eamque substantialem, non enim accidentalem, quae pro voluntate ejus et gradus quosdam et quasi impensionem quandam et remissionem admittat, virtutem hanc omnimodam et substantialem iniquam non intra se comprimere, sed emittere, propagare, atque extendere quatenus et quomodo ipse vult, quid aliud nisi summae potentiae summaeque benignitatis est? neque enim materia illa res mala est, aut vilis existimanda, sed bona, omnisque boni postmodum producendi seminarium; substantia erat, nec aliunde quam ex fonte omnis substantiae derivanda, indigesta modo et incomposita, quam Deus postea digessit et ornavit. (*de doctrina*, pp. 128-130.)

Sumner's expression in his English translation, 'digested into order by the hand of God,' is an excellent phrase for conveying the idea of Creation which Milton was describing in the *de doctrina* passages.

Milton very fully carried out this idea that Creation was an *ordering* of the elements of Chaos in *Paradise Lost*. He followed it very closely in his description of the appearance of the various parts of the Universe and of the forms of life on the Earth itself. The Universe, in the poem, was an arrangement of a certain portion of Chaos. In the same manner, Hell in its creation was an *ordering* of another portion of Chaos, which, personified, complains to Satan that its realm has been encroached upon,

> 'I upon my Frontieres here
> Keep residence; if all I can will serve,
> That little which is left so to defend,
> Encroacht on still through our intestine broiles
> Weakning the Scepter of old *Night*: first Hell
> Your dungeon stretching far and wide beneath;
> Now lately Heaven and Earth, another World
> Hung ore my Realm,'
> —Book II:998-1005.

But in Milton's discussion of the Creation of the Visible Universe, while the whole process is represented as one which produced *order* in a portion of Chaos, the priority of the parts of the Visible Universe in their creation is never indicated. Hell was created before the Universe; but so far as the various parts of the Universe were concerned, Milton carefully refrained from pointing out the priority of any one of them at the expense of any other. Thus, as already stated, we cannot tell whether the Heavens or the Earth came into being first. It is interesting to note in this connection that Rashi was very explicit on this particular point, denying priority to any part of the Universe in Creation over any other part. His commentary is very

suggestive of the idea of Creation that Milton presented.
Rashi thought of Creation as having taken place all at
once, with no priority between any of the various parts of
the Universe, and then each of these parts being put into
their places as the work of the Six Days. This is clearly
discernible in the following portion of his commentary,
especially his denial of priority to any one part of Creation
at the expense of another:

בראשית ברא'...ויאמר אלהים יהי אור' ולא בא המקרא להורות סדר הבריאה לומר
שאלו קדמו שאם בא להורות כך היה לו לכתוב בראשונה ברא את השמים וג' שאין
לך ראשית במקר' שאינו דבוק לתיבה של אחריו כמו בראשית ממלכת יהויקים ראשית
ממלכתו ראשית דגנך אף כאן אתה אומר בראשית ברא ה' את השמים וג' כמו בראשית
ברוא ודומה לו תחילת דבר יי' בהושע כלומר תחילת דבורו של הקב"ה בהושע ויאמר
יי' אל הושע וג' ואם תאמר להורות בא שאלו תחילה נבראו ופירושו בראשית הכל
ברא אלו ויש לך מקראות שמקצרים לשונם וממעטים תיבה אחת כמו כי לא סגר
דלתי בטני ולא פי' מי הסוגר וכמו ישא את חיל דמשק ולא פירש מי ישאנו וכמו אם
יחרוש בבקרים ולא פירש אם יחרוש אדם בבקרים וכמו מגיד מראשית אחרית ולא
פירש מגיד מראשית דבר אחרית דבר אם כן תימה על עצמך שהרי המים קדמו שהרי
כתוב ורוח ה' מרחפת על פני המים ועדיין לא גילה המקרא בסידור הקודמים
המאוחרים כלום ברית המים מתי' הא למדת שקדמו לארץ ועוד שהשמים מאש
וממים נבראו על כרחך לא לימד המקרא בסדר המוקדמים והמאוחרים כלום:

in the beginning created . . . And God said Let there be light. This
verse does not intend to teach the order of Creation, or to indicate
which of these (creations) was first. For if it did intend to teach
that, it should read *at first* (בראשונה) *he created the Heavens etc.*
For the word *beginning* (ראשית) never appears in the text of Scripture unless it connects with a noun following it, as (cites a number
of illustrations from Scripture with quotation). So here, you
might say, *in the beginning God created the Heavens and the Earth etc.*
meaning *in the beginning of Creation,* as in (Hosea 1:2) *when the
Lord spake at the first to Hosea,* meaning *in the beginning of the
speech of the Holy One blessed be he to Hosea, and God said etc.*
And if you say that the verse (in Genesis) teaches that these
(Heaven and Earth) were created first, meaning that he created
them in the beginning of it all, (follow reasoned examples from
Scripture). . then you may be astonished to discover that water

was first, for it is written, *and the Spirit of God moved on the face of the waters*. For the text has said nothing as yet concerning the priority, whether earlier or later, of the Creation of land or water. This apparently shows that water preceded earth, and yet the Heavens [which apparently were created first of all in verse 1] were created from fire and water [which is not mentioned until the following verse]. Hence you are forced to admit that the verse teaches nothing about the order, earlier or later, of anything created.   —(Commentary on Genesis 1:1.)

Rashi's definiteness in denying the possibility of determining the order in which the parts of the Visible Universe were created is in marked contrast to Milton's ambiguity on the same point; but it is important to notice that neither poet nor rabbi permits priority to any one part of Creation at the expense of any other. Milton's very ambiguity on the point perhaps best indicates that he had some reason for refraining from being more clear, namely, that all parts of the Universe were created at the same time. But the ambiguity was studied; for according to Milton and as we have seen in a previous chapter, Creation took place as a quickening, an impregnation of matter by the Spirit of God. Before this took place, matter was neither good nor evil, but possessed of the capacity for good, or capable of being *arranged* by the Spirit of God. But before this arrangement, that is, before Creation, the condition of this primeval matter is interesting: it existed *sine* dimension and *sine* time. Ibn Ezra explained that time was among those things that were created, and Milton subscribed to the same idea. The condition of Chaos before Creation was explained as an existence *sine* time because *sine* space. Satan, Sin, and Death gazed on

> the hoarie deep, a dark
> Illimitable Ocean without bound,
> Without dimension, where length, breadth, and highth,
> And time and place are lost;   —Book II:891-894.

Creation itself, the Act whereby God arranged the hitherto chaotic elements, dealt with timeless material, and was itself timeless because it was instantaneous:

> 'Immediate are the Acts of God, more swift
> Then time or motion,'
> —Book VII:176-177.

Thus, as to Rashi, there could be no priority *in time* between the various parts of Creation.

Milton followed very strictly this idea of Creation in the poem, representing the Act of Creation as being instantaneous and creating everything at once. But he also pointed out very carefully that after the Act of Creation, the various created things took their places as the Works of the Six Days. Many of his details in the descriptions of various events of those Days are also very strongly suggested by Rashi. For instance, Milton said that the sun, though created in the beginning, was kept hidden until it was 'transplanted' to its permanent place in the firmament on the fourth day. While the Works of the first three Days were being accomplished, the sun

> 'in a cloudie Tabernacle
> Sojourn'd the while.'
> —Book VII:248-249.

Of course the origin for the idea of the disposition of the sun in a 'cloudy tabernacle' is the fourth verse of the nineteenth Psalm, *in them* (the heavens) *hath he set a tabernacle for the sun*. But the idea that the sun was created on the first day, or at the beginning of all things, and then hidden away until it was time to put it in its place is not found in the Bible. But Rashi's commentary expressly accounts for just such a procedure with the sun, indeed, with all the luminaries of heaven. The rabbi commented on the fourteenth verse of the first chapter of Genesis as follows:

יהי מאורות וגו' מיום ראשון נבראו וברביעי צוה עליהם להתלות ברקיע וכן כל
תולדות שמים וארץ נבראו ביום ראשון וכל אחד ואחד נקבע ביום שנגמר עליו הוא
שכתוב את השמים לרבות תולדותיה' ואת הארץ לרבות תולדותיה:

let there be lights. On the first day the lights (sun, moon, and stars) were created, and on the fourth day he (God) ordered them to be placed in the firmament. So with all the Creations of Heaven and Earth: they were created on the first day, and every one of them was put in place on the day that was determined for it. Hence את (the sign of the direct object) is written with *Heavens* and with *Earth* to indicate their specific creations.

Such a conception of God's Creation of everything at once, then putting each item into place at its proper time after having kept it 'hidden' until then, throws unexpected light on a difficulty often noted but still unexplained in the Creation of Christ. Without entering fully into the discussion of Milton's peculiar Arianism, it is well known that with some modifications he held to this doctrine throughout the later part of his life, particularly in *Paradise Lost* and the *de doctrina*. But in the poem he has apparently contradicted himself. In Book V, Raphael relates to Adam how Christ was announced to Heaven as the Son of God:

> 'As yet this world was not, and *Chaos* wilde
> Reignd where these Heav'ns now rowl, where Earth
> now rests
> Upon her Center pois'd, when on a day
> (For time, though in Eternitie, appli'd
> To motion, measures all things durable
> By present, past, and future) on such day
> As Heav'ns great Year brings forth, th' Empyreal Host
> Of Angels by Imperial summons call'd,
> Innumerable before th' Almighties Throne
> Forthwith from all the ends of Heav'n appeerd
> Under thir Hierarchs in orders bright
> Ten thousand thousand Ensignes high advanc'd,
> Standards, and Gonfalons twixt Van and Reare

Streame in the Aire, and for distinction serve
Of Hierarchies, of Orders, and Degrees;
Or in thir glittering Tissues bear imblaz'd
Holy Memorials, acts of Zeale and Love
Recorded eminent.   Thus when in Orbes
Of circuit inexpressible they stood,
Orb within Orb, the Father infinite,
By whom in bliss imbosom'd sat the Son,
Amidst as from a flaming Mount, whose top
Brightness had made invisible, thus spake.
     ' "Hear all ye Angels, Progenie of Light,
Thrones, Dominations, Princedoms, Vertues, Powers,
Hear my Decree, which unrevok't shall stand.
This day have I begot whom I declare
My onely Son, and on this holy Hill
Him have anointed, whom ye now behold
At my right hand; your Head him I appoint;
And by my Self have sworn to him shall bow
All knees in Heav'n, and shall confess him Lord:" '

                              —Book V:577-608.

Much later in the same Book, when Abdiel answers Satan
concerning the revolt, another statement about the Creation of the Son is made:

     ' "Thyself though great and glorious dost thou count,
Or all Angelic Nature joind in one,
Equal to him begotten Son, by whom
As by his Word the mighty Father made
All things, ev'n thee, and all the Spirits of Heav'n
By him created in thir bright degrees,
Crownd them with Glory, and to thir Glory namd
Thrones, Dominations, Princedoms, Vertues, Powers,
Essential Powers, nor by his Reign obscur'd,
But more illustrious made, since he the Head
One of our number thus reduc't becomes,
His Laws our Laws, all honour to him done
Returns our own." '

                              —*ibid.* 833-845.

It is difficult to see how the Son could have been the instrument for the Creation of the Hosts of Heaven, and at the same time have first been announced to them as Son of God long after their Creation. Various explanations of this point have been attempted, Masson, unable to cope with the difficulty otherwise, suggesting that Christ, to Milton, had two aspects, the one the Divine Logos, and the other the announced Son of God.[1]   Saurat has uncon-

---

[1]Masson, *Poetical Works*, vol. III:362-63, commenting on lines 579-583: Here, at the outset, Milton's or Raphael's, plan of narrating the events of the eternal or transcendental world so as to make them analogically conceivable by the human mind involved him in a daring image, with a perplexing theological consequence. Heaven has its "great year,"—perhaps that "great year of the Heavens," imagined by Plato, which is measured by one complete revolution of all the spheres, so that all are brought back to the exact condition of mutual arrangement from which they set out, and are ready to begin a new repetition of their vast courses. Well, on a day such as this great year brings forth,—the first day of one such enormous Heavenly revolution,—there was an assembling of the Heavenly hierarchies, by summons, to hear a grand new announcement of the will of the Infinite Father. It was that on that day had been begotten the only Son, and that he was consti-tuted and anointed Head and Lord over all things. Now, as the Angelic hosts were assembled to hear this decree, they had indefinitely pre-existed the day so splendidly marked, and it came as a kind of interruption or new epoch in their existence. This seems farther hinted in a subsequent speech of Satan (lines 853-863), where it is implied that, in Satan's view at least, the Angels had come into being at the beginning of a *previous* great year or natural cycle of the Heavens. Now, though Milton was an Arian, as is proved by his *Treatise of Christian Doc-trine*, yet his Arianism, as avowed in that treatise, was of the kind called High Arianism, which would not have been content with imagining the as-cendancy of the Son as subsequent to the creation of the Angels. Accord-ing to Bishop Sumner's summary of the portion of the treatise referring to this subject, Milton asserted that "the Son of God existed in the be-ginning and was the first of the whole creation," and that "by his delegated power all things were made in heaven and earth." There might seem to be an incon-sistency between this and what is suggested in the present passage. But see the speech of Abdiel (lines 835-840), where the seeming inconsistency is provided for by the assertion that, although the Son had been begotten on that day of the as-sembling of the Angels, yet by Him originally had all things, including the Angels themselves, been made. It seems unavoidable to suppose that Milton drew a dis-tinction between the essential existence and power of the Divine Logos and "his being begotten as the Son," dating the first as from the beginning, or at least from before all Creation and all Angels, but placing the last within the limits of created time and of angelic history, and so denying what theologians call "the Eternal Sonship."

vincingly connected these two passages with the Book of Enoch.[1] Unfortunately, the Enoch fragment contained in Syncellos, so far as is known the only form in which Milton could have known the Book of Enoch, does not contain the very verses that would have been of most value to the poet in this connection.[2] It is, therefore, extremely doubtful if he took from the Book of Enoch the idea of such a creation and subsequent 'hiding' of the Son until the Great Day of Assembly in Heaven when he was announced as the Son of God, first begotten and ruler over all of God's works in Heaven and Earth.[3]

However, Rashi's explanation of the Creation of the various parts of the Universe is entirely adequate to explain Milton's conception of the Creation of the Christ and the announcement of him as Lord of the Universe. Rashi says that God created everything all at once, at the very beginning, and then put each part in its proper place at the appointed times. Thus the Sun, created at the very beginning, was kept hidden until the fourth day, when it was put in its place in the heavens. We have found Milton using precisely this same notion regarding the Sun. The

[1]Denis Saurat, *La Pensée de Milton* (Paris, 1920), p. 245, 'Milton nous présente Dieu intronisant son Fils: (*P.L.*V:600 et suiv.) Or, ce Fils n'avait pu être conçu "en ce jour" et présenté aux anges, puisque c'était lui-même qui avait, dès l'origine, crée et le monde et les anges.

Le Livre d'Hénoch nous propose une solution ingénieuse de la difficulté: (v. R. H. Charles, *The Book of Enoch*, Clarendon Press, 1912, p. 93, notes sur le verset a du chapitre XLVIII.) Le Fils existait bien dès avant la création, mais Dieu l'avait tenu caché jusqu'au jour choisi pour sa révélation.'

[2]Saurat himself has evidently taken cognizance of this point by omitting all reference to it in *Milton: Man and Thinker* (New York, 1925).

[3]I had already written the above when there came to hand Kathleen Ellen Hartwell's *Lactantius and Milton* (Harvard University Press, 1929). In this work it is suggested (pp. 100 ff.) that Milton may have used as source the Jewish פסיקתא רבתי and ילקוט שמעוני in both of which occurs the same idea of the creation of the Messiah used in *P.L.* It seems most unlikely to me that Milton knew either of these two works directly. It would be necessary to connect him with either, or with both, before it would be possible to assume that he secured his conception of the creation of the Messiah from them. But it is certain that the origin of the idea is rabbinical.

rabbi denies priority of any part of the Universe at the expense of any other part.   If this conception of Creation be applied to Milton's discussion of the Creation of the Son, the difficulties pointed out before disappear.   The Christ, the creating Principle, the Logos, was the means by which all Creation took place, and thus was clearly, as stated by Abdiel, 'the Word by whom the Mighty Father made all things.'   Existent from the very beginning of Creation, but not coexistent with God, the Creating Principle, the λόγος, was not revealed as such until 'the day' in Heaven when God announced him as the Son.   This is exactly Rashi's idea of all Creation, and Milton has applied it to the Christ.   Strangely enough, it makes Satan's revolt more reasonable.   The Word, the Christ, was created at the very beginning of all things; but so too were all the other hosts of Heaven.   The Creating Principle contained in itself all of the other elements of Creation—thus, in a sense, Satan was as early created as the Logos because when the Logos or Idea of Creation came into existence, with it there came also into existence the ideas of everything it was to create.   And just as with the word, there was a delay or a long period following his creation before the λόγος was announced to the Hosts of Heaven in its proper condition of the Christ, the Son of God, only begotten, by means of which all things were created, so too with Satan, there was a delay between his creation and his appearance in his proper condition, that of the leader of the Revolting Angels.   Milton has treated them alike, following Rashi's suggestion regarding the mode of Creation that caused everything to be created at once but not to appear in its proper place or condition until the time appointed for such manifestations.   Instead, therefore, of having been inconsistent in his treatment of the Creation of the Christ, Milton has been most consistently faithful to that conception of Creation as a whole he was using throughout the poem. Just as the Sun was created when the heavens and the earth were created, and then put in its place on the proper day, so too the Son, created at the very beginning of Creation, indeed, the Principle on which Creation proceeded, was not announced as such until the appointed time.

Returning for a moment to the creation of the 'lights' Milton has paraphrased Scripture thus:

> 'let them be for Signes,
> For Seasons, and for Dayes,'

He then added, what Scripture only provided,

> 'and circling Years;'
> —Book VII:341-342.

Repeatedly elsewhere he has called attention to the 'circling' idea as the basis of time, notably in the following:

> they (the stars) as they move
> Thir Starry dance in numbers that compute
> Days, months, and years, towards his (the sun's) all-
> chearing Lamp
> Turn swift thir various motions, or are turnd
> By his Magnetic beam,
> —Book III:579-583.

Verity has suggested that the phrase 'circling years' is of classical origin, and perhaps it was;[1] but Rashi affords more than a hint of its origin for Milton, at least for the first of the two passages quoted above. The rabbi continued his comment on the 'lights' by saying further of them,

ושנים' לסוף שלש מאות וששים וחמשה ימים יגמרו מהלכתם בי"ב מולות המשרתים
אותם והיא שנה

---

[1] Verity, *op. cit.*, p. 541, 'circling'; cf. *P. R.* i. 57, 'the circling hours,' and Greek κυκλεῖν (sic)—'to revolve,' as in Sophocles, *Electra*, 1365. Perhaps Milton has in mind Homer's περιπλομένων ἐνιαυτων (as the years go round).

and years. At the end of three hundred sixty-five days, they (the lights, sun, moon, and stars) finish their circle with the twelve planets that serve them, and this is a year.

Another similar detail employed by Milton in working out the process of Creation as the arrangement in their places of the various created things was that of the origin of plants. His idea of their creation is most unusual, and in his statement concerning them occur the following perplexing lines:

> 'and each
> Plant of the field, which e're it was in the Earth
> God made, and every Herb, before it grew
> On the green stemm;'
>
> —Book VII:334-337.

Without the idea of Creation as a process of arrangement of its separate parts, it is extremely difficult to explain the meaning of these lines, and even more difficult to understand why such a statement as this should ever have been made. But with the idea of Creation as a process of arrangement clearly in mind, the lines take on a significance otherwise impossible. They are further redeemed from obscurity, and the reason for Milton having used them made clear, by the following direct comment by Rashi on the same point:

טרם יהיה בארץ' כל טרם שבמקרא לשון עד לא הוא ואינו לשון קוד' ואינו נפעל
לומר הטרים כאשר יאמר הקדים וזה מוכיח ועוד אחר כי טרם תיראון עדיין לא
תיראון ואף זה תפרש עדיין לא היה בארץ כשנגמר' ברית עולם בששי קודם שנברא
אדם

and not yet was in the earth. Always in Scripture the word טרם means *not yet*, and not *at first* or *before*. The verb form הטרים does not occur as does הקרים *to precede*. This is one reason; and another is (Ex. 9:30) *ye will not yet fear*, meaning *as yet will ye not fear*. And so the phrase is explained in the case before us, *not yet was in the earth*, means on the sixth day, after the Creation of the world was entirely completed but before, or while not yet was man created.

Rashi's time-concept and his explanation are complicated; but to understand them makes the intent of Milton's lines perfectly clear, and likewise helps to understand the whole process the poet had in mind.

Rashi meant that the plants had been created as had everything else in the narrative of the first chapter of Genesis. But, as he said, though Milton did not follow him entirely in this, after everything else except man had been created, they, the plants, were not yet in the Earth although they were in existence. That is, God caused the plants to appear, not by having them first spring from the Earth, but by first creating them; and then, after having brought them into existence, putting them into the Earth. In other words, they were not put into their proper places until the day appointed for doing this, as with all other created things. But they had been, as had everything else, created at the very beginning. This is an idea strange to us who have forgotten many of the explanations necessary to the whole doctrine of special Creation. We have even forgotten the necessity for such an explanation which arose from the misunderstanding of the relationship between the two parallel but different accounts of Creation in Genesis. We today experience no particular difficulty in reading the first two chapters of Genesis and realizing that they are two distinct though similar accounts of the same events. We no longer need insist that all differences between the two passages must be explained as actual differences between actual events, for we realize that the differences are due to two separate narratives, each with different interests. But in Rashi's time, and indeed in Milton's, the events of the two chapters were carefully integrated with respect to each other and to each account, as always it was necessary to preserve the distinct priority of the first chapter over the second. Indeed, Milton's perplexing lines about the plants having been created before they were in the earth, are but one of a number of instances that demonstrate his meticulous care for the letter of Scripture. Rashi's comment in the case of the plants may have so emphasized the matter that Milton deliberately worked into his poem the apparent perversity contained in the fifth verse of the second chapter of Genesis. But other similar instances occur to demonstrate the tremendous authority possessed for him by all Biblical statements. We have already seen that Biblical authority for Milton meant the authority of the originals. Milton, of course, was only sharing in the general 'jot or tittle' attitude toward the Bible of the age in which he wrote.[1] On the matter of the plants, Rashi might have confirmed Milton's opinion, but he could scarcely have created it. I should prefer to believe that the rabbi's comment aided Milton in clarifying his thoughts on Creation as much as the same comment aids us in understanding Milton. Nevertheless, it is apparent that there is more than a mere resemblance between the two writers here, and the significance of the resemblance strikes deep because of the virtual identity of their ideas on the point in question.

Before leaving the general subject of the plants and their Creation, it is most interesting to note another instance of the influence of Rashi's commentary upon Milton's treatment of vegetation in general. There is no more charming embellishment of Scripture in *Paradise Lost* than the representation of the Earth being clothed as with a garment

---

[1]Other instances in *Paradise Lost* of the same attempt to preserve both of two mutually exclusive Biblical passages may be seen in the animals and birds entering the Ark 'in sevens and pairs' (Book XI:735), and the careful preservation of the two accounts of the creation of man contained respectively in the first and second chapters of Genesis (Book VII:530, and Book VIII:333).

by the plants as they sprang forth from the ground at the command, *let the Earth put forth grass.* Milton has had much to say of this, in part

> 'and said, "Let th' Earth
> Put forth the verdant Grass, ..."
> He scarce had said, when the bare Earth, till then
> Desert and bare, unsightly, unadornd,
> Brought forth the tender Grass, whose verdure clad
> Her Universal Face with pleasant green,'
>
> —Book VII:309-316.

The suggestion for this elaboration is contained in Rashi's commentary. His comment is brief, but pointed; suggestive rather than complete; but it supplied the idea:

תדשא הארץ' תמלא ותתכסה לבוש עשבים

let the earth put forth grass, meaning, let it be filled and clothed as with a garment of herbs.

Another curious detail of Creation employed by Milton is to be noted among the animal forms. This is his description of the worms, which were created, according to Milton and following Genesis, along with the insects. That is, Genesis has said they were created together: Milton would say that they made their appearance together. But it is his description of the appearance of the worms and their physical characteristics that is remarkable. He described their creation and followed this with a suggestive and curious picture of them:

> 'These (the worms) as a line thir long dimension drew,
> Streaking the ground with sinuous trace;'
>
> —Book VII:480-481.

The figure used to describe them is that they draw their lengths along the ground, and as a descriptive figure, it is

certainly effective.   This likewise is found in Rashi in the
following form:

ורמש' הם שרצים שהם נמוכים ורומשים על הארץ ונראים כאילו נגררין שאין הלוכן
ניכר

creeping thing.   These are the worms that are low and creep on the
earth, appearing as if they were dragging themselves along, for
their walking is not apparent.

This curious and interesting bit of rabbinical natural history, Milton has worked into his description of the
'minims of nature.'

A similar bit has to do with the origin of birds.   This not
only indicates a point of origin for the idea, but is very
informative as to the manner in which Milton was using
Rashi's commentary in connection with his poetical account of the Biblical story of Creation.   It is clear that
Milton's account of the origin of birds makes out that they
were of a muddy, miry beginning.   The whole passage in
which he described their origin indicates this:

> 'Mean while the tepid Caves, and Fens and shoares
> Thir Brood as numerous hatch, from the Egg that soon
> Bursting with kindly rupture forth disclosed
> Thir callow young; but featherd soon and fledge
> They summ'd their Penns, and soaring th' air sublime
> With clang despis'd the ground,'
>
> —*ibid*. 417-422.

Why are all the points of origin of birds of the same earth-
water mixed nature?   'Cave' and 'fen' and 'shoare' all
imply mud and mire as having been their place of origin.
One can, of course, go to classical and medieval ornithol-
ogy for this point, but Rashi was at hand to give it scriptural authority with his comment:

Comment on Genesis 2:19

ויעש ה' את חית הארץ וגו' אלא בא ופירש שהעופו' נבראו מן הרקק לפי שאמר
למעל' מן המי' נבראו וכאן אמר מן האנץ נבראו

and God made the beasts of the earth etc. Now it is clear as to how
the birds were created from the mire, for earlier it was stated that
they were created from water, and here it is said that they were
created from the earth.

Of course, if we were logical, as were Rashi and Milton, we
could very readily see that if the Bible says in one place
that birds were created from water, and later that they
were created from earth, they must have been created from
a mixture of earth and water, or mud. Rashi has earlier in
the commentary to the same chapter said that birds were
created from such a mixture:

Comment on Genesis 2:8

וללמד על העופות שנבראו מן הרקק

and also to teach that the birds were created from a mixture of
earth and water.

It was this earlier comment that he was explaining in connection with the eighteenth verse.

However, this whole point concerning the muddy origin
of birds is of greater importance than the connections it
has with Rashi. It arises from the same difficulty that
was encountered with the two opening chapters of Genesis
noted in connection with the creation of plants. In the
first chapter, the birds were apparently put forth by or
from water; but in the second chapter, they were formed
from the ground, hence mud was their origin. This is a
very small point; but when coupled with the full cognizance shown by the poet to the creation of plants under
similar conditions of relation, the point is peculiarly important because of the indication it affords of the infinite
care Milton was exercising in his use and manipulation of
details in his account of Creation. Literally every line of

Books seven and eight was written with the utmost care and precision. No work of Defoe's was ever prepared with greater care of detail for the purpose of securing verisimilitude than were these two Books of *Paradise Lost* to preserve every possible vestige of scriptural authority. No point was too small to overlook; nothing in an account of the Creation of the Cosmos could be regarded as insignificant; the result being that, if it were not for the immense change which has taken place since Milton's day in our attitude toward the material, we should be able to read this account of Creation as if and with the feeling that we were perusing a report of something that actually took place. Unfortunately, or, from our point of view, fortunately, the entire cosmological theory on which Milton's account of Creation rested has been irretrievably swept away into the lumber-room of discarded ideas, destroying all of the value and hence much of the appeal of much of his elaborate panorama of Creation. But it is nevertheless salutary to pause here and remember that, if granted his premises, Milton's treatment of Creation is stupendous in its complexity and grandeur of structure, and that this effect is gained primarily by never-ceasing attention to details. Rashi's contributions to those details or to the understanding of them are, therefore, of more importance to us in helping us to realize the bewildering intricacy of Milton's structural attainment in his account of Creation than they are in connection with any light they may throw upon outmoded ideas of Creation.

Before leaving Milton's account of the Creation of the Universe and turning to the story of man's Creation and subsequent life in the Garden, there are one or two other details used by Milton to which I wish to call attention because they were suggested in Rashi's commentary. Thus, Rashi furnished a suggestion for Milton's conception of how and in what circumstances God ordained the World, man, and all created things, which He knew must fall.

In *Paradise Lost*, before Satan had reached the Universe on his evil journey, God points him out to Heaven, flying toward this World, and discourses with the Son on the future of man and of all created things. He declares that He has created man 'just and right'; but unable to withstand temptation, almost fated to fall. And fall he would, for 'justice alone' was too great a burden for the World to bear, as bear it must if it and man remained free to choose:

> 'I formd them free, and free they must remain,
> Till they enthrall themselves: I else must change
> Thir nature, and revoke the high Decree
> Unchangeable, Eternal, which ordain'd
> Thir freedom, ...
> . . . . Man therefore shall find grace,
> The other (Satan) none: in Mercy and Justice both,
> Through Heav'n and Earth, so shall my glorie excel,
> But Mercy first and last shall brightest shine.'
>
> —Book III:124-135.

Man's only salvation lay in God's grace, freely given:

> 'Man shall not quite be lost, but sav'd who will,
> Yet not of will in him, but grace in me
> Freely vouchsaft;'
> —*ibid.* 173-175.

That is, God ordained Creation

> 'In Mercy and in Justice both,
> Through Heav'n and Earth,'
> —*ibid.* 132-133.

After man's foreseen Fall, God again voiced this principle of the union of Mercy with Justice as the basis of all Creation. This was announced to the Hosts of Heaven as the plan of Man's salvation. Man has fallen, just as God had said he would; now he is so treated, not with Justice alone, which would utterly and forever ruin him, as it was his own and not God's fault that he fell. Not Justice alone; but Justice tempered with Mercy:

> 'Easie it might be seen that I intend
> Mercie collegue with Justice sending thee
> Man's Friend, his Mediator, his design'd
> Both Ransom and Redeemer voluntarie,
> And destin'd Man himself to judge Man fall'n.'

—Book X:40 58-62.

Creation was originally effected in Justice; but Justice alone was not enough, and Mercy was added.

This is curiously suggested, without speculative theological adornment, by Rashi's comment on the original ordination of Creation. He commented on the Hebrew form of the name of God that creates in the first verse of the first chapter of Genesis; but his comment was not so much concerned with a discussion of the names of God as it was with the bases on which the World was ordained, as these grew out of the names of God. There is no need here to explain Rashi's discussion of the qualities that pertain to the different names of God in Hebrew, only his statements regarding the qualities of Justice and of Mercy through which the World was ordained being of direct consequence here. The rabbi said

ברא אלהים' ולא נאמר ברא יי' שבתחלה עלה במחשבה לבראתו במדת הדין וראה
שאין העולם מתקיים והקדים מדת רחמים ושתפה למדת הדין'

God (אלהים) *created*. It is not said that "י (the Tetragrammaton) created. At first, there was the intention to create it (the World) with the quality of Justice only. But He saw that the World would not be able to exist on Justice alone. So He let the quality of Mercy precede, and associated with it the quality of Justice.

Rashi's statement 'so He let the quality of Mercy precede' is too much like Milton's 'but mercy, first and last,
shall brightest shine' for us entirely to ignore this comment in connection with Milton's conception of the ordained arrangement for the World's Fall and the possibility of redemption. In fact, the whole idea of the rabbi
finds a remarkable echo in Milton's words. Of course,
several centuries of theological discussion lie between the
rabbi and poet, and the rabbi's ideas had been caught up
into the stream of conventional speculation. Milton has
still further developed the idea by embodying in it the
Christian ideal of the Christ as Mediator, not only between
God and man, but also between the two principles, Justice
and Mercy. Through the Son, at once Justice is maintained
and Mercy administered. Rashi's commentary directly
on the relationship between Justice and Mercy and the Creation of the Universe is apparent in Milton's account.

I wish again to call attention to Milton's Crystalline
Sphere as he described and used it in his cosmological system, this time in connection with Rashi's commentary.
We have already seen that Ben Gerson's commentary also
provided such a sphere, and it was one common to all medieval thought about the Cosmos. That is, it was found too
in the works of the medieval rabbis. It is not surprising,
therefore, to find Rashi discussing it, and his discussion
throws some light on Milton's description and use of the
same sphere. For this reason, before leaving those portions of Rashi's commentary which deal with the Creation
of the Visible Universe, I shall here discuss what the rabbi
had to say of the sphere.

The ninth, 'crystalline' sphere had been added to the
Ptolemaic system of spheres in order to account for the
precession of the equinoxes. Milton described this sphere
as a vast expanse of waters:

'and God made
The Firmament, expanse of liquid, pure,
Transparent, Elemental Air, diffus'd
In circuit to the uttermost convex
Of this great Round: partition firm and sure,
The Waters underneath from those above
Dividing: for as Earth, so he the World
Built on circumfluous Waters calme, in wide
Crystallin Ocean,'

—Book VII:263-271.

That is, just as there were waters above and below the
Earth, so too there were waters above and below the
crystalline sphere of the Universe; and as those earthly
waters were separated from each other by the Earth itself,
so those cosmic waters were separated from each other by
the 'partition firm and sure, the waters underneath from
those above dividing.'   Although the peculiar cosmology
of the poem was more or less the conventional Ptolemaic
system of the Middle Ages and earlier, nevertheless in this
detail, as in others, there is amplification of the convention
due to some discernible factor, in this case perhaps, Rashi.
The rabbi offered direct comment on this point when he
described the nature of the Firmament in his commentary
on the sixth verse of the first chapter of Genesis:

בתוך המים' באמצע המים שיש הפרש בין מים העליוני' לתחתוני לרקיע כמו בין הרקיע
למים שעל הארץ

in the midst of the waters, meaning placed between the waters. For
there is a separation between the upper and lower waters of the
Firmament as there is between the waters that are on the Earth.

Of course, Renaissance cosmology would have supplied the
same point; but doubtless Milton was influenced to employ it as he has because he found it in rabbinical comment
directly upon Scripture.   And Rashi provides further information of the kind Verity has assembled in connection

with the Crystalline Sphere. Verity has devoted an entire appendix to the discussion of Milton's Cosmology, and has this to say of the Ninth Sphere:

The Crystalline Sphere and the *Primum Mobile* were not included in the original Ptolemaic system. They were added later, to explain certain phenomena which the earlier astronomers had not observed, and for which their theories offered no explanation. Thus the supposed swaying or 'trepidation' of the Crystalline Sphere was held to be the cause of the precession of the equinoxes. This Sphere was described as a great expanse of waters. There are waters in the Universe because Chaos, of which it was a portion, was a kind of sea. At first these waters formed one great 'Deep:' now they are divided. Part are collected round the Earth, the middle point of the Universe, and cover it. Part are placed in the Ninth or Crystalline Sphere, i.e. in the uttermost but one of the regions of space that surround the Earth. The 'firmament,' according to Milton, is the expanse of air, stretching from the Earth to this Crystalline Sphere. Hence the 'firmament' intervenes between and 'divides' the waters that flow immediately round the Earth and the waters of the Crystalline Sphere: the former being 'the waters which were under the firmament,' the latter 'the waters which were above the firmament' (*Genesis* i. 7); as Milton says, 'The waters underneath' and 'those above.' It (the Crystalline Sphere) encircles the eight inner Spheres. The original notion may perhaps be traced to the waters 'above the firmament' in *Genesis* i. 7. Compare the picture in VII. 270, 271 of the World

> 'Built on circumfluous Waters calme, in wide
> Crystallin Ocean,'

The main purpose that this 'ocean' serves is to protect the Earth from the evil 'influences' of Chaos; those 'fierce extremes' of temperature which might penetrate through the outside shell (the *Primum Mobile*) and 'distemper' the whole fabric of the Universe, did not this wall of waters interpose.[1]

This comment by Verity, the fullest of all comments on the Crystalline Sphere, is typical of what annotators and com-

---

[1] Verity, *op. cit.*, pp. 665-666, and 539-540.

mentators have said of the nature of the Sphere. Rashi's commentary may be looked upon as a medieval account in connection with Scripture of how this Sphere came into existence. Milton's description of its Creation is in full accord with Rashi's commentary, and it is clear that both poet and rabbi had in mind the same idea.

Immediately following the account of the Creation of the Crystalline Sphere in the poem, Milton described the formation of the Earth itself, calling attention to the fact that it was at first entirely covered with water until the seas were created,

> 'over all the face of Earth
> Main Ocean flow'd,'
> —Book VII:278-279.

Rashi's commentary pointed to precisely the same condition as this having existed before the Earth was made to appear in the process of its Creation:

Comment on Genesis 1:9

יקוו המי' היו שטוחין על פני כל הארץ והקוom באוקיינוס

he gathered the waters. They had been spread out over the face of the whole Earth, and he gathered them into the Ocean (the Mediterranean אוקיינוס).

The point is small; but valuable as an indication of how carefully Milton worked out the whole presentation of Creation, neglecting nothing that could be of the slightest consequence.

When we come to consider Milton's treatment of Adam, we find that many details of that treatment were anticipated by Rashi's commentary.

One of these details is the manner in which Milton represented Adam as having been created outside of the Garden of Eden and after his Creation being brought to it. Genesis (2:8) says only, *and the Lord God planted a garden eastward in Eden; and there he put the man whom he had formed.* This, indeed, suggests that Adam was created outside of the Garden and then placed therein. But Milton supplied more information about the occurrence than is found in the Biblical text itself. Following the suggestion of the text, or some other suggestion, Milton explained at some length how Adam was first created and then brought to the Garden afterwards:

> 'One came, methought, of shape Divine,
> And said, "thy Mansion wants thee, *Adam*, rise,
> First Man, of Men innumerable ordain'd
> First Father, call'd by thee I come thy Guide
> To the Garden of bliss, thy seat prepar'd."
> So saying, by the hand he took me rais'd,
> And over Fields and Waters, as in Aire
> Smooth sliding without step, last led me up
> A woodie Mountain; whose high top was plaine,
> A Circuit wide, enclos'd, with goodliest Trees
> Planted, with Walks, and Bowers, that what I saw
> Of Earth before scarce pleasant seemd.'
> —Book VIII:295-306.

The chief basis for this was doubtless Biblical, the verse quoted above and the fifteenth of the same chapter affording much of the underlying suggestion. But the address to Adam by his guide, with its trace of persuasion, is not to be found in the text. It is, however, directly indicated by Rashi, who explained how it was that Adam was induced to enter the Garden. In his comment on the fifteenth verse of this chapter, the rabbi said:

ויקח' לקחו בדברים נאים ופתהו ליכנס

he took, by means of fine words he persuaded [Adam] to enter the Garden.

Milton supplied a short speech by the vague form that led Adam to Eden, using the suggestion with which Rashi had provided him.

One of the most notable instances in which Rashi very obviously supplied Milton with an idea of importance is to be found in the poet's account of why, how, and under what circumstances Adam came to be provided with a wife.

The account of Eve's Creation contained in the second chapter of Genesis clearly implies that the Lord God observed Adam alone of all the forms of life on the Earth without a mate: *and the Lord God said, It is not good that man should be alone; I will make him an help meet for him.* That is, the account in Genesis implies that it was the Lord God who first realized Adam's need for companionship, and the desire to remedy the situation is entirely a desire on the part of the Deity, and not at all of Adam. But Milton did not follow this. He placed the first realization of Adam's loneliness, not in the mind of God, but in the mind of Adam. Elaborately the poet built up the account of how Adam, by naming the animals, first became aware of his lack of human companionship. The man then reflects on the matter, and his lonely condition without another of his kind becomes for him a highly significant psychological fact. Desire for companionship is next awakened in him through further reflection, and he finally and very hesitatingly asks the Deity to afford him relief, although he is not just certain what it is he wants or what he will receive, even if his request is granted.

Milton has apparently adorned the Biblical passage with great splendor having deviated from it by making Adam rather than God rationalize the situation. This is indicated by the following extracts from the whole passage:

> ' "each Bird and Beast behold
> After thir kindes; I bring them to receave
> From thee thir Names," . . . .
>
> . . . .

As thus he spake, each Bird and Beast behold
Approaching two and two, ...
    . . . .
I nam'd them, as they pass'd, and understood
Thir Nature, ...
   . . . . but in these
I found not what methought I wanted still;
And to the Heav'nly vision thus presum'd.

(*Adam addresses God*)
  . . . . "but with mee
I see not who partakes,"

(*They converse*)

(*Adam says*)
  . . . . "they rejoyce
Each with thir kinde, Lion with Lioness;
So fitly them in pairs thou hast combin'd;"
   . . . .
(*They further converse*)
Hee ended, or I heard no more, for now
  . . . . overpowerd,
. . . . sunk down, and sought repair
Of sleep, which instantly fell on me,
  . . . . and clos'd mine eyes." '
       —Book VIII:342-459.

As a matter of fact, the basis for the whole account was
supplied by Rashi's commentary, and especially for the
discontent and longing aroused in Adam by being obliged
to name the animals. As they came to him, male and
female in pairs, there was induced in him an awareness of
his own need for a mate. Rashi's comment on the twentieth verse of the second chapter of Genesis is as follows:

ולאדם לא מצא עזר ויפל ה' אלהי' תרדמה' כשהביאן הביאן לפניו כל מין ומין זכר
ונקבה אמר לכולם יש בן זוג ולי אין בן זוג מיד ויפל

*but for man there was not found a help meet. . . . .and God caused a
deep sleep to fall.* When God brought the animals to Adam to be
named, he brought them before him in pairs, a male and a female.
And Adam said, 'For all of them there is a help meet; but for me
there is no help meet!' And immediately God caused a deep
sleep to fall on him.

It is evident that Milton took this over whole. The man
observed as he named the animals that they were in pairs,
a male with a female of its kind, and he understood why,
'and understood their natures.'

> ' "but in these
> I found not what methought I wanted still;" '

He therefore appeals to God, voicing the longing and
unrest induced in him by his observation of the mated
animals. The single statement put into the mouth of
Adam by Rashi has been augmented by Milton into a
dialogue between Adam and God. But the result is the
same, and immediately as the conversation ceases, a deep
sleep falls suddenly upon Adam. This is most striking,
for Scripture itself supplies none of the embellishments
which Milton made the basis for Adam's naïve account of
his state of mind, and for the entire series of events connected with the Creation of Eve. However, Rashi's
cryptic commentary explaining the process of naming the
animals provided a basis for Milton's whole treatment of
the entire episode, although his poetical treatment of it
was of considerable length.

Milton was very much interested in the phrase *help meet*,
which occurred in the Biblical verse telling of the result of
Adam's naming of the animals. The phrase gave Milton
great concern in his divorce writings, and he found in it an
opportunity to expound his ideas on divorce for reasons of
incompatibility. In the *Tetrachordon*, he took special
pains to explain the full meaning of the expression as part

of his comment on the eighteenth verse of the second chapter of Genesis, *and the Lord God said, it is not good that the*
man should be alone; I will make him an help meet for him,
devoting several pages to the discussion of the expression,
I will make him an help meet for him.[1] His entire discussion
was an attempt to show the full meaning of the Hebrew
phrase עזר כנגדו *help meet*, of which he said, 'The originall
heer is more expressive then other languages word for word
can render it.' He tried chiefly to show how full of chance
is marriage, and how woman, the *help meet*, can be man's
greatest joy or his greatest sorrow. He pointed out that a
man and his wife might be on the one hand 'pious Christians together, they may be loving and friendly, they may
be helpfull to each other in the family,' or, on the other
hand, 'they can neither serv God together, nor be at peace
with the other, nor be good in the family one to the other,
. . . . or live as they were deadly enemies.' He continued in the same vein, pointing out that 'there is nothing in the life of man . . . . made more uncertain, more
hazardous and full of chance then this divine blessing with
such favorable significance heer conferr'd upon us, which
if we do but erre in our choice the most unblamable error
that can be erre but one minute, one moment after those
mighty syllables pronounc't which take upon them to joyn
heavn and hell together . . . . this divine blessing that
lookt but now with such a human smile upon us, and spoke
such gentle reason, strait vanishes like a fair skie and
brings on such a scene of cloud and tempest, as turns all to
shipwrack without havn or shoar.' Milton was here
pointing out in connection with the phrase *help meet* that
there are two conceptions involved in the expression, one
of which he said was 'another self, a second self, a very
self it self.' In the discussion that follows, he managed to

[1] *Tetrachordon*, vol. IV:157-160.

get in a full account of what chance can do in marriage, together with the resulting conflict if the arrangement is unfortunate. All of this discussion grew out of his attempt to explain the phrase *help meet*. His statement concerning the word in the original clearly shows that it was the Hebrew phrase that he was trying to explain. It is, therefore, interesting and highly suggestive to find that Rashi has explained the phrase in a way that would have been most welcome to Milton in his spirited exposition of the Biblical passage. That is, while Milton doubtless arrived at the general conception of the marriage relation through long reflection and reading on many and varied phases of the matter, when his discussion turns on the point of the meaning of the Hebrew phrase עזר כנגדו *help meet*, Rashi furnished in his commentary precisely the same point that Milton finally set forth concerning the two directly opposed possibilities in marriage. Rashi's statement is cryptic and epigrammatic, but because it is comment upon the same verse and the same words in that verse on which Milton commented in the *Tetrachordon*, had undoubtedly struck home to him. Rashi, indeed many rabbis, had been struck by the two words in the Hebrew which express what God saw was lacking to Adam. And like Milton, or rather Milton like Rashi, felt called on to explain the phrase. Rashi's comment is:

עזר כנגדו' זכה עזר לא זכה כנגדו להלחם

help meet (literally, *help as-over-against-him*). This means if he is lucky, a help (עזר); if unlucky, an antagonist (עזר) with whom to fight.

In *Paradise Lost*, Milton has used the same idea of the dire possibilities contained in the Hebrew phrase עזר כנגדו (*help as-over-against-him*). In the midst of the terrible quarrel between Adam and Eve after the Fall, Milton had Adam say of marriage:

'for either
He never shall find out fit Mate, but such
As some misfortune brings him, or mistake,'
—Book X:898-900.

Adam later expresses a realization that they have quarreled:

'let us no more contend'
—*ibid.* 958.

And again later, Eve returns to the same thought:

'To me transgressour, who for thee ordaind
A help, became thy snare;'
—Book XI:164-165.

An even fuller statement by Adam of the unfortunate possibilities contained in the marriage relationship, a statement which not only recognizes to the fullest extent how
uncertain and treacherous marriage can be, but which also
re-states in a few lines of verse whole pages of the *Divorce*
tracts, is contained in the following lines:

'linkt and Wedlock-bound
To a fell Adversarie, his hate or shame:
Which infinite calamitie shall cause
To Humane life, and houshold peace confound.'
—Book X:905-908.

Adam has just before this called woman a snare to man,
man's natural enemy, (lines 880-900) and Eve, as already
pointed out, made use of the same term. That is, woman,
who was created to be man's help, because she is so close
and necessary to him, by circumstantial necessity may become man's greatest enemy. Milton was careful to point
out that an unfortunate outcome to the marital relation is
entirely the result of chance; but he was equally insistent
that such a possibility always exists, its appearance in any
marriage depending wholly upon fortune. He conceived

of woman as man's greatest blessing and need under perfect circumstances, and in Book IV has so depicted the utter felicity, before the Fall, of Adam and Eve under such circumstances. But under other circumstances, Adam's greatest solace, his *summum bonum* on earth, becomes his greatest enemy, the cause of his greatest trouble and confusion.

It is never entirely possible to determine how far Milton's statements regarding the marriage relationship are to be taken as reflections of the actual conditions he encountered in his own first marriage. It is dangerous to speculate too much upon his statements accurately reflecting conditions he had actually experienced. But there can be no doubt whatever that all of his statements in prose or verse connected in any way with marriage were an outgrowth of his thought and reflection on the subject, and all of his thought, all of his nature must have given itself up to the struggle and great spiritual strife laid upon him by the actualities of his unfortunate experiences with Mary Powell.

In the *Tetrachordon* also occurs that strange statement by Milton about the possibility of man having been created hermaphroditic which he forthwith rejected, after having noted that it was a Jewish fable occurring also in Plato. He said:

Created he him. It might be doubted why he saith, *In the Image of God created he him*, not them, as well as *male and female* them; especially since that Image might be common to them both, but *male and female* could not, however the Jewes fable, and please themselvs with the accidental concurrence of Plato's wit, as if man at first had bin created *Hermaphrodite:* but then it must have bin male and female created he him.[1]

[1]*ibid.*, p. 147.

Milton would have encountered one form of this 'Jewish fable' in Rashi's commentary. The rabbi commented upon the twenty-seventh verse of the first chapter of Genesis as follows:

זכר ונקבה ברא אות' ולהלן הו' או' ויקח אח' מצלעותיו וגו' ומדרש אגדה שבראו
שני פרצופים בריה ראשונה ואחר כך חלקו ופשוטו של מקר' כאן הודיעך שנבראו
שניהם בששי ולא פירש לך כיצד בריייתן ופירש לך במקו' אחר:

male and female created he them. But later it is said that *he took one of his ribs.* The Agada explains that at the first Creation, two faces were created (to one body) and afterwards these were divided. According to the plain meaning of the verse, Scripture makes known to you that on the sixth day, both (man and woman) were created, but it does not explain to you the manner of their Creation, which will be explained to you in another place.

This is so much like Milton's statement, especially in its suggestion and then rejection of the possibilities of the creation of man as an hermaphroditic creature, that it is apparent why it caught Milton's fancy.

However, Rashi's statement concerning the hermaphroditic nature of man as first created is very cryptic and entirely negative. A much fuller statement of the Jewish notion of the androgynous nature of man as first created is to be found in the Midrasch Rabba to Genesis (מדרש בראשית רבה). There the whole idea of such a creation is very clear and unmistakable, as the following quotation demonstrates:

ויאמר אלהים נעשה אדם בצלמנו כדמותנו' רבי יוחנן פתח אחור וקדם צרתני וגו'
אמר רבי ירמיה בן אלעזר בשעה שברא הקב"ה את האדם הראשון אנדרוגינס בראו
הדא הוא דכתיב זכר ונקבה בראם א"ר שמואל בר נחמן בשעה שברא הקב"ה את
אדם הראשון דיו פרצופים בראו ונסרו ועשאו גביים גב לכאן וגב לכאן איתיבון ליה
והכתיב ויקח אחת מצלעותיו אמר להון מתרין סטרוהי היך מה דאת אמר ולצלע
המשכן דמתרגמין לסטר משכנא וגו'

'And God said, Let us make man in our image, after our likeness:' Rabbi Jochanan opens his exposition with (Ps. 139:5) 'Thou hast

beset me before and behind' etc. . . . . Rabbi Jeremiah ben Eleazer
said that in the hour when God created the first man, he created
him androgynous, אנדרוגינס because it is written 'Male and female
created he them.' Rabbi Samuel bar Nachman said that in the
hour when God made the first man, he created him with two faces,
and then he split him in halves and made two backs, one back for
this one and another back for that one (i.e. one for the man and the
other for the woman). Does this mean then that he took one of
his ribs? No, [explains Samuel, it means] he took one of his two
sides, as (Ex. 26:20) 'the second side of the tabernacle' which the
Targums translate as לסטר משכנא.[1]

In this passage, the 'Jews' fable' is unmistakably the
creation of man as a hermaphrodite, and then the cutting
apart of the two faces, the male and the female to create
man and woman. This is similar to Plato's fable of the
same occurrence in the *Symposium*.

It is also significant here to note how, in the same
Tetrachordon passage, Milton followed his discussion of the
possibility of man having been created hermaphroditic
with the earliest and original statement of the famous line
'He for God only, she for God in him.'[2] The basis of his
whole conception of the relation of the man and woman to
God was chiefly due to what was said about the matter by
Saint Paul, as Milton's own statement indicates:

So had the Image of God bin equally common to them both, it had
no doubt bin said, In the Image of God created he them. But
St Paul ends the controversie by explaining that the woman is not
primarily and immediately the image of God, but in reference to
the man. *The head of the woman*, saith he, 1 Cor. 11. *is the man:
he the image and glory of God, she the glory of the man:* he not for her,
but she for him. Therefore his precept is, *Wives be subject to your
husbands as is fit in the Lord*, Coloss. 3:18. *In every thing*, Eph.
5:24. Neverthelesse man is not to hold her as a servant, but re-
ceives her into a part of that empire which God proclaims him to,

מדרש בראשית רבה[1], (Wilna, 1911, 2 vols.), vol. 1, p. 40b. (כא)
[2]*Paradise Lost*, IV:299.

though not equally, yet largely, as his own image and glory: for it is no small glory to him, that a creature so like him, should be made subject to him.[1]

But the woman has been subject to the man since her creation, and the reason for this is partly due to the reading of the Hebrew of Genesis. Milton meant by St. Paul settling the matter that here in Scripture definite warrant is provided for the idea that man rules over woman, and thus the relations of the two to Deity are through the superior of the two, the man. This difference between man and woman, and their respective relations to each other and hence to God is also explained by Rashi as part of his commentary to the verse that has already been discussed in connection with hermaphroditism. If Milton read that commentary, he could have hardly escaped the following:

וכבשה' חסר וי"ו ללמדך שהזכר כובש את הנקבה שלא תהא יצאנית ועוד ללמדך שהאיש שדרכו לכבוש מצווה על פריה ורביה ולא האשה

and subdue it. The ו after the שׁ is missing to teach you that the male subdues the female that she be not headstrong or wanton. (Rashi's point is that the verb *subdue*, intended to have *the Earth* as its object, actually refers to the subjection of the female by the male because the ו after the שׁ is missing, making the expression read in the text *subdue-ye-her*.) And further to teach you that it is the man whose way is to predominate that is commanded concerning the command *be fruitful and multiply*, and not the woman.

Thus, Rashi's explanation of this phrase provides a statement regarding the man's rulership over the woman, growing directly out of the very texts in Genesis that deal with the Creation of man and woman. Man's mastery is, therefore, as old as Creation.

Rashi also provided Milton with another curious bit of information regarding Adam and Eve in the Garden that

[1] *Tetrachordon*, vol. IV:147.

Milton has used.   In *Paradise Lost*, Adam and Eve before
the Fall and during their life in the Garden were exclusively vegetarians, as were all the beasts of the Earth.
The only food afforded man or beast was vegetable: Raphael calling Adam's attention to the food permitted them:

> 'the Trees of God,
> Delectable both to behold and taste;
> And freely all thir pleasant fruit for food
> Gave thee, all sorts are here that all th' Earth yields,
> Varietie without end;'
>   —Book VII:538-542.

Earlier in the poem we have been given an account of one
of the meals partaken of by Adam and Eve in Eden:

> to thir Supper-Fruits they fell,
> Nectarine Fruits which the compliant boughes
> Yielded them,
>   —Book IV:331-333.

Also, an inventory of Adam's food before the Fall is provided in the account of the preparations to entertain the
visiting Angel, Raphael.   As the Angel approached, Eve
was preparing the noon-day meal:

> For dinner savourie fruits, of taste to please
> True appetite,
>   —Book V:304-305.

On sight of the visitor, Adam admonishes her to 'go with
speed, and what thy stores contain bring forth, and pour
abundance, fit to honour and receive our heavenly
stranger;' but none of the foods mentioned in the long list
that follows is other than vegetable.   Adam speaks with
wonder of Raphael's appetite, and is told, among other
things, that 'flowers and fruit' are 'man's nourishment.'
It is obvious that Milton intended to indicate that before
the Fall, the human pair ate only vegetables, as did the

animals. He deliberately pointed out later and after the Fall, that the animals before that time had also been subsisting on vegetables only; for one of the consequences of the Fall was that

> Beast now with Beast gan war, and Fowle with Fowle,
> And Fish with Fish; to graze the Herb all leaving,
> Devourd each other;
> —Book X:710-712.

This detail of life in the Garden is also to be found in Rashi's commentary. Commenting on the twenty-ninth verse of the first chapter of Genesis, he said:

לכם יהיה לאכלה ולכל חית הארץ' השוה להם בהמות וחיות למאכל ולא הרשה
לאד' ולאשתו להמית להמית בריה ולאכול בשר אך כל ירק עשב יאכלו

and to you it shall be as meat, and to all beasts of the field. He allowed them the same food as for animals. He did not permit Adam and his wife to kill any creature or to eat flesh. All of them (mankind and animals) ate only of all the green herbs.

Thus Rashi provided Milton with another detail of Adam's life in the Garden before the Fall, and Milton has carefully worked it into his poetic account of that life.

Rashi's commentary also supplies the immediate cause for Satan's seduction of the human pair. In the Bible, there is no explanation whatever of the reason why the serpent desired to succeed in getting Eve to eat of the forbidden fruit. In *Paradise Lost*, the animosity of Satan and his cohorts toward man, a creature whom they had never seen, was only indirect. The Fallen Hosts hoped to secure revenge or otherwise injure God through his newest creature man, but toward man himself they felt no particular hatred, nor when Satan set out upon his mission to find man was there any clear idea of what he would do when he found him. The Arch Fiend had left the 'Stygian council' filled with high ambition to wreak vengeance for the plight of the Fallen Angels upon man. Perhaps the amazing adventures that had beset him while journeying to 'this pendent world' had somewhat shaken this high resolve; perhaps a fuller realization of the difficulties confronting him caused him to despair. For, as he reached his goal, he found himself beset by doubts and fears for his course of action. He approached Earth

> Yet not rejoycing in his speed, though bold,
> Far off and fearless, nor with cause to boast,
> Begins his dire attempt, which nigh the birth
> Now rowling, boiles in his tumultuous brest,
> And like a devillish Engine back recoiles
> Upon himself; horror and doubt distract
> His troubl'd thoughts, and from the bottom stirr
> The Hell within him, for within him Hell
> He brings, and round about him, nor from Hell
> One step no more than from himself can fly
> By change of place: Now conscience wakes despair
> That slumberd, wakes the bitter memorie
> Of what he was, what is, and what must be
> Worse; of worse deeds worse sufferings must ensue.
>
> —Book IV:13-26.

He fortified himself at this point by declaiming that remarkable soliloquy, the famous address to the Sun, one of the earliest portions of the poem to be written. In this, Satan reminds himself of his original purpose and is able to proceed.

But after he had gained entrance to the Garden, his first observation of the human pair so wrought upon what still remained of his better nature that he regretted his mission and was almost ready to forego the accomplishment of their ruin. Although he had come to Eden for the express purpose of effecting some sort of ruinous connection with newly created mankind, as he watched Adam and Eve in the early part of Book IV, his heart misgave him concerning them:

'whom my thoughts pursue
With wonder, and could love,'
—*ibid.* 362-363.

So greatly do they attract and appeal to him that he re-
grets his mission, and is able to hold to his original design
only by remembering that he will thereby be revenging
himself through mankind on God. After having exhibited
wonder, admiration, and pity for the human pair, Satan
concludes the speech that begins 'O Hell! what do mine
eyes with grief behold?' with the words

'And should I at your harmless innocence
Melt, as I doe, yet public reason just,
Honour and Empire with revenge enlarg'd,
By conquering this new World, compels me now
To do what else though damnd I should abhorre.'
—*ibid.* 388-392.

The possibility that the innocence and loveliness of the
human pair might have so much further worked upon his
better nature as to have completely ruined his purpose is,
at this point, very great. But the problem of motivation
of Satan's enmity is almost immediately solved, for Milton
realized that at least a certain amount of hatred must be
aroused in Satan toward mankind. Satan continues to
watch them, taking on the forms of various beasts in order
to approach nearer to them. Milton suggested that a
half-formed idea of seizing them while in the guise of a
beast of prey passed through Satan's mind while he ca-
vorted as first this animal then that. But as he approached
nearer and nearer to them, he began to listen to their conversation. This incidentally provided him with much
information; but it remained for their actions when they
ceased speaking to provide him with all the bitterness
toward them necessary to carry out his nefarious intention.
For as they ceased speaking to each other, they embraced:

> he (Adam) in delight
> Both of her Beauty and submissive Charms
> Smil'd with superior Love, as *Jupiter*
> On *Juno* smiles, when he impregns the Clouds
> That shed *May* Flowers; and press'd her Matron lip
> With kisses pure: aside the Devil turnd
> For envie, yet with jealous leer maligne
> Ey'd them askance, and to himself thus plain'd.
> 'Sight hateful, sight tormenting! thus these two
> Imparadis't in one anothers arms
> The happier *Eden*, shall enjoy thir fill
> Of bliss on bliss, while I to Hell am thrust,'

—ibid. 497-508.

Later in the poem, Adam specifically mentions the basis of Satan's enmity toward the human pair, although Milton did not explain how Adam knew what this was:

> 'Conjugal Love, then which perhaps no bliss
> Enjoy'd by us excites his (the Devil's) envie more;'

—Book IX:263-264.

There is thus provided throughout the remainder of the poem and of Satan's speech begun in the lines quoted above, *because of jealousy of their conjugal bliss*, more than enough malice toward and envy of the human pair to insure Satan's lasting enmity. Having observed them 'imparadised in one another's arms,' Satan is now so envious of their bliss that, fully purged of his regret that he must cause their ruin, he leaves them; and the outcome of his venture is never again in doubt.

Milton has now succeeded in motivating Satan's ruin of the human pair, not only on the basis of his desire to revenge himself on God by accomplishing the ruin of his latest creatures, but likewise by inciting Satan to jealousy of the pair themselves. The direct cause of this jealousy was the openly amorous dalliance of the man and woman in their perfect innocence.[1]

The suggestion for such a motivation of Satan against Adam and Eve is furnished directly by Rashi, who, in his commentary contributes the following in discussing the first verse of the third chapter of Genesis:

והנחש היה ערום' מה ענין זה לכאן היה לו לסמוך ויעש יי' אלהים לאדם ולאשתו כתנות עור וילבישם אלא למדך מאי זו עצה קפץ הנחש עליהם ראה אותם ערומים ועוסקי' בתשמיש לעין כל ונתאוה להם:

the serpent was more subtle. How does it happen that this verse is here where the reading should have continued with (3:21) *and God made for the man and for his wife coats of skin and clothed them?* In order to teach you in what manner the serpent seized on them. The serpent saw that they were naked and going about in wedded bliss (בתשמיש) before all eyes, and it was envious of them.

[1]Satan's jealousy of Adam as the cause for the devil's seduction of mankind is very frequently found in the writings of the rabbis. The reason why Satan was jealous of newly created man is met with in widely varied forms in an equally wide variety of rabbinical works. Sometimes Satan is jealous of Adam because he was ordered to worship the man; sometimes because Adam was able to name the animals after all the Angels had failed; sometimes because of Adam's beautiful appearance, having been created in God's image; and sometimes merely because man had been created. The rabbinical legend that Satan was jealous of Adam because of the latter's creation and position, favored as in *Paradise Lost* by life in the Garden, *may* have been responsible for the use in the poem of the analogy of Satan's jealousy of Christ as the announced Son of God for the basis of the Revolt of the Angels. However that may be, it is certain that Milton has represented Satan as being jealous of both the Christ and of Adam—jealous of the superiority of the one and of the 'amorous dalliance' of the other, dalliance curiously denied to Satan. I see in this basis for Satan's jealousy of Adam an attempt by Milton to employ the story of the Angels contained in the fragmentary beginning of Genesis 6. He never quite used the story of how the Sons of the Elohim saw the daughters of men that they were fair, but he often referred to it. In some curious manner, sexual desire entered into the warfare between good and evil. Perhaps Milton at some time or other intended to do more with the idea; but he never did. Or perhaps he came to feel that he must always represent the ideal possibilities in perfect marriage in such a way that, in accord with the reasoning of the divorce tracts, conjugal bliss was an ideal of conduct always to be sought in distinction to promiscuity in sexual relations. Perhaps he found himself unable to use the implications of the story in Genesis 6 in accordance with his carefully defined modes of human conduct. But strange vestiges of various rabbinical conceptions of Satan's jeal-

That is, the serpent's desire to bring about the ruin of the man and the woman was due to jealousy of the conjugal relations enjoyed by them. Both Satan in *Paradise Lost* and the serpent in Rashi's commentary become jealous at the sight of the couple 'imparadised in one another's arms' and desire, because of that jealousy, to inflict suffering upon them. Thus there is a remarkable identity between the motivation of the serpent and the motivation of Satan so far as their animosities toward Adam and Eve are concerned. Rashi then becomes a source for a large and important portion of Book IV, the entire episode of Satan regretting his mission and being restored to his former eagerness for the ruin of man by becoming intensely jealous of man's enjoyment of a bliss denied to the Fallen Angels. In addition to this, Rashi's commentary supplies an explanation for Milton's careful provision of Satan with direct, personal malice toward the pair in the Garden. Apparently, sexual jealousy was a feeling that could be aroused only in a Fallen Angel, for when Milton presented Eve serving her husband and Angel guest, she 'ministered

ousy of Adam, and of an almost Dionysiac treatment of sexual relations are to be found in Milton's verse, both early and late.

But Satan's jealousy of the innocent dalliance of the human pair is the only use Milton made of all the rabbinical stories of jealousy between devil and mankind. Just why Satan was more jealous of conjugal bliss than anything else (Bk. IX:263-64) is not made clear. It may be noted that according to Milton's highly fantastic conception of adultery, set forth in the divorce tracts, Eve, in her defection from Adam and her waywardness, was actually guilty of adultery with the serpent when she ate of the Forbidden Fruit. Symbolically at any rate, she was seduced by Satan. The rabbis frequently relate that such a seduction took place, and that Cain was the result of this illicit union. Others state that sexual relations were taught to Eve by Satan after she had eaten of the fruit. The only vestige of this in Milton is that to him the fruit was an aphrodisiac for the human pair. Consistently, he represents their actions after eating it as no different sexually from what they had been before eating, but quite differently motivated. Unrestrained, untempered action was obnoxious to him; and it is this quality in him more than anything else that has caused him to be regarded as an arch Puritan.

naked,' and the poet takes advantage of the occasion to exclaim:

> O innocence
> Deserving Paradise! If ever, then,
> Then had the Sons of God excuse to have bin
> Enamour'd at that sight; but in those hearts
> Love unlibidinous reign'd, nor jealousie
> Was understood, the injur'd Lovers Hell.

> —Book V:445-450.

However, if, as has already been suggested, Rashi's comments on various details of the Creation and Garden of Eden narratives found in the opening chapters of Genesis are important as sources for Milton, they are even more important in helping us to understand what Milton was attempting to do with these materials. This is perhaps especially true of what Rashi had to say of Adam's intelligence in the state of innocence.

Sumner, in his notes to his English translation of the *Christian Doctrine*, has called attention to the stress Milton laid upon Adam's ability immediately to give names to the animals as they were brought to him in the Garden. Sumner pointed out that Milton, on three distinctly different occasions, has emphasized Adam's ability to give names to the animals the moment he first saw them. This immediate ability seemed to Milton to have been the most striking fact connected with the naming of the animals as that process is described in Genesis. But Sumner also pointed out that Scripture itself does not supply any comment or suggestion of Adam's 'sudden' ability to name Earth's creatures.[1]

---

[1] Sumner refers to *de doctrina*, p. 139, 'Sine permagna autem sapientia ita subito nomina animalibus dedisse non potuit; Gen. 2:20.' *The Christian Doctrine*, (London, 1904, Bohn edition), vol. 1:195n. 'In this illustration the chief stress is laid upon the suddenness with which Adam was enabled to give appropriate names

The passage in the *de doctrina* to which Sumner has thus called attention reads *sine permagna autem sapientia ita subito nomina animalibus dedisse non potuit; Gen. 2:20,* which Sumner has translated as *Certainly without extraordinary wisdom he could not have given names to the whole animal creation with such sudden intelligence, Gen. 2:20.* In addition to this, Milton, in the *Tetrachordon*, first expressed the idea as follows:

But Adam who had the wisdom giv'n him to know all creatures, and to name them according to their properties, no doubt but had the gift to discern perfectly.[1]

The same idea occurs again in *Paradise Lost*, in the speech by Adam to Raphael, telling of how the animals were named,

> 'I nam'd them, as they pass'd, and understood
> Thir Nature, with such knowledg God endu'd
> My sudden apprehension:'
> —Book VIII:352-354.

A possible place of origin for Milton's obvious emphasis upon Adam's remarkable and unaccountable knowledge of the beasts is afforded by Rashi. This rabbi in his comment on the twenty-sixth verse of the first chapter of Genesis points out how God gave man dominion over the beasts of the Earth and over the fish of the sea. He said of this matter,

ורדו בדג' הים' יש בלשון הזה לשון רידוי ולשון ירידה זכה רודה בחיות ובבהמות
לא זכה נעשה ירוד לפניה' והחיה מושלת בו

let him have dominion over the fish of the sea. There is in this phrase the meaning of rulership and dethronement: if man is worthy, he

to the brute creation, as it passed in review before him. Milton has two other allusions to this event, and the same circumstance is marked as the prominent feature of the case in both passages. There is nothing in the scriptural narration to suggest the particular idea, or the coincidence would have been less remarkable.'

[1] *Tetrachordon*, vol. IV:161.

rules over beasts: if he is unworthy, he becomes inferior to them, and the beast rules over him.

This is his preparation for the discussion of the naming of the beasts by Adam, for Rashi continues:

וייצר מן האדמה'... ועוד למדך כאן שבשעת יצירתן מיד בו ביום הביאם אל האדם
לקרות להם שם' ובדברי אגדה יצירה זו לשון רדוי וכבוש כמו כי תצור אל עיר'

out of the ground God formed etc. . . . . Also, this verse is to teach you that in the hour of their formation, at once on that day, they were brought to the man for him to give them their names. And in the words of the Agada, יצירה means to assume domination and control over, as in (Deut. 20:19) *when you beseige (capture, possess, subdue, seize, wholly take control of) a city.* So he (God) subjugated [them (the animals) to the hand of man].

That is, Rashi points out how immediately after their formation, the animals were brought to Adam for naming. There was no time afforded Adam in which to have become acquainted with the animals before naming them: he simply knew their names because of the perfect knowledge given to him in his state of innocence. This is the same point that Milton made in his use of the phrase, 'sudden apprehension.' That is, Adam was immediately possessed of a perfect knowledge of nature.

But the most important observation on this point made by Rashi, and the one which most emphasizes Adam's endowment with perfect natural knowledge, is contained in his comment on the twenty-fifth verse of the second chapter of Genesis. He is therein commenting upon the fact that Adam and Eve were naked in the Garden and were not ashamed. He says:

ולא יתבוששו' שלא היו יודעים דרך צניעות להבחין בין טוב לרע ואע"פ שנתנה בו
דעה לקרוא שמות' לא נתן בו יצר הרע עד אכלו מן העץ ונכנס בו יצר הרע וידע
מה בין טוב לרע

and were not ashamed. For there was not known to them any way of being able to distinguish between good and evil. Although

Adam was given knowledge enough to name the animals, the instinct or knowledge of evil was not given to him until after they (the man and the woman) had eaten from the tree. Then the knowledge of evil entered, and then he knew the difference between good and evil.

That is, before the Temptation and Fall, Adam knew virtually everything except the difference between good and evil. He was possessed of all natural knowledge, as his ready naming of the animals attested. For Milton also, there were no limits with respect to what Adam could know before his Fall, except how to distinguish between good and evil. In the *Tetrachordon* he said, *man in his original rectitude, in whose breast all that was naturall or moral was engrav'n.*[1] Certainly the discourses of Adam and Raphael in Books six, seven, and eight of *Paradise Lost* cover all conceivable subjects except those that would have involved a knowledge of good and evil. Adam, like a brilliant student, followed his heavenly mentor with alacrity and eagerness.[2] He appeared perfectly capable of understanding the difficult matters of which Raphael speaks, and follows with equal ease of comprehension the highly involved explanations and reasonings employed by the Angel. So greatly has Milton equipped Adam with natural knowledge that the latter is even able to ask questions of Raphael which the Angel either cannot or will not answer. Adam's questions are the most difficult and the most intelligent questions about nature and man's relations to it that the race has ever asked, and they are asked by a being who had had at most but a few hours or a day and a night in which to have become aware of such knowledge. That he apparently knows so much, although he

[1] *ibid.*, p. 161.

[2] For the parallel between Raphael and Adam, and a teacher and a pupil, cf. M. L. Bundy, 'Milton's View of Education in *Paradise Lost*,' *Journal of English & Germanic Philology*, XXI (1922) pp. 127-152.

had been afforded no opportunity to have become acquainted with such a store of knowledge, may seem incon-
gruous. But actually, Milton's elaborate presentation of
the encyclopedic range of Adam's natural knowledge contained in the fifth, sixth, seventh, and eighth books of the
poem is thereby made to serve a dual purpose. Its first
purpose, of course, is to serve as an epic convention, or to
present a summation through the mouth of a character or
of characters of past events and impending action of importance to the whole poem. But the second purpose of
the contents of these two books is to serve as the means of
presenting the most intrinsically difficult problem which
confronted Milton—that of adequately accounting for the
Fall of Man.

Milton's problem in the poem was to account for the
Fall of Adam as a fact. His problem almost immediately
solved itself because of the basic idea which he had of
Adam's supreme natural knowledge of everything the
human mind can grasp, except the knowledge of the difference between good and evil.

The psychological processes through which Milton had
Adam pass in order to add to his stock of natural knowledge a way of knowing the difference between good and
evil, are long and involved. The poet began with the idea
that Adam was remarkably endowed with an almost mi-
raculous mental equipment. Raphael casually informs
Adam that of course he is eloquent, for

> 'God on thee
> Abundantly his gifts hath also pour'd
> Inward and outward both, his image faire:
> Speaking or mute all comliness and grace
> Attends thee, and each word, each motion, formes,'

> —Book VIII:219-223.

Added to this equipment was a mind possessed of great intellectual acumen and vigor, a mind at once able to grasp and to understand all natural knowledge. As Adam himself expressed his peculiar mental abilities, immediately after his creation,

> 'To speak I tri'd, and forthwith spake,
> My Tongue obey'd and readily could name
> What e're I saw.'
> —*ibid.* 271-273.

It is this remarkable mental endowment of Adam which, as Sumner has pointed out, Milton in a number of places in his works has so repeatedly stressed. In fact, so greatly did he stress it, that he felt the necessity for elaborating and explaining the whole process of Adam's becoming aware, following the Fall, not only of what had taken place, but also of that knowledge that had been heretofore withheld from him, the knowledge of the difference between good and evil. So greatly had Milton stressed the range and acumen of Adam's intellect, and the high quality and remarkable amount of his knowledge, that the poet found it necessary to explain in great detail how an individual so well equipped could possibly fall. Consequently, the whole process through which Adam's mind passed has been set before us in the poem. The outcome is never in doubt, and it is clear enough at all times that Adam is unable to cope with the Tempter because of the lack of a knowledge of good and evil. But the process itself through which his mind passed in order to reach an understanding of all that had taken place through the eating of the Forbidden Fruit, and an attainment of the ability to distinguish between good and evil, is long drawn out.

Beginning with the half-quarrel between Adam and Eve, their first, the morning after Eve's disturbing dream, which neither of them was able to interpret, there enter elements which are vaguely alarming. But Adam, although somewhat uneasy, does not know of any reason for their being alarmed. He attempts to reason with Eve about her separating herself from him, but is unable fully to refute her arguments because he is totally ignorant of what to tell her to expect if she does separate herself from him. He feels that she may then be in some danger, but aside from a general and very vague notion that somehow or other they must implicitly obey God, he is completely unaware of what the future may have in store for either of them. He knows, because Raphael has so informed him, that they undoubtedly will be tempted in some manner by their Adversary. But Adam has no idea whatever of what Temptation is, nor does he in any way know his Adversary except for that slight knowledge he gained from Raphael's account of the Warfare in Heaven. With only his reason to guide him, he manages to arrive at the conclusion, which is a most remarkable achievement in view of his total ignorance of the facts, that he and Eve must most fear fraud. But he is not very certain as to what fraud is. Eve makes the statement that it is not violence that Adam need fear,

> 'As wee, not capable of death, or paine,
> Can either not receave, or can repell.'

She then reasons that it must be the Adversary's 'fraud is then thy fear.' Adam answers her by pointing out that whatever else the vague 'enemy' may be, this aspect of him must be kept in mind.

> 'Nor thou his malice and false guile contemn;
> Subtle he needs must be, who could seduce
> Angels, nor think superfluous others aid.'

Further discussion serves still more to show and to emphasize Adam's intellectual acumen, which throws off the suggestion that after all what they have most to fear from the Adversary is due to the presence of a danger that lies within themselves:

> 'Against his will he can receave no harme.
> But God left free the Will, for what obeyes
> Reason, is free, and Reason he made right,
> But bid her well beware, and still erect,
> Least, by some faire appeering good surpris'd
> She dictate false, and missinforme the Will
> To do what God expressly hath forbid,'
>
> —Book IX:350-356.

> 'Reason not impossibly may meet
> Some specious object by the Foe subornd,
> And fall into deception unaware,
> Not keeping strictest watch, as she was warnd.'
>
> —*ibid.* 360-363.

It is remarkable here to see how Milton has made Adam rationally anticipate precisely what was about to take place, and yet in no way be directly conscious of what he was saying. Adam lacked all knowledge of the vague 'evil' of which he was speaking. He reasons well enough about what may take place, but he has no way of knowing the truth or falsity of what he says.

Now Eve leaves him, going abroad into the Garden to encounter the Serpent, and to pass through the very experiences that Adam has described, but which neither he nor Eve would have known the full meaning of when they encountered them. Adam discovers Eve after she has eaten of the Forbidden Fruit, still by the tree. It is significant that she immediately begins to tell Adam of what has happened. She is in this recital unaware even yet that she has met with and been conquered by the Adversary, although she has finished eating of the fruit. She tells Adam that the fruit is good to eat, her reason being that the

Serpent has eaten, or at least told her that he had, and did not die,

> 'the Serpent wise,
> Or not restraind as wee, or not obeying,
> Hath eat'n of the fruit, and is become,
> Not dead, as we are threatn'd, but thenceforth
> Endu'd with human voice and human sense,'

> —*ibid.* 867-871.

She in no way identifies the Serpent with Satan, any more than either she or Adam had when Satan previously appeared before them in the forms of various beasts. They had failed completely to recognize him before when

> from his loftie stand on that high Tree
> Down he alights among the sportful Herd
> Of those fourfooted kindes, himself now one,
> Now other, as thir shape servd best his end
> Neerer to view his prey, and unespi'd
> To mark what of thir state he more might learn
> By word or action markt: about them round
> A Lion now he stalkes with fierie glare,

> —Book IV:395-402.

Nor is Eve at all aware of the fact that she has sinned. Adam's reaction to her announcement that she has eaten of the forbidden fruit is most peculiar, but most consistent. He likewise in no way identifies her having eaten of the fruit with her seduction by Satan. At first, Adam is tremendously concerned only with the fact that she has transgressed the Divine command:

> 'how hast thou yeelded to transgress
> The strict forbiddance, how to violate
> The sacred Fruit forbidd'n!'
> —Book IX:902-904.

His questioning of her leads him to suspect that something

more than mere transgression has occurred, but he is not certain as to what it is,

> 'som cursed fraud
> Of Enemie hath beguil'd thee, yet unknown,
> And mee with thee hath ruind'
> —*ibid.* 904-906.

Then begins in Adam that most curious process of ratiocination which endeavors to reason out what has taken place. Before eating of the fruit, he attempts to reach some conclusion, but misses the point when he says:

> 'yet so
> Perhaps thou shalt not Die, perhaps the Fact
> Is not so hainous now, foretasted Fruit,
> Profan'd first by the Serpent, by him first
> Made common and unhallowd ere our taste;
> Nor yet on him found deadly, he yet lives,
> Lives, as thou saidst, and gaines to live, as Man
> Higher degree of Life,'
> —*ibid.* 927-934.

It is clear here that Adam does not even dimly suspect that the Serpent is any more than he appears. He has not the slightest suspicion that he and Eve have been trapped by the Adversary of whom Raphael warned him. He is unaware that the complete ruin of Eve has already taken place—that she has met the Adversary and has fallen. Nor is there any reason at this point why he should be so aware, for he has not yet eaten of the fruit. He is not yet possessed of the knowledge of good and evil, hence his futile, specious argument, logically correct enough, but worthless because he does not know whether what he says is true or false. But the marvellous intelligence with which he was equipped darts forward then, and he almost, without the aid of the fruit, cuts through to the reality when he becomes involved in the idea that God cannot possibly allow his 'prime creatures' thus to be ruined. His reason tells him that somehow God would thereby be defeated by the Adversary, but it is clear in the following lines that he has not yet made the necessary connection between the Adversary and what has taken place, because he cannot yet discern clearly the evil that has entered Eden:

> 'Nor can I think that God, Creator wise,
> Though threatning, will in earnest so destroy
> Us his prime Creatures, dignifi'd on high,
> Set over all his Works, which in our Fall,
> For us created, needs with us must faile,
> Dependent made; so God shall uncreate,
> Be frustrate, do, undo, and labour lose,
> Not well conceav'd of God, who, though his Power
> Creation could repeate, yet would be loath
> Us to abolish, least the Adversary
> Triumph and say; "Fickle their State whom God
> Most Favors, who can please him long; Mee first
> He ruind, now Mankind; who will he next?"
> Matter of scorne, not to be given the Foe,'
>
> —*ibid*. 938-951.

In this statement, he is very near the truth; but unwittingly, for he has not yet eaten of the fruit of the Tree of the Knowledge of Good and Evil and cannot quite make the connection. Nevertheless, he has here intellectually reached so far forward that almost he has made the necessary step.

Then he eats of the fruit; amorous desire overcomes him; the debauch of sense follows, terminating in sleep.

Upon awakening, his mind unhappily returns to the problem of what has taken place. In his first speech after awakening from the eating and its effects, he has evidently slipped back again in his mind, probably because of the intoxicating effect of the eating, to the mental position he occupied much earlier. But there is also to be considered the fact that the human mind works 'in fits and starts,' and it is with remarkable fidelity to observable mental phenomena that Milton has him, immediately after recovering his senses from debauch, begin to retrace his mental steps of explanation. He speaks first of the Serpent:

> 'O *Eve*, in evil hour thou didst give eare
> To that false Worm, of whomsoever taught
> To counterfet Mans voice,'
> —*ibid*. 1067-1069.

The word 'whomsoever' indicates that he is again as far away as before from his thought of God being overcome by the Adversary: that at this particular moment, he is just as uncertain as ever about the connection between the Serpent and Satan. But in the next breath he shows that he now possesses a knowledge that he did not before possess, a knowledge of the difference between good and evil:

> 'we know
> Both Good and Evil, Good lost, and Evil got,'
> —*ibid*. 1071-1072.

Shame now comes to the aid of the man and the woman, who have been enduring the keenest mental agonies, and they plunge into the forest to hide themselves and find coverings for the nakedness of which they are now conscious.

Then begin the recriminations. Adam turns on Eve for having been the cause of their troubles. Her retort contains an amazing indication of why the Serpent's attempt was successful:

> 'hadst thou been there,
> Or here th' attempt, thou couldst not have discernd
> Fraud in the Serpent, speaking as he spake;
> No ground of enmitie between us known,
> Why hee should mean me ill, or seek to harme.'
> —*ibid*. 1148-1152.

She points out what was precisely the fact—that it was impossible for them to have detected fraud in the Serpent, because they were not equipped with the ability to distinguish between good and evil. She makes the same point in this connection that Adam had made to her in their morning argument about separating for the day. That is, Milton repeats the point that their knowledge simply did not include this ability, although in other matters they were most adequately equipped.

Adam retorts to Eve with the time-honored plaint of the injured male, 'I told you so.'

> 'I warn'd thee, I admonish'd thee, foretold
> The danger, and the lurking Enemie
> That lay in wait;'
> —*ibid*. 1171-1173.

This was only partly true, for he had but repeated to Eve the warning that Raphael had given him. He in no way knew nor did he warn Eve of precisely what to expect, for such knowledge was not given to him. As Eve told him, neither of them was equipped with a knowledge that would have warned them of the nature of the temptation.

Next, they are compelled again to talk with a Heavenly messenger, the Christ, and when asked who tempted her to eat of the Forbidden Fruit, Eve replies, not that it was Satan, but that it was the Serpent. And not only is she totally unaware at this point of the connection between the Serpent and Satan, but to make the point doubly certain, Milton takes the trouble to point out that God then cursed the Serpent:

> though brute, unable to transferre
> The Guilt on him who made him instrument
> Of mischief,
> —Book X:165-167.

Man, Adam and Eve, at the time of the curse laid upon

them had not yet come to realize the connection between the two, nor were they fully aware that anything more had happened than that they had eaten of the Forbidden Fruit:

> more to know
> Concern'd not Man (since he no further knew)
>
> —*ibid*. 169-170.

After the relation of the delayed and mysterious curse of Satan mentioned a few lines later, the poet again returns to Adam and the problem of his comprehension of what had taken place. Adam is discovered near the close of the tenth book in the depths of despair, ruminating on his fate, what Death is like, when he will die, and other chimeras. As Eve timidly approaches him, he turns on her the full force of his wrath, and begins again to express his thoughts about what has actually happened. He tells her once more that if she had listened to his warning, all would have been well with them, but she, he says,

> 'Rejected my forewarning, and disdain'd
> Not to be trusted, longing to be seen
> Though by the Devil himself, him overweening
> To over-reach, but with the Serpent meeting
> Fool'd and beguil'd, by him thou, I by thee,'
>
> —*ibid*. 876-880.

Here is a return to the speech made just before Adam ate of the fruit. He is here again linking the Serpent and Satan together, though in no clear fashion, but nevertheless linking them. Again, he almost discovers their connection, but is too incensed at Eve to continue his thought.

Then follows the tremendous scene introduced by this speech of Adam's, the most adequately motivated, and hence the most compelling scene in the entire poem. The scene itself is made up of a synthesis of human emotions.

Such peaks of emotional fervor would have been utterly impossible to Adam and Eve before the Fall, because the whole scene springs from and owes its power to those overwhelming emotional depths of human nature employed by the great tragedians—utter despair and self-loathing. As the unhappy pair run the gamut of mental suffering, Adam's intellectual processes apparently take on greater depth and consequently deeper penetration. Turning to the almost hopeless task of comforting Eve, who has suggested suicide for them both, there comes to Adam a clearer, more sustained vision of what has occurred. And suddenly he almost blurts out the truth, so startlingly does it dawn on him. He reasons aloud:

> 'Then let us seek
> Some safer resolution, [than suicide] which methinks
> I have in view,'

Then the clear vision breaks upon him:

> 'calling to minde with heed
> Part of our Sentence, that thy Seed shall bruise
> The Serpents head;'

That would be 'piteous amends' indeed! But wait! An idea occurs to him!

> 'unless
> Be meant, whom I conjecture, our grand Foe
> *Satan*,'

Then comes to him the great conclusion of his whole mental agony:

> 'who in the Serpent hath contriv'd
> Against us this deceit:'

Now he begins to see a future, although not yet very clearly, and it is toward a realization of a future that the whole poem is now turned:

> 'to crush his head
> Would be revenge indeed; which will be lost
> By death brought on our selves, or childless days
> Resolv'd as thou proposest; so our Foe
> Shall scape his punishment ordain'd,'

Now at last is Adam aware of the whole relationship between the Serpent and Satan which, for Milton, symbolized discrimination between good and evil. That is, when Adam knew the precise relationship of Satan to the Serpent, he knew the difference between good and evil; and until he had become aware of that relationship, he could not distinguish between what was good and what was evil. From this point on in the poem, Adam remains sure of that relationship, again expressing it in the eleventh book when he informs Eve of the results of his prayer to God. It is remarkable to notice that the results of that prayer were peace of mind, brought about apparently by the memory of the promise that in the future, the grand foe was in some manner to be dealt with:

> 'For since I saught
> By Prayer th' offended Deitie to appease,
> Kneel'd and before him humbl'd all my heart,
> Methought I saw him placable and mild,
> Bending his eare; perswasion in me grew
> That I was heard with favour; peace returnd
> Home to my Brest, and to my memorie
> His promise, that thy Seed shall bruise our Foe;
> Which then not minded in dismay, yet now
> Assures me that the bitterness of death
> Is past, and we shall live.'
>
> —Book XI:148-158.

Adam's attitude now is that he desires to live and to continue living, because he clearly understands the actual cause of his downfall. He also knows that the cause of his downfall will in some manner be 'bruised.'

Milton at this point was preparing for the inculcation of the idea of the Messiah, the Christ who is to come. When Michael, following the Fall, descends to Earth in order to instruct Adam further in the way in which he should go after the expulsion from the Garden, he tells Adam that the most important result of the eating of the forbidden fruit is the acquisition of the capacity to know the future. As he tells Adam to ascend the hill in order to be shown the future, he says:

> 'Ascend
> This Hill; let *Eve* (for I have drencht her eyes)
> Here sleep below while thou to foresight wak'st,'
> —Book XI:366-368.

This 'foresight' was completely unknown to Adam before, and now the true purpose of it is to enable him to realize the full import of what he is to behold in order that he may grasp the idea of the Messiah. The Messiah, the 'one greater Man' of the opening lines of the poem, as a conception in the mind of Adam, is the direct outcome of the rational processes through which his mind has passed in its efforts to understand the significance of all that was involved in the Temptation and Fall. It is amazing to observe all this development. In order to become aware of the connection between the Serpent and Satan, Adam had first to learn or acquire a knowledge of the difference between good and evil. In doing this, through his own mental processes, God's promise that the seed of the woman should bruise the head of the Serpent came to mean to him the hope of and for the future. He now understood how the Fall took place, and knew also that without it, he would never have had any thought for the future. The great promise of the future then becomes the idea of the Messiah, the 'greater Man' who shall restore mankind to complete salvation.

It is a little difficult to realize that Milton meant all this
to come out of Adam's acquisition of the knowledge of
good and evil, but such was what he intended, as the discussion of the same point in the *de doctrina* bears witness.
He therein himself discussed, as he has Adam discuss in
the poem, the meaning of the Fall and all that it implied.
He connected the whole matter with man's mental wel-
fare, as is well-known, and suggested that man was perhaps better off after the Fall than before, because after it
his knowledge was complete, and he was in addition supplied with the idea of the Messiah.[1] Milton here was not
in complete agreement with the discussion of the same
point, the end of knowledge, by Francis Bacon, who
pointed out that it 'is a restitution and reinvesting (in
great part) of man to the sovereignty and power (for
whensoever he shall be able to call the creatures by their
true names he shall again command them) which he had in
his first state of creation.'[2]

This is a far cry from Rashi's rather restrained statements about Adam having been endowed with all natural
knowledge, so much of it indeed that he was able at once
to name the animals, although they were brought to him
almost as fast as they were created. But Adam, before the
Fall, lacked completely a knowledge of the difference between good and evil. Milton's interest in Adam's state of
knowledge before the Fall, and the mental processes
through which he passed as a result of the Fall, has been
found to have been the basis of the development within

---

[1] *de doctrina*, p. 161, 'Arbor scientiae boni et mali non erat sacramentum, ut
vulgo statuitur: sacramenta enim sunt ad usum, non ad abstinentiam: sed erat
veluti pignus et monumentum quoddam obedientiae. Dicta est autem scientiae
boni et mali ab eventu: post eam enim degustatam, non malum tantummodo
scimus, sed ne bonum quidem nisi per malum. Quis enim fere virtutis usus, quae
lux est, nisi in malo?'

[2] Francis Bacon, *Works*, edited by James Spedding, R. L. Ellis, and D. D. Heath
(Boston, 1863), vol. VI:34.

the poem of the conception of the Messiah as the result and outcome of Adam's acquisition of the knowledge of good and evil. Adam's state of knowledge before the Fall, nearly perfect so far as it went, was, nevertheless, without a way to distinguish between good and evil, a barrier between him and the use of his fullest capacities. His mental development leading to his acquisition of the knowledge he formerly lacked not only reconciled Adam to his fate by explaining it to him, but also, through the effects of the mental processes that lead him to accept that fate, both he and the reader are brought to a full realization of all that has taken place in the Temptation and Fall.

We have now traced Milton's development of Adam's mental or intellectual equipment and capacities before the Fall, through the Fall itself, and into the period of half-regretful reconciliation following it. Milton has set forth this development by giving us the actual thought processes themselves through which Adam passed or which he experienced. The result of all this is that we are thereby afforded a remarkable opportunity to observe Milton's actual working out of one of the most important aspects of the whole poem. Rashi has furnished some of the bases on which Milton's whole development of Adam's mind has been found to rest; but the poet has also drawn heavily upon the aims of Christian theology.

Allied with this similarity of idea between rabbi and poet is their full agreement concerning the marital relations of Adam and Eve before the Fall. To neither was the Fall the beginning of sexual relations. Milton affirmed the complete, but ideal and pure, relations of man to woman, affording perfect union to them in the Garden. Thus Satan's jealousy was of their innocent enjoyment of a relationship denied to him. This was always a highly disputed point, many divines contending that the Fall consisted in

the discovery of sexual relations.   But Milton was very
explicit on the matter,[1] and Rashi was equally as explicit,
taking special pains to point out how it was possible for
the Serpent to have been jealous of them.   Expressly of
their conjugal relations, the rabbi said in his comment to
the first verse of the fourth chapter of Genesis:

והאדם ידע' כבר קודם ענין של מעל' קוד' שחט' ונתרד מן עדן וכן ההריון והליד'

שאם כת' וידע אדם נשמע שלאחר שנתרד היו לו בנים

and the man knew his wife.   Already, before the matters just mentioned (i.e. the Fall and Expulsion from the Garden).   Before he
had sinned and had been banished from the Garden of Eden, even
then had conception and birth (begun).   Had it been written *and
then the man knew* (וידע אדם) it would then be understood that only
after having been banished were children possible for him.

Thus both writers are most effectively able to employ the
same and in many ways the most adequate basis for
Satan's jealousy of the human pair—his jealousy of their
conjugal happiness—and explicitly to point out the conjugal relationship of Adam and Eve before the Fall.

From Rashi also may have come Eve's chief reason for
desiring after she had eaten of the Forbidden Fruit, that
Adam also should partake of it.   Almost immediately
after eating the fruit, she decided that she must persuade
Adam also to eat of it in order that, if she died, he might
not live forever and marry another woman.   The *Zohar*
and *Josippon* have been suggested as possible sources for
this motivation;[2] and, while Rashi adds nothing to these
suggestions, he provides for such motivation of Eve,
another source whose text can be definitely connected
with Milton.   Rashi is very brief on this point; but he is
as explicit as brief; in his comment on the sixth verse of the
third chapter of Genesis he said:

[1]Cf. the famous passage in Book IV:741 ff.
[2]Denis Saurat, *op. cit.*, p. 284, and my *Milton's Semitic Studies*, p. 132.

ותתן גם לאישה' שלא תמות היא ויחיה הוא וישא אחרת

and she gave also to her husband—so that she would not die while he lived and took another wife.

We have now examined Rashi's commentary to the opening chapters of Genesis for details that find an echo in Milton's treatment in *Paradise Lost* of the Creation, and of Adam and Eve in the Garden, together with the Temptation, Fall, and Expulsion. Many of Rashi's details, not found in the scriptural text, have been found in Milton's treatment of these subjects, and many of these details of that source unmistakably make their appearance in the poem. The rabbi's commentary has been found to be rich in suggestion for the very striking kind of changes and additions Milton has employed to round out the material found in the text of Scripture. Several of these details, more or less minute in Rashi, have been elaborated by Milton into large and important portions of the poem. Thus, Rashi's discussion of Adam's intelligence before the Fall, becomes in *Paradise Lost* one of the most important ideas of the whole medial portion of the epic. In this case, it is not so much that Rashi's comment yielded Milton a ready-made treatment of this subject as that the rabbi has indicated very clearly his use of the same basic assumption regarding Adam's intellectual nature before the Fall, and the intellectual result of the Fall, as have been set forth by the poet. The rabbi's suggestion, in other words, greatly aids our understanding of what Milton was attempting.

The greatest number of details from Rashi which Milton has used are those connected with the Creation of this Earth and of its various forms of life. These are highly informative of the care that Milton expended on those parts of the poem dealing with Creation. The amount of preparation Milton devoted to his account of the events connected with Creation must have been enormous. His

elaborate and precise treatment of the events of the Six
Days was made up of a mosaic-like fitting together of an
almost infinite variety of minor details. The result might
well have been a lesson to Defoe in how to secure verisimilitude in a fictional piece of literary work. Milton's
sources for these details very obviously included Rashi's
commentary. In many cases, such as Milton's statement
about the 'green herbs,' the rabbi actually throws light
upon what Milton had in mind. This is perhaps less because of Milton's direct borrowing in this case from Rashi
than because the rabbi's comment represents a point of
view in connection with Creation, very much older than
Milton's own, which makes the later, similar, but not
identical view more comprehensible.

CHAPTER VI

SOME LOYAL ANGELS

Thus far in this work we have confined our examination of Milton's acquaintance with rabbinical materials almost entirely to his use of rabbinical commentaries on Scripture. For the most part, these commentaries have been those found in Buxtorf's *Biblia Rabbinica*, and our examination has been of various portions of those commentaries on parts of Scripture in which Milton was very obviously interested. Not all such passages have been examined, but enough of them have to show the kind of material contained in the commentaries and how useful this material was to Milton. We have seen how those scriptural passages which he listed in the *de doctrina* as dealing with Creation held a curious but easily understood fascination for him in connection with his own account of Creation, particularly in *Paradise Lost*. We have likewise seen how richly suggestive are the rabbinical commentaries on such passages. Their examination results, as we should expect it would, in the discovery of his use of many details in his account of Creation that have been taken over with only the slightest of changes from those commentaries. And many of the details found in *Paradise Lost* but not found in Scripture were, as we have seen, supplied by the same rabbinical commentaries.

However, because of the nature of the material employed in *Paradise Lost*, many of the details used therein appear to have been drawn from the Bible. But by no means all of them, whether used in the account of Creation or in other parts of the work, are to be found either in the scriptural text or in the rabbinical commentaries upon that text. Milton depended upon Scripture as far as Scripture would supply him with the materials he needed. But, in the very nature of the case, in working with scriptural materials, he encountered various traditional treatments that had developed very early in the rise of Christianity and of the Church, of ideas primarily scriptural or perhaps derived from Scripture, but which were entirely separated from commentaries. The same kind of development had begun several centuries before the Christian era among the Jews, and as a consequence, a large literature other than Scripture itself had been built up, supplementing it and sometimes providing an entire development of a subject almost wholly unmentioned by Scripture. Thus, the development of the synagogue among the Jews was a subject on which the Old Testament itself is almost entirely silent; but a whole literature came to be written on and about this subject by the rabbis. In the same way, the Christian Church developed a literature about its own origin and growth which attempted to justify both on scriptural bases, although Scripture itself had little or nothing to say of either.

Then the rabbis, whether those who lived and wrote so long ago that even their names have been forgotten or have become traditional, or later and better known rabbis, developed and discussed many subjects that were very imperfectly if at all dealt with by Scripture. Although whatever topic so discussed might have been of scriptural origin, often so little did Scripture offer or so ambiguous were the various Biblical mentions of it, that the work of the rabbinical, or of Christian writers for that matter, on that particular topic became a literature wholly separated from commentaries on Scripture. Nevertheless, this literature often, in fact usually, drew and depended greatly on the text of Scripture for support or confirmation of its various points. The rabbis very early developed works, which,

like the Talmud, were anything but scriptural commentaries, and which included the discussion of a wide variety
of topics very imperfectly dealt with by Scripture.

In his foreword to the *de doctrina*, Milton protested that
he had used very little of such material, whether Jewish or
Christian, in building his theological treatise. But he has
left us plenty of evidence of his use of Christian material of
the nature we are now discussing. His use of rabbinical
works of a like nature is most apparent in connection with
his treatment of such ideas as the Angels, whether in
Paradise Lost or in the *de doctrina*. There is very little
systematic treatment of Angels in the Old Testament.
Vague references are common enough, but the nature of
Angels was a topic that developed apart from scriptural
commentary. Material concerning Angels is originally to
be found in other types of works than commentaries, and
for this reason Milton's Angelology necessitates the investigation of other kinds of rabbinical works than the commentaries. It also affords an opportunity to discover what
some of these other rabbinical works were with which he
was acquainted.

It therefore becomes necessary to examine some of these
works here, but not in any haphazard manner. Rather,
such works will be considered only in connection with
Milton's definite treatment of certain material, in this
case, Angels.

But it will first be necessary to survey the sources and
the development of Milton's general ideas about Angels,
together with his general system of Angelology used in
Paradise Lost, and the general doctrine as found in the
de doctrina. Such a survey will not only provide us with a
knowledge of his system and doctrine in general, but will
also acquaint us with those details he has used which do
not strictly belong to the more general source-material on

which he drew.   In making such a survey, it will be neither
necessary nor possible in so brief a space as this to become
precise, for the development of Christian Angelology, to
say nothing of Jewish, is too large and difficult a subject to
discuss here in detail.   Indeed, for our purposes here, the
more general the survey of the development of Angelology
and what it included, the better.   For Milton was usually
thoroughly orthodox in his use of Angels, both in the poem
and in his discussion of them in the theological treatise.
Let us therefore look briefly at what was the more or less
conventional opinion of his day regarding Angels, and how
it arose.

The sources on which Milton drew for his Angelology
were primarily Christian and scholastic.   For the most
part, his system, with its rather vague outlines, and its
individual members are conventional in substance and in
treatment.

The development of the scholastic Angelology is, as
already stated, too large a subject to be treated here in any
great detail; but its main outlines may be rapidly sketched.
The Apostolic Age in the main and in general looked to
Judaism for its ideas about Angels and their various relationships whether to God, to each other, or to men.   The
age in which Christianity began universally admitted the
existence of an invisible world composed of good and bad
spirits.   This could hardly have been otherwise.   The development of such an idea had begun among the Jews with
the Captivity, some centuries before the Christian era.
With the Jews, the basis of this development was, of
course, the Bible.   Throughout the Old Testament there is
mention of Angels performing the services of God, and
demons grouped about Satan, their chief.   The pre-Christian Jew, and later the early Christian, in reading the
Bible could scarcely fail to believe that behind the veil of

sense-phenomena there existed intelligent beings, some
animated by good and some by evil intentions toward
man. At the same time, the definite information afforded
by the Bible regarding the world of the Angels was insufficient to satisfy man's curiosity concerning them. Many
questions about Angels arose, both before and during the
beginnings of Christianity, to which Scripture could give
no certain answer. The result was that answers to these
questions came, as such answers always come, from philosophical conjecture or theological necessity.

The Apostolic Age itself depended largely, if not wholly,
upon Jewish speculation for its ideas of Angels. The
angelology of the New Testament is, as should be expected, entirely Jewish in origin.[1] Not until Christianity
reached the relatively non-Jewish centers of the Graeco-
Roman world did a recognizably Christian angelology begin to develop; and even when this took place, the bases of
the angelological system were still Jewish in nature, although differences almost immediately developed.

But even the early Fathers themselves were greatly concerned with the nature of Angels, and had much to say on
the subject. They very early developed schisms over the
true nature of Angels. But by the end of the fifth century
after Christ, while angelology had developed considerably
since the Apostolic Age among Christians, having taken on
decidedly Christian and non-Jewish aspects, it was still far
from assuming the definite form known to the Middle
Ages. In particular, there remained two points still to be
determined. These concerned the nature and the organization of the Angelic World.

Particularly was the latter point undetermined, for
Scripture itself is especially vague regarding the orders of

[1] Cf. especially H. L. Strack and P. Billerbeck, *Kommentar zum Neuen Testament* (München, 1922-), *passim*.

Angels. Sometimes seven, sometimes eight, sometimes nine or ten orders of Angels are mentioned in the Old Testament. But up to the fifth century, no one had apparently attached any importance to these numbers. Some Christians thought that the same category reappeared in different numbers under different names. Others thought, on the contrary, that the numbers furnished by Scripture were merely to give some idea of the innumerable classes or ranks of Angels which made up the celestial company.

This matter of the Angelic orders suddenly became of great importance at the beginning of the sixth century. There then appeared the work *De caelesti Hierarchia* attributed, though erroneously, to Dionysius the Areopagite which was to play so large a part in the development of Christian angelology. In it were found all the essential lines of organization of the Angelic World, and these were to be retained in all future speculation on the subject. The Angels were divided in this work into three Hierarchies, each of which was in turn subdivided into three orders or choirs. The first Hierarchy was made up of Seraphim, Cherubim, and Thrones. The second was made up of Dominations, Virtues, and Powers. And the third was made up of Principalities, Archangels, and Angels. None of the elements of this system was original to this work; but the definite organization of the whole Angelic World upon previously provided and well-recognized bases was a distinct and welcomed innovation. The fundamental scheme of this organization was never successfully attacked, and the system of Pseudo-Dionysius passed into the Middle Ages practically unchanged.

By the end of the thirteenth century, the theory of Angels formulated by Dionysius, or in the work that passed under his name, had become a fully recognized system. Such discussion of it as still went on was confined mainly to details, such as the nature of the Angelic substance and its relation to matter and quantity. Various speculations that need not be reproduced here were put forward in connection with the material or non-material nature of Angels. But in the main, the organization of the Angelic World had become a settled and well-recognized doctrine or principle.

One other aspect of the scholastic discussion of the subject of Angels, perhaps its most important aspect, is of interest here. This was the quarrel over the nature of Angels. Certain philosophers of the Middle Ages distinguished between a number of kinds of matter, or material substance. They said that there was an elementary matter of which terrestrial, mundane beings are made; secondly, a celestial substance of which the stars are made; and thirdly, a substance of a wholly metaphysical nature. The chief characteristic of this third matter was its ability to possess distinct qualities without being subject to the restrictions of quantity. That is, this third kind of substance was postulated as matter that existed without being spread out or extended. The French school sought to introduce this substance into the world of Angels. Alexander of Hales and Saint Bonaventura upheld the idea that Angels were doubtless completely spiritual and incorporeal; but at the same time, they possessed a substance and a form. In other words, this theory maintained that the Angelic form rested on a matter not subject to *quantity*, and the form found in such matter was merely its principle of individuation.

But this theory was not very successful. Albertus Magnus energetically attacked it. Saint Thomas maintained that matter that was not subject to quantity was fantastical and absurd, and in addition pointed out that an intellectual *substance* must be foreign to and independent of any kind of matter. The scholastics in general ranged themselves with Saint Thomas, and the doctrine of the Spirituality of Angels was thenceforth safe from all attack, at least within the Church.

Such was the general status of the theory of Angels, their nature, being, and organization, at the close of the Middle Ages. And such it virtually remained, for the Renaissance became interested in other matters than such purely academic discussions.

For his purposes in *Paradise Lost*, Milton accepted these well-known and relatively long-established ideas of Christian Angelology. The system he employed, in so far as it may properly be called a system, was particularly based upon the hierarchical arrangement already outlined. He occasionally inserted fragments caught from the minor scholastic quarrels over special aspects of Angels. But in general the more or less conventional Christian tradition is the basis for all the Angelic machinery of *Paradise Lost*. And the hierarchical arrangement of the Angels Milton fully accepted, although he did not make use of all of it in the poem. His two prose discussions of Angels, the one in the *Reason of Church Government*, and the other in the *de doctrina*, clearly follow and take into account the same system.[1]

However, an examination of Milton's angelology, whether in his poetry or in his prose, strongly suggests that extreme caution should be exercised when speaking of his 'system.' In the first place, it is impossible to determine

---

[1] *The Reason of Church Government urg'd against Prelaty*, vol. III:98, 'Yea the Angels themselves, in whom no disorder is fear'd, as the Apostle that saw them in his rapture describes, are distinguisht and quaterniond into their celestiall Princedomes, and Satrapies, according as God himselfe hath writ his imperiall decrees through the great provinces of heav'n.' Cf. also *de doctrina*, Book I. Chapter ix. 'De Gubernatione Speciale Angelorum' *et passim*.

with any degree of precision just what his system is. In its larger aspects, it is extremely vague and shadowy, especially in what it comprises. Only in a general way can it be discerned as a system at all. In the *de doctrina*, where we should naturally expect a rigorous and sharply defined treatment of Angels if anywhere in Milton's work, the vagueness of the 'system' is perhaps more strikingly apparent than in any other of his works. His Angels are, it is true, surrounded by all of the hierarchical machinery extant in his time; but we rightly feel that we are told little or nothing of the significance of such machinery. It results in groupings of the Angels which are not constant. That is, Milton fails to be precise about the way in which his Angels are organized. In general, he informs us that they are organized on a hierarchical basis; but then we find that any single Angel whose name the poet mentions cannot be exactly placed in the hierarchy. He fails also to tell us much about the nature of his Angels. They are at once corporeal and non-corporeal: possessed of substance and not possessed of substance. Satan is, when first Abdiel, and then Michael smite him with their swords, at least quasi-material in nature. But Milton's Angels are also, as the embarrassed and blushing Raphael explains to Adam, wholly spiritual when 'if Spirits embrace, total they mix.'[1]

Many more angelological elements are to be found in *Paradise Lost* than in the *de doctrina* or elsewhere in Milton's works. But in each of his various treatments of Angels, two major facts are markedly apparent. The first of these is the eclectic nature of the angelological material he presents; and the second is the loose and amorphous nature of his angelological 'system.' There is, I believe,

---

[1] *Paradise Lost*, Book VIII:626-627. Cf. also Origen *De principiis*, IV. 35; and *In Matth.* XXII:30.

a relation existing between these two facts connected with Milton's angelology which is of considerable and general importance. The second of them, the loose and amorphous nature of his system, was due to the same factors which caused his similar and repeatedly manifested failures to become definite on many subjects. There are numerous instances in *Paradise Lost* of Milton's reluctance to make a choice among various and sometimes dissimilar possibilities. Among these, everyone is familiar with the vacillation between the selection of the Ptolemaic and the Copernican cosmological systems as basic conceptions of the Universe. Although the poem is clearly based upon the Ptolemaic, Milton could not refrain from having Raphael set forth the Possibility that the Copernican might be a truer cosmology, being apparently unwilling to give up either theory. Another such instance of the same lack of precision is the equally well-known attempt to convey an indeterminate idea of the use of artillery by the Rebel Angels in the phrase 'brass, iron, stony mould,' as indicating all kinds of cannon. These are instances of the same reluctance to become definite and precise that may be noted in connection with his angelological system.

His perfectly apparent reluctance to become completely systematic in his treatment of Angels belongs to the Renaissance, although all the elements of angelology which he employs in all their wide variety are thoroughly medieval or earlier. His poetic treatment of this material, as is so often the case with Milton, is the result of the warfare between the Medieval material and the Renaissance point of view, both of which struggle in Milton for expression. Perhaps, in so far as he was able to resolve in poetry the clash between that material and that point of view, we should say that he approached a more modern solution of the problem of adapting the one to the other. But in order to understand more completely how his treatment of this particular material came about, it is necessary to know a great deal more about the material with which he was working. Without comprehension of both his material and his treatment of it in poetry, appreciation of his poetic achievement is impaired if not made impossible.

It therefore becomes necessary to examine more fully the material on which he drew for his angelology in order to understand the significance of the eclectic nature of the whole.

We have already seen that for the most part and in general outline, his angelology was derived from the conventional Christian ideas about Angels of the Middle Ages. But if this is true for the general outlines of it, it is not true for many of its details. Milton is often found to have deviated from conventionally Christian conceptions of Angels and of the system to which they belong. Some of these deviations are due to Apostolic, Patristic, or other Christian variations from the conventional treatment of Angels, variations forgotten or otherwise excluded from the ultimate scholastic scheme. But certain other deviations are obviously and unmistakably of direct Jewish origin, and a few of them come directly from the medieval rabbis or kindred sources.

It will be the purpose of this and of the following chapter to point out and partially at least to determine how Milton drew on rabbinical sources for some of his conceptions of Loyal and of Fallen Angels. As already stated, this work will in no wise constitute a complete account of Milton's angelology. Such a work, fascinating as it is and would be, would necessitate the examination of the whole range of Christian, to say nothing of the Jewish, treatment of Angels, from its rise in the Apostolic Age through its complete development by the Scholastics. Such a study should some time appear; but I shall confine myself here entirely to a few rabbinical contributions to Milton's treatment of Angels. Nor will these rabbinical sources herein pointed out be in any sense exhaustive treatments of all rabbinical contributions to Milton's ideas of Angels. I intend, rather, to point out a method of procedure and a few actual borrowings from rabbinical materials, with their implications. In other words, this and the following chapter will provide some materials for the investigation of Milton's rabbinical readings with special reference to Angels.

Having set forth some of the more general characteristics and aspects of Milton's angelology, let us now turn to a more definite consideration of the matter, keeping in mind, however, all that has been said so far of its fundamentals.

In his angelology, one of Milton's chief variations from the conventions of the basic Christian traditions, which he accepted, appears in the names he chose to use for his individual Angels, and in the ranks with which he endowed those Angels. For this reason, I insert here a digest of his actual treatment of Angels in *Paradise Lost* so far as their rank was concerned.

A survey of the distribution of Angels' names by rank in *Paradise Lost* reveals what was meant by the earlier and previous statement to the effect that the 'system' of angelology employed in the poem is very loose and unschematic. Thus, Raphael is found to have been assigned to all three hierarchies, and appears in two orders of one of them. Abdiel also exhibits an astonishing variety of classification, appearing in both the highest and the lowest order of Heavenly Beings, and thus in two distinct hierarchies. It is unnecessary here to enter into explanations of the distinctions between the hierarchies and the orders found within them, it being sufficient to remark that there is no particular principle of gradation among the hierarchies or the orders.[1] That is, a particular Angel might by virtue of his rank in the order of Seraphim, be treated as a member of any other order. But on the whole, gradations of rank had some meaning.

Milton had plenty of adequate authority for these shiftings; but this authority need not be cited here. The real reason for such shifting in *Paradise Lost* apparently was not due, however, to the fact that authorities differed, but occurred because of a very real need in the poem itself. This need was to secure equal rank for certain of the individual Angels, in particular, Satan, Raphael, Michael, Gabriel, and Uriel.

The most remarkable result of securing equality between certain of the individual Angels is to be seen in connection with the conventionally prominent Michael, Ra-

[1]Seraphim	Cherubim	Thrones	Domina-tions	Virtues	Powers	Prin's.	Arch-Angels	Angels
1:324	1:324	2:310	3:392	2:15	2:11	6:447	Uriel	1:593
6:579	:665	3:320	5:601	:311	:310		3:648	3:325
7:113	:794	:399	:772	5:601	3:320		(Christ)	:445
:198	2:516	5:749	:840	:773	5:601		4:712	:446
Uriel	3:636	6:199	10:87	:840	:772		Gabriel	6:594
3:667	:666	:723	:460	7:199	:840		4:865	Satan
Raphael	4:778	7:198		10:460	10:86		Raphael	1:243
5:277	6:102	9:232		Raphael	:460		5:385	:600
Abdiel	:771	10:86		5:371			7:41	5:660
5:875	7:198	:460					Michael	:694
:896	:218	11:296					6:257	Uriel
	9:61						Satan	3:648
	11:100						1:243	Michael
	:128						:600	6:257
	12:628							11:238
	Beelzebub							:884
	1:157							12:2
	Azazel							:466
	1:534							:626
	Satan (as disguise)							Raphael
	3:636							7:41
	Zephon							Gabriel
	4:844							4:549
	Zophiel							:561
	6:535							:781
	Gabriel							:865
	4:971							:877
	Ithuriel							
	4:788							
	:810							
	Uzziel							
	4:782							

Compiled from Laura E. Lockwood, *Lexicon to the English Poetical Works of John Milton* (New York, 1907). I have checked each of these references, but have included only a single indication of the rank of Arch-Angel for each of the proper names in that column.

phael, and Gabriel. These three Angels form the basic triad of scholastic angelology. They had gradually come to be accepted alike by those who were willing to go to any lengths in the use and designation of Angels, and by those who strove to minimize such use for fear of charges of polytheism. All agreed that these three Angels could be and were recognized. Their names and employment as a triad were at least as old as Jerome, and their citation throughout the Middle Ages and later a commonplace.[1]

Milton's general representation of these three Angels in *Paradise Lost* is to all appearances in accordance with the stereotyped Judaeo-Christian tradition. Each of the three in the poem exhibits the well-known and recognized char-

---

[1]Jerome, (Migne, vol. 25:537-538 (5:676-677)) *Commentarium in Danielem Liber*. 'Virum istum qui praecepit Gabrieli ut Danielem faceret intelligere visionem, Judaei Michaelem autumant. Consequenter autem quia visio de praeliis erat, regumque certaminibus, immo regnorum successionibus, Gabriel, qui praepositus est praeliis huic officio mancipatur. *Gabriel* enim in linguam nostram vertitur *fortitudo*, vel *robustus Dei*. Unde et eo tempore quo eart Dominus nasciturus, et indicturus bellum daemonibus, et triumphaturus de mundo, Gabriel venit ad Zachariam, et ad Mariam (Luc. 1.) Et postea in Psalmis legimus de Domino triumphante: *Quis iste rex gloriae?* etc. (Ps. 23:8.) Ubicumque autem medicina, et sanatio necessaria est, *Raphael* mittitur, qui interpretatu *curatio*; vel *medicina Dei:* si cui tamen placet Tobiae librum recipere. Porro ubi populo prospera promittuntur, et quod nos vel *propitiationem*, vel *expiationem* possumus dicere, necessaria est, *Michael*, dirigitur, qui interpretatur *quis sicut Deus?* hoc videlicet nominis interpretatione significante, quod in Deo sit medicina vera.'

Cf. also S. Bonaventura, *Opera Omnia*, edited by A.C. Peltier (Paris, 1866, 15 vols.), vol. 8, chap. xx., p. 100a. *Compendium Theologicae Veritatis*, 'De his nominibus, *Michael, Gabriel, Raphael*, sciendum est, quod haec sunt propria nomina Archangelorum, licet eorum interpretationes aliis sunt communes; sed eorum propria sunt, quia his horum nominum interpretationes conveniunt excellentius. Michael interpretatur, *quis ut Deus?* hic est de ordine Principatuum, et attribuuntur ei quatuor, scilicet esse praepositum paradisi, id est, Ecclesiae, sicut et olim fuit princeps Synagogae. Item deferre animas in paradisum; sed hoc intelligas, quod gloriosius deferat quam alii. Item, pugnare cum dracone, id est, diabolo, sicut legitur in Apocalypsi (xii:7). Item, venire in adjutorium populo Dei.

Gabriel interpretatur *fortitudo Dei*. Hic est de ordine Archangelorum, et merito quia magna annuntiavit.

Raphael interpretatur *medicina Dei*, et est de ordine Virtutum, quia mirabilia magna fecit.'

acteristics that were usually associated with him in current traditions.

But Milton's further treatment of them is not so conventional. In assigning them to the various hierarchies and their orders, the assignment is conventional enough, but its results cause certain variations from traditional Christian procedure to appear which should be mentioned. And by observing some of the results of how Milton grouped the three Angels, Michael, Raphael, and Gabriel, it is possible, perhaps, to discover certain relationships between his Angels which have not heretofore been pointed out.

First, it should be noted that these three Angels appear together in the same general orders of the hierarchy. All three are named as Angels and as Archangels.[1] They occur also singly or in pairs in other orders in other hierarchies. But only as Angels and as Archangels do all three of them find a completely common classification. It is obvious, then, that they are recognized by Milton as three Angels or Archangels possessed of the same or of equal rank. He has, as it were, equated them with each other. In all this he has been thoroughly conventional.

But when we examine the orders in which these three Angels appear together, we make another discovery. Milton's group of great and important Angels is not the triad more or less conventional to Christian angelology. When the three Angels, Michael, Raphael, and Gabriel, appear in the same orders, they always appear in Milton's work with a fourth Angel. If we look more closely at the two orders of the third hierarchy that are called Archangels and Angels, we find, not three but four Angelic Beings

[1]Verity, *Paradise Lost*, p. 509, note to VI:45-46, states that Gabriel is inferior to Michael, because *only an angel*. This is not only misleading, but untrue. Cf. IV:865.

with specific names and of equal rank included in both orders. These are the four Angels, Michael, Raphael, Uriel, and Gabriel. Each of these four appears, it is true, in other orders. But only in the orders of Archangels and Angels do all four appear together. They form the only group of three or more loyal Angels in *Paradise Lost* who appear in more than one order.

That is, when the three Angels, Michael, Raphael, and Gabriel appear in the same order, they appear always with the Angel Uriel. Then all four are of equal rank. This means that Milton's group of important Angels or Archangels is not the same as the conventional Christian group of the most important Angels. For the Scholastics, and for even earlier Christian theologians, the most important group of Angels was a triad made up of those three greatest Angels of the Heavenly Hosts, Michael, Raphael, and Gabriel. Over and over again one finds the medieval angelologist listing these names as the names of those Angels who made up the triad for the entire system of Angels. For Milton, however, the most important Angels were not a triad, but a quadrumvirate. According to the digest of Milton's Angels in *Paradise Lost*, his quadrumvirate of the greatest Angels is made up of Michael, Raphael, Uriel, and Gabriel.

The reasons for his selection of a quadrumvirate rather than the conventional triad are complicated, but, I think, perfectly clear. As some of these reasons are apparent in portions of his treatment of Uriel, let us first examine that Angel as he appears in *Paradise Lost*.

As Satan, in his search for the dwelling-place of man, approached the Sun, a magnificent description of the nature and function of that great orb prepares us for what he encountered when he finally alights on its sphere. As he surveyed the Sun,

> he soon
> Saw within kenn a glorious Angel stand,
> The same whom *John* saw also in the Sun:
> His back was turnd, but not his brightness hid;
> Of beaming sunnie Raies a golden tiar
> Circl'd his Head, nor less his Locks behind
> Illustrious on his Shoulders fledge with wings
> Lay waving round; on som great charge imploy'd
> He seemd, or fixt in cogitation deep.
> —Book III:621-629.

Extremely glad was Satan to find someone who could direct him toward his goal. But before addressing the bright and thoughtful Angel of the Sun, Satan took the form of a stripling Cherub, and drew near the Angel:

> He drew not nigh unheard, the Angel bright,
> Ere he drew nigh, his radiant visage turnd,
> Admonisht by his ear, and strait was known
> Th' Arch-Angel *Uriel*, one of the seav'n
> Who in Gods presence, neerest to his Throne
> Stand ready at command, and are his Eyes
> That run through all the Heav'ns, or down to th' Earth
> Bear his swift errands over moist and dry,
> O're Sea and Land: —*ibid.* 645-653.

Satan immediately accosts him, and his words supply a little more information about Uriel:

> '*Uriel*, for thou of those seav'n Spirits that stand
> In sight of God's high Throne, gloriously bright,
> The first art wont his great authentic will
> Interpreter through highest Heav'n to bring,
> Where all his Sons thy Embassie attend;
> And here art likeliest by supream decree
> Like honours to obtain, and as his Eye
> To visit oft this new Creation round;'
> —*ibid.* 654-661.

Satan's disguise was not discerned by Uriel, who took him

for the Cherub he appeared to be, but in pointing this out to us, Milton contributes a bit more to his full conception of Uriel when he says of him that he is

> Regent of the Sun, and held
> The sharpest-sighted Spirit of all in Heav'n;
> —*ibid.* 690-691.

Uriel appears again in Book Four, when, at the close of day, he hurries to Gabriel with important information. After Satan had received directions from Uriel as to how to reach this Earth, the false Cherub continued on his journey, and Uriel watched him as he sped on his way. When Satan reached the Earth, he put off his disguise, and the all-seeing and watchful eye of Uriel which could discover all but fraud, discovered the Cherub to be 'alien from Heaven.' We are afforded no further information regarding Uriel in this passage; but in Gabriel's reply to Uriel's eager speech, we have a confirmation of information previously gained. Gabriel opens his reply with the words:

> '*Uriel*, no wonder if thy perfet sight,
> Amid the Suns bright circle where thou sitst,
> See farr and wide:'
> —Book IV:577-579.

Uriel is, therefore, conceived of as Angel of the Sun, its regent, residing in it in order to keep watch over the newly created Universe. He is an Archangel, and one of the seven Angels of the Presence who are nearest to God's throne. This group stands ready at God's command to do his bidding, and are his eyes. They see and report what they see. They are also ready to run on 'his swift errands' through the Heavens or down to Earth. Uriel, especially, is the first Interpreter of God's will, and he brings this will to the other Angels of Heaven. This had been his function long before the World was created. He had been one of the Angels present at Creation, and this fact helped Satan's disguise to succeed, for Uriel thought it not at all strange that such 'a stripling cherub' should not have been present at Creation. He even commends the disguised Satan for wishing to see the newly created Universe at first hand:

> 'To witness with thine eyes what some perhaps
> Contented with report hear onely in heav'n:'
>
> —Book III:700-701.

And Uriel, conscious of his own greatness and in a rather condescending manner, is only too pleased to tell about Creation. His account is the account of an eye-witness. After Creation, he has taken his place in the Sun, and occupies a position with respect to the Universe similar to that he had heretofore occupied in Heaven. He is the sharpest-sighted of all the Angels, and being so, is admirably equipped to watch over and report on all happenings in the Visible Universe. He travels through the Universe on the Sun's rays, being at once the Angel of Light and the Angel of the Sun.[1] He takes his place quite naturally with Raphael in the battle with the Rebel Angels, these two captaining the wings of the Loyal Army.[2] The Loyal Army as a whole is in command of a staff made up of Michael, Gabriel, Uriel, and Raphael, with Michael commander-in-chief. Thus these four are Archangels and of equal rank and station. Such is Milton's conception of the Archangel Uriel. But we are concerned here with his origin and the reasons for his employment.

Milton's conception of 'those seven Spirits that stand in sight of God's high throne,' 'ready at command,' 'and

[1] Book IV:555-556.
[2] Book VI:363.

are his eyes that run through all the Heavens, or down to the Earth bear his swift errands,' is likewise presented in the *de doctrina* in much less detail. The origin of the conception is Biblical. The primary basis of the seven ministering Angels, the seven 'eyes of God,' is to be found in Zechariah. The formation of Milton's full conception is, as already suggested, a little complicated, but to follow it through is enlightening with respect to Uriel.

The first statement referring to the 'seven eyes' is found in the ninth verse of the third chapter of Zechariah, *for behold, the stone that I have set before Joshua; upon one stone are seven eyes.* Apparently there is little or nothing concerning Angels here; but this passage has always been interpreted allegorically. The first step in making the 'seven eyes of the stone' the 'eyes of God,' which are the Seven Angels of the Presence, is found in standard expositions of the verse of Milton's day. In Tremellius's Bible, the verse carries several marginal notes. The first of these explains the nature of the stone itself. The first note reads:

lapis, altera allegoria, significans firmitatem Christi, et Ecclesiae superaedificatae Christo.

Of the seven eyes upon the stone, he says

apponens lapidi unico septem oculos, id est, perfectissime adhibens ei absolutissimam providentiam meam, ut infra 4. 10. et in eo collocans ipsam, ut perfungatur administratione sua ex voluntate Patris. Nam providentia Dei, oculis; perfectio septenatio numero figuratur. De lapide autem vide Psal. 118. 22. et Jeschah. 28. 16.

The two cross-references cited by Tremellius are important in making the 'seven eyes' the 'seven eyes of God' or the seven Angels. The Psalms reference is to the famous *The Stone which the builders rejected is become the head stone of the corner.* The verse referred to in Isaiah is *Therefore thus saith the Lord God, Behold I lay in Zion for a foundation a stone, a tried stone, a precious corner stone of sure foundation.* The stone, in both of these cases, was, of course, held to be Christ by all Christian commentators. Tremellius says of it in the Isaiah passage, '*lapidem*, Christum, ut Psalm. 118. 22.'

Zechariah furnishes more information about the 'seven eyes,' in the tenth verse of the fourth chapter, *For who hath despised the day of small things? for they shall rejoice, and shall see the plummet in the hand of Zerubbabel, even these seven, which are the eyes of the Lord; they run to and fro through the whole earth.* Tremellius's translation of this verse and his notes to it are suggestive. His translation reads:

Nam quis spreverit diem parvorum operum? nam laetantur aspicientes ad lapidem illum perpendiculum in manu Zerubbabelis septem isti, oculi inquam Jehovae, ipsi peragrantes terram?

His notes to this verse are as follows:

Nam quis, alterum argumentum a providentia et studio Dei patris. Deus (inquit Christus) non tantum dixit, sed etiam procurat infinita providentia sua: quis ergo interverterit? Deus delectatur eo, quis spreverit?

Parvorum, id est, tenuium principiorum istorum, quae ducta sunt in extruenda domo.

oculi, id est, infinita Dei providentia.

The meaning of the stone with its seven eyes begins to appear from a consideration of these notes. The stone was God (*inquit Christus*) and the 'eyes' were the seven spirits who surrounded him, one conception growing out of the other, then merging with it forming the whole idea of God surrounded by seven ministering Spirits.

These seven ministering Angels are further explained in the apocryphal book of Tobit. In the fifteenth verse of the twelfth chapter occurs the statement, *I am Raphael, one of*

*the seven holy Angels, which present the prayers of the Saints,
and which go in and out before the glory of the Holy One.*
Junius has much to say of this verse which is of direct
interest here. His Latin translation of the verse reads:

Ego sum Rephael, unus ex septem Angelis illis sanctis qui referunt preces sanctorum, et egrediuntur coram gloria sancti.

His long note on this verse follows:

unus ex septem Angelis, si unus hic locus exstaret ad revincendam
libri istius impuritatem, mihi quidem satis futurus esset; nihil enim
profecto in toto orbe terrarum magicum dici potest, aut hoc ex
principiis magiae petitum est, quorum doctores primarii ex India
et Bactriana profecti cum Judaeis suum virus communicaverunt:
Nam statuunt illi Angelos horatios, diarios, et alios coeli regionibus
attributos, principes, ministros, etc. ex quibus Zoroastres Bactrianus, Menaster Indus, et alii scelerum concinnatores suas magiae
observationes elaboraverunt. Atque hoc quidem vitio Judaeos
fuisse non mediocriter inquinatos ostendit Epiphanius tomo I. sui
Panarii, ubi de Pharisaeis agit; et ipsorum quoque libri diurnaeque
observationes testantur, quibus diem Solis Rephaeli, diem Lunae
Gabrieli, diem Martis Sammaeli, diem Mercurii Micaeli, diem
Jovis Tzidkieli, diem Veneris, Hanaeli, diem Sabbathi Kepharjeli
tribuunt, eosque dominos staruunt totius administrationis in diem
illum necessariae. Quamobrem ita statuimus, qui ex hoc libro
veritatem petunt, aut se confirmaturos putant, eos perinde facere,
atque si molem gravissimam statuminare velim arundine.

At this point may be noticed the beginnings of Milton's
defection from the conception of the seven Archangels
which he had evidently begun to set up when he composed
the early part of the poem. In the account of Uriel in
Book III, are the vestiges of a system of Angels which he
had begun to work out. But after examining Junius's note
to the verse from Tobit, and the verse itself, we find that
Milton disregarded what he found therein and eventually
ignored the whole idea of the seven ministering Angels so
far as *Paradise Lost* was concerned. The verse in Tobit

names only Raphael as one of the seven Angels; but Junius's note provides us with names for all seven of these Angels. The same note further states that Raphael is Angel of the Sun; but Milton has used neither of these suggestions.

If we examine the treatment of Uriel in *Paradise Lost* in connection with the statements already quoted about him from the third Book, we have at least a hint of what happened to the system of seven Angels. Uriel, as the digest of Milton's Angels shows, is named as an Archangel with three others. He appears in two orders of Angels with Michael, Raphael, and Gabriel, these two orders being respectively the order of Archangels and that of Angels. Milton never carried out his idea of giving names and offices to the 'seven eyes of God' suggested by the early chapters of Zechariah and announced in connection with Uriel's introduction in the third Book of the poem. The Archangels in charge of the Heavenly troops in the battle with the Rebels are four in number, unless Milton intended to imply that Abdiel was also partially in command by what was said of his fighting.[1] Otherwise, Uriel is one of *four* chief Angels, not one of *seven*. Milton never reconciled the number of Archangels set down in the third Book with the number he actually employed in the later books of the poem.

On the basis of Scripture, it is impossible to tell how many Archangels there were, and Milton has consequently refrained from being explicit or even consistent in the matter. That is, he announced in connection with Uriel that this Angel was one of the seven Angels of the presence who were nearest God's bright throne. Then he makes this Angel actually one of four such Angels. The reason for this is to be found in another verse also contained in

[1]Book VI:369 ff.

the book of Zechariah. This is the fifth verse of the sixth
chapter, and in so far as it is in direct contradiction with
the statement that there are seven ministering Angels of
the presence, this verse effectively prevented Milton from
being either explicit or consistent. The verse in question
reads, *And the angel answered and said unto me, These are
the four winds of heaven, which go forth from standing before
the Lord of all the earth.* The word *winds* in the Hebrew is
רוחות, which is usually translated *spirits*. Tremellius's note
on this verse is important, for it illustrates how the verse
came to be responsible for the number of important Angels,

venti, id est, angeli ex quatuor coeli partibus se sistentes Deo,
et ab illo excurrentes ad exsequenda mandata illius.

These two contradictory verses from Zechariah furnished
Milton with both of the arrangements of Angels found in
the poem. From the verse in the third chapter and from
the statement found in the book of Tobit, Milton apparently set out to build up a system of seven Archangels.
We find such a system in the discussion and description of
Uriel in the third book of the poem. There, Uriel is one of
seven Archangels and in addition is 'regent of the Sun.'
But later in the poem, only three other Archangels of equal
importance with Uriel are named, and in action, the four
function as a quadrumvirate, the 'seven' of the third
Book not being used.

Scripture alone will and does account for certain elements in this complication. The reasons for Milton's apparent vagueness about the number and function of the
Archangels can be explained by the apparently contradictory statements in Zechariah and Milton's attempts to
agree with both. This is similar to his attempt to include
all that Genesis had to say of the creation of the plants.
But there is nothing in Scripture which helps to explain

why Milton selected Uriel as one of these principal Archangels, nor why he made him 'regent of the Sun.' In fact
the Tobit passage, and Junius's note to it, would appear to
have been good reason for Raphael and not Uriel being
named to that office. But Milton has actually selected
Uriel as one of the four great Archangels and made of him
the figure that we have just described. Let us turn now to
the origins of the figure Uriel, and the reasons why Milton
has selected him for the part this Angel plays in the poem.[1]

The name *Uriel* does not occur in Scripture as the name
of an Angel.[2] It does, however, occur therein four times as
the name of a man.[3] But the name occurs at least three
and possibly four times in the apocryphal book of second
Esdras.[4] In Esdras, Uriel is mentioned three times distinctly as an Angel. The fourth mention calls him an
Archangel. But there is nothing in any of these passages
in Esdras to suggest the Uriel of *Paradise Lost*. In fact,
the current treatment of this name as it occurred in Esdras
was to assume that it meant Christ. Junius's comment
does this for the first occurrence of the name,

Uriel, Hac voce significatur Christus, lux et sapientia Dei, cum hoc
loco, tum etiam in sequentibus: quamobrem deinceps domina
appellatur, ut sup. 1. 4.

[1]Verity, *op. cit.*, p. 449, offers a number of suggestions for the source of Uriel as
an Angel and Archangel, such as Heywood's *Hierarchie of the Blessed Angels*,
Scot's *Discourse on Devils*, and More's *Song of the Soul*. These literary usages of
Uriel would be very valuable were there not more authoritative sources all of
which were available to Milton.

[2]This is the most constant and conventional statement made about the name
Uriel by Milton's commentators. The most important of these for this name are
Hume, Keightley, Masson, and Verity, who was mentioned in the previous note.
I omit their comment here, as I shall return to some of it *infra*. Keightley is the
most learned of them all, and his comment the most detailed.

[3]1 Chron. 6:9; 15:5, 11; 2 Chron. 13:2. The Hebrew form is the same in all
three chapters.

[4]2 Esdras 4:1; 4:36; 5:20; 10:28. The name in 4:36 is sometimes *Ieremiel*. It is
this verse, and only this one that calls him an Archangel.

Junius uses the name *Ieremiel* in the text of the thirty-sixth verse of the fourth chapter of second Esdras, and says of it

Ieremiel, hoc nomen in totis Bibliis non exstat: sed apud phanaticos Judaeos est cognitum, et a magis decantatum. Docti viderint.

Of the other occurrences in the same book of this name *Uriel*, Junius says nothing, having indicated in his note to its first occurrence that they mean, as did that, Christ.

But Milton had plenty of authority for using Uriel as an Angel and attributing to him the various characteristics and the office which he did. Although, as already stated, the Western Church had very early made the usual basis of its angelology the three Angels, Michael, Raphael, and Gabriel, the Eastern Church had evidently continued to employ the fourth Angel, Uriel.[1] But he had apparently dropped out of the angelology of the Western Church at a very early date, and never reappeared therein as an important Angel.

The origin of the name and conception, Uriel, for the Eastern fathers and later ecclesiastical historians was Jewish. In the recently discovered remains of the Jewish angelological Apocrypha, Uriel is found very often. And he did not disappear or tend to disappear in the Jewish literature written about the beginning of the Christian era, as he disappeared in the later literature of the Western Church. The Jewish angelology of those centuries just before and just after the birth of Christianity, found expression in the large amounts of angelological literature of the time. Some of this material naturally found its way into the Targums, which were then being written down in

---

[1]Cf. Georgius Cedrenus in *Corpus Scriptorum Historiae Byzantinae*, ed., Niebuhr (Bonnae, 1838), vol. 34, p. 17, 'ab Urielo, qui angelorum princeps (archangelum Graeci vocant)' p. 21, 'Urielum angelum Enocho indicasse quid mensis sit, quid solstitium quid annus;'

forms at least very similar to those preserved to us. Perhaps the greatest amount of such Jewish angelology was stored in those almost wholly angelological works which were lost for so many centuries. Undoubtedly much of this literature has never been and will never be recovered, and much that has been recovered was almost unknown from the third to the nineteenth century. But many of its ideas, and much of its lore was caught up into other literature which was not lost, and found its way into Jewish midrasch and commentary.

In Milton's day, although there was distinctly less of such material in its source-form available than today, most of this Jewish angelology was readily accessible in various secondary forms to the educated reader. Some of it had, indeed, become so only during his century, while some had always been reasonably accessible. The chief variation in the degree of accessibility was whether or not it had been translated from its original rabbinical language into Latin or a European vernacular. By 1650, a considerable amount was available in Latin translation and in such remarkably supplemented lexicons as Buxtorf's.[1] Other portions were less accessible except to those who were able to read it in the original.

Heretofore, two commentators have supplied us with the major portion of our information regarding the details of Milton's angelology. These commentators were Patrick Hume and Thomas Keightley.[2] Both of these commentators have virtually assumed that whenever Milton used angelological material not to be found in Scripture he had invented it. Their contributions, therefore, to our understanding of Milton's Angels have not been very valuable.

---

[1] Johann Buxtorf I, *Lexicon Chaldaicum, Talmudicum et Rabbinicum* (1639).

[2] Patrick Hume's annotated edition of *Paradise Lost* first appeared in 1695. His notes on the various angelic names have been almost slavishly followed by later commentators, including Keightley, whose work first appeared in 1851.

Nevertheless, for the whole conception of the Angel, Uriel, as found in *Paradise Lost*, nothing has been added to the seventeenth century work of Hume since his day. Keightley's treatment of the same Angel is but an amplification of Hume's, and proceeds in exactly the same manner. The detailed information regarding the name and other matters which follow are, then, the first addition to our knowledge of this Angel in Milton's work that has been made in over two centuries. Moreover, to assume with Hume or Keightley that Milton invented the details of his angelology is to misunderstand the great range of his reading and his whole attitude toward authority.

So far as the use of the name *Uriel* as that of an Angel was concerned, Milton had ample authority. But it was not only authority for the use of the name that led him to use it, but the whole conception of the Angel which lent itself so admirably to his purposes. While the name, as already stated, does not occur as the name of an Angel in the canonical books of the Bible, the name *Uriel* (אוריאל) as the name of an Angel is dealt with, however, at some length in a number of works available to Milton. The first of these to be noticed here is Buxtorf's *Lexicon Chaldaicum*, which has been described in some detail in an earlier chapter. As stated there, this work first appeared at Basel in 1639, and for the same reasons that gave such a prominence and wide circulation to its compiler's *Biblia Rabbinica*, the *Lexicon* likewise received wide-spread notice and use. Because of the remarkable amount of information it contained, some entries running to hundreds of words, even today this work remains extremely valuable as a Talmudical and general rabbinical lexicon. Its critical apparatus is full; its citation remarkably reliable; and its general usefulness very great, even to the modern student. As an epitome of rabbinical lore accessible to European

Christians during the first half of the seventeenth century, it is even of greater value.

The entry under the name Uriel (אוריאל) is typical of what may be expected of Buxtorf's *Lexicon* in connection with any important proper name, unless it is wholly Biblical. I include here the entire entry, primarily in order to present all that Buxtorf has to say of the name *Uriel*. But in addition to this, the entry gives a good idea of the nature of the information one may expect to find in this lexicon.

אוריאל *Uriel, angeli nomen. Unus est quatuor angelorum, qui circumstant solium majestatis divinae, ad ministeria ejus semper parati.* Sunt autem hi: מיכאל גבריאל אוריאל רפאל Michael stat ad dexteram ejus ad vexillum tribus Ruben, versus meridiem. Quare vocatur nomen ejus Michael? quando transivit populus Israeliticus mare rubrum, Moses aperuit or suum, et dixit: מי כמכה באלים יי' Exod. 15. 11. Et alibi: אין כאל ישרון Non est sicut Deus Jeschurun, Deut. 33. 26. (Ecce dicitur מי & dicitur כאל, unde מיכאל). *Uriel* stat ad sinistram ejus, da vexillum tribus Dan, versus septentrionem. Quare vocatur nomen ejus אוריאל? propter Legem, Prophetas & Hagiographia. Unde contigit Israelitis, ut ad eos dictum sit: קומי אורי כי בא אורך Surge, luce, quia venit lux tua, Jesa. 60. 1. Et David dixit: אל יי ויאר לנו Benedictus sit Deus Dominus, qui lucem praebuit nobis, Psal. 118. 27. Ecce hinc est nomen אוריאל. Ulterius Scriptura dicit: כי אשב בחשך יי אור לי Quando sedeo in tenebris, Dominus lumen mihi est, Mich. 6. 7. (7:8) (Testimonium ex lege omissum est). *Gabriel* stat ante conspectum ejus ad vexillum tribus Jehudae, juxta Mosen & Aharonem versus orientem. Quare dictum est nomen ejus גבריאל? De Jehuda scriptum est: Nam Jehuda גבר praevaluit fratribus suis, 1 Paral. 5. 2. Et de Mose scriptum est ויקרא אל משה. Et vocavit ad Mosen, Levit. 1. 1. Ulterius scriptum est, Et vocavit nomen ejus פלא יועץ אל גבור Jesa. 9. 6. Ecce hinc est nomen גבריאל. *Raphael* (stat a tergo ejus) pro vexillo Ephraim. Quare vocatur nomen ejus רפאל Raphael? כדי לרפאות Ad sanandum fracturas Jeroboam, qui ortus fuit ex tribu Ephraim, que habitavit versus occidentem. Dictum etiam est, אל נא רפא נא לה O Deus, sana quaeso eam, Numer. 12. 13. Hinc est nomen Raphael. Leguntur haec

in Bemidbar rabba sect. 2. Vide & R. Bechai in scet. Bemidbar.[1]

I wish to point out here certain facts about this lexicon
and Milton's use of it. The direct connection of this work
with him is not clear. But that he made use of it is, it
seems to me, beyond conjecture. All of Milton's references directly to rabbinical material are to be found in
those works written within the decade after his return from
Italy, that is, the decade immediately following the appearance of this great lexicon. The same lexicographer's
Lexicon Hebraicum, known and used by students of Hebrew throughout Europe since its appearance in 1607,
together with his Hebrew grammars, had caused the name
of Buxtorf to be known wherever the Semitic languages
were studied. The products of his labors, his *Biblia Rabbinica*, grammars, lexicons, and editions and translations
of various medieval Jewish writers, were perhaps better
known to Christians of the first half of the seventeenth
century than were the Jewish publications of any other
European editor. One may reasonably presume, in the
case of any Gentile student of *Semitica* or *Judaica* after
1600, that he knew the works prepared, edited, or composed by the various Buxtorfs, who, beginning with the
editor of the *Lexicon Chaldaicum*, continued to produce
works in this field until the eighteenth century.

Milton's use of this lexicon is, therefore, more than a
mere hypothesis. We know that he was a rather close
student of Hebrew and of *rabbinica*. In addition to this,
he has mentioned Buxtorf as the editor and translator of
Maimonides' *Doctor perplexorum*.[2] And, still more important in connection with his use of this lexicon, he has dis-

---

[1] Johannis Buxtorf, *Lexicon Chaldaicum, Talmudicum, et Rabbinicum* (Basileae
1639) col. 46.
[2] *Doctrine and Discipline of Divorce*, vol. IV:34.

cussed Semitic lexicography in such a way as to indicate his possession of a rather wide acquaintance with it.[1] In general, I should say that Milton's knowledge and use of Buxtorf's *Lexicon Chaldaicum* are as certain and as inevitable as his knowledge and use of any book that he has actually said he used.

Buxtorf's account of Uriel supplies an authority for his angelic nature, and further supplies a conception of him as an equal to Michael, Raphael, and Gabriel. The four Angels constitute, according to Buxtorf, precisely the kind of quadrumvirate Milton has employed in *Paradise Lost*. Uriel, according to Buxtorf again, is one of the four Angels (*unus est quatuor angelorum*) who *circumstant solium majestatis divinae, ad ministeria ejus semper parati*. Some more precise information regarding his nature and function is supplied, but Milton has gone much beyond this and made him Angel of the Sun. This he did, quite evidently, on some other basis than anything found in Buxtorf's *Lexicon*. This lexicon did, however, supply him with a basis for making Uriel an Archangel, and equal in rank with Michael, Raphael, and Gabriel. Thus Buxtorf is one authority for the use of the quadrumvirate made up of those three Angels plus Uriel.

Another work, already definitely connected with Milton, in which the grouping of Uriel, as an Angel, with Michael, Raphael, and Gabriel was pointed out, was the *Biblia Polyglotta Waltoni*.[2] This work, mentioned elsewhere in connection with an appeal by Milton to a reading of a particular verse in the Syriac New Testament, contains much very early rabbinical lore. A systematic investigation of its contents in connection with Milton and other writers of the second half of the seventeenth century is

[1] *de doctrina*, p. 78.
[2] Cf. *The Use of the Bible in Milton's Prose*, pp. 86-88.

greatly needed. But for our purposes here, we need only note that the *Polyglotta* contains a portion of a work that is more or less packed with Jewish lore of the first and second centuries of the Christian era. This is the *Targum of Jonathan Uziel*. Walton did not print all of this Targum; but he did include all of the Targum to the Pentateuch in his fourth volume. We need notice here only a single treatment of the Angel Uriel found in the Targum to the Pentateuch. In this Targum, Milton would have found a treatment of Uriel as an Angel. Not only that, but the Targum connects and gives him equal rank with the same three Angels that are his equals in *Paradise Lost*. In the Targum of Jonathan to the sixth verse of the thirty-fourth chapter of Deuteronomy, which deals with the burial of Moses, the quadrumvirate of Angels that Milton used is found. We need not pause here to examine the full treatment of Moses' burial contained in the Targum, as apparently it constitutes one of those rabbinical treatments of Biblical material to which Milton obviously had access but which he failed, for some reason, to use. It is unnecessary to speculate upon Milton's use of this material in its original tongue, and entirely unnecessary to suppose that after Walton's Bible had appeared that there would have been any difficulty whatever for Milton to have had ready access to the Targum in question. In the *Polyglotta*, the original of the Targum is paralleled by a Latin translation. Because of this, the whole matter of Uriel as an Angel who contended with Satan for the body of Moses as set forth in the Targum of Jonathan would have been readily accessible to Milton at least as early as 1655, the year in which the *Polyglotta* appeared.

The passage from the Targum, original and Latin translation follows:

אליף יתן למפרנסא מסכנין מן דאחית לבני ישראל לחמא מן שמיא' אליף יתן למקבר
מיתיא מן משה דאתגלי עלוי במימריה ועמיה חבורן דמלאכי שיריתא' מיכאל וגבריאל
אצעון דרגשא דדהבא מקבעא ביורכין וסנדלכין ובורלין ובורלין מתקנא בבסתרקי מילת
וסובנין דארגוון ואוציטילין חוורין מיטטרון ויופיאל ואוריאל ויפיפיה רבני חכמתא
ארבעון יתיה עלה ובמימריה דבריה ארבעתי מילין וקבר יתיה בחילתא כלו קבל
בית פעור דכל אימת דזקיף פעור למדכר לישראל חובתהון מודיק בבית קבורתיה
דמשה ומתכביש ולא חכים בר נש ית קבורתיה עד ומן יומא חדין:

docuit nos alendos esse pauperes, ex quo demisit filiis Israel panem
e coelis; docuit nos sepeliendos esse mortuos ex Mose, quia ipsi
manifestatus est per sermonem suum, et cum eo societates angelorum ministerii: Michael et Gabriel sternebant lectum aurem
distinctum margaritis, corallio, et beryllo, ornatum stragulis sericis
et sabanis purpureis, et stolis albis; Mitatron, et Jophiel, et Uriel,
et Jephepija sapientiae doctores jacere fecerunt ipsum in eo, et per
verbum suum duxit ipsum per quatuor milliaria, et sepelivit ipsum
in valle e regione Bethpeor (ut quotiescunque elevaret se Peor ad
revocandum in memoriam Israelitis peccata sua, prospiceret in
domum sepulchri Mosis, et reprimeretur) neque quisquam novit
sepulchrum ejus usque ad tempus diei hujus.[1]

An even more direct statement regarding the relationships
between these Angels, with special reference to Uriel,
occurs in the Supplement to the *Polyglotta*. This was the
learned *Lexicon Heptaglotton Castelli*, which appeared in
two enormous volumes in 1669. Of course this was much
too late to have had any direct influence upon Milton's use
of the name in *Paradise Lost*, but Castell's definitions re-
flected very largely the lexicography of the time. His
definition of the word אוריאל (*Uriel*) is

אוריאל Uriel, angeli nomen. *Unus est quatuor Angelorum qui cir-
cumstant solium majestatis Divinae ad ministeria ejus semper parati.
Sunt autem hi Michael, Gabriel, Uriel, Raphael, v. Bemidbar Rab.
S. 2.*

This is very similar to the earlier definition and account of

---

[1]Walton, *Biblia Polyglotta*, vol. IV, p. 389.

the word found in Buxtorf's Chaldaic lexicon, and, together with that work, it emphasizes the fact that the quadrumvirate of important Angels, made up of Michael, Raphael, Uriel, and Gabriel, is characteristic of Jewish angelology. The Jews tended to use a quadrumvirate instead of a triad of great Angels, and this quadrumvirate was usually made up of the four Angels already mentioned.

The rabbis in Buxtorf's *Biblia Rabbinica* have little or nothing to say of the Angel Uriel. They could, therefore, have furnished Milton with little or no information concerning the grouping of the four great Angels. Certainly they have nothing at all to contribute toward Milton's conception of Uriel as 'regent of the Sun.'

In fact, none of the references cited so far has in its treatment of Uriel had much to say of that meaning of the name. None of those just cited in any way explains this Angel as the Angel of the Sun. True, in the derivation of his name, as Buxtorf recounted it, following certain rabbinical authorities, there is a connection of Uriel with light. But no authority thus far cited has indicated any reason for employing him as 'Angel of the Sun.'

But such a conception of Uriel, a conception that made of him the great Angel of the Sun and of the Day, actually existed.

The name אוריאל *Uriel* is supposedly made up of two distinct elements, אור *light* and אל *God*. This composition of the name was hinted at by Buxtorf in his long discussion of the name, reflecting the opinion of the rabbis. Now, as a matter of fact, we know little or nothing about the actual origins of those names of Angels which end in אל-*el*.[1] Based on the two supposed elements, אור *light* and אל *God*,

---

[1] Cf. E. Kautzsch, *Die Apokryphen und Pseudopigraphen des Alten Testaments* (Tübingen, 1900), 2 vols., vol. II:355 note b, 'Die Engelnamen, sämtlich auf–'el (אל–)- gebildet, sind bis jetzt ein ungelöstes, schwieriges religionsgeschichtliches Problem.'

the name was taken and still may be taken today to mean *God's light*, or *light of God*; or, there may be substituted for the word *light*, the word *flame*.[1]   But it cannot be too strongly emphasized that in such matters, modern knowledge or lack of it is of no consequence whatsoever, the real question being what seventeenth century scholarship knew or thought it knew of such names.   It is unfair to Milton or to any other man under similar circumstances to find fault with his knowledge or scholarship when these are but the reflection of the best knowledge and opinion of his day.   That is, the important question here is, what did the seventeenth century think that the name *Uriel* meant?

It is not difficult to see how a conception of this Angel as the Angel of the Sun could have grown out of the name alone, but, as a matter of fact, probably the intrinsic meaning of the name was insufficient for periods later than the very beginnings of Jewish angelology.   For there appears in Jewish literature a full discussion of the Angel Uriel which not only ranks him in a quadrumvirate with Michael, Raphael, and Gabriel, but also makes of him the great Regent of the Sun, casting his beams over the whole of Creation.   This composite discussion is to be found in ספר מדרש רבה במדבר' פרשה ב (*the Midrasch Rabba to the book of Numbers*).   The passage in which he is described as one of the Four Presences that surround כסא הכבוד (*the Throne of Divine Majesty*) is the original of the passage cited by Buxtorf and Castell in their lexicons.   Not all of it need be cited here, but the following extract contains what we need for the quadrumvirate:

כשם שברא הקב"ה ד' רוחות וכנגדן ד' דגלים אף כך סיבב לכסאו ד' מלאכים מיכאל
וגבריאל ואוריאל ורפאל

---

[1]Cf. Brown, Driver, and Briggs, *op. cit.*, p. 22a-b, *flame of El* (God) or *my light is El* (God).

Translation: 'So the Holy One blessed-be-He created the Four Spirits, ruling over and having charge of the Four Divisions (the points of the compass). These are the same as surround his throne, the Four Angels Michael, and Gabriel, and Uriel, and Raphael.'[1]

In the same work occurs another passage concerned with Uriel's function and nature as an Angel. This passage supplies the other characteristics with which Milton has endowed him in *Paradise Lost*, including his station and his regency of the Sun. This passage, with original and translation, follows:

אוריאל משמאלו כנגד דן שהוא בצפון למה נקרא שמו אוריאל בשביל תורה נביאים
וכתובים שהקב"ה מכפר עליו ומאיר להם לישראל שנאמר קומי אורי כי בא אורך

'Uriel is at his (God's) left, toward Dan, which is in the North. Why is his name called Uriel? Because of the Torah, the Prophets, and the Writings (כתובים). For the Holy One blessed-be-He through Uriel (as through the Sun) spreads his light over Israel and over them (the other nations) as it is said (Isaiah 60:1) *Arise, shine for thy light is come.*'[2]

Here, then, is the origin of the conception of Uriel as Angel of the Sun, shedding his light and letting his rays travel over the whole of the Created Universe.

However, the most remarkable characteristic of Milton's figure of Uriel is the complexity of its structure. It will be noticed that no single source is sufficient to supply all phases of the idea of the Angel found in the poem. Milton's figure begins with the idea of the Angels of the Presence as presented in Zechariah, with conflicting statements as to their number. Scripture is silent as to the names of these Angels, but very early, in Midrasch and Targum, the Jewish rabbis supplied them. These Angels in Scripture are God's eyes. Milton selected Uriel because of rabbin-

---

[1] מדרש רבה במדבר פרשה ב ספר, וילנא, 1911, vol. II., p. 10, col. 2.
[2] *ibid.*

ical development of the nature of this Angel, particularly in the *Midrasch Rabba*, as Angel of the Sun. In him was then centered the whole Biblical conception of the 'eyes,' and in *Paradise Lost* Uriel is endowed with the keenest eyesight of all the Angels. Being possessed of such eyesight, he is the official Watchman of all that goes on in the Universe, his eyesight symbolizing the penetration of the Sun's rays, spread over and searching out all parts of the Universe. The full understanding of his origin for Milton impresses us with the variety of material on which the poet very often drew for such a conception as that of Uriel.

Growing out of this discussion of Milton's Uriel is a point connected with Gabriel which, so far as I know, has never before been noted or explained. In his depiction of Gabriel, the Archangel second in command to Michael, Milton has followed Christian tradition almost entirely. There is very little that may be added to what has long since been said or noted of him in connection with that tradition. His nature and function in *Paradise Lost* were derived almost wholly from patristic and scholastic Christian commentary and doctrinal exposition.

There is, however, one small portion of his actions in the poem which remains entirely unexplained. This is the station in the Universe to which Milton has assigned him. This station is not only difficult to explain, but Milton's use of it is also difficult to discover unless the reader is fully aware of just what is implied. In addition, more knowledge of Gabriel than is supplied by the ordinary Christian traditions connected with him is needed for complete comprehension of what Milton had in mind.

In the fourth Book of *Paradise Lost*, certain directions are given out by Gabriel which make it possible to determine his location while he is speaking, and also the location of his definite station in the Universe. It is apparent from what he says that his station is one of the four cardinal points of the compass, the East. Now of course, we are not concerned here with the location of the compass-point known as the East, but we are concerned with what Milton meant by such a statement. Let us look at what Gabriel says of his station.

In the fourth Book, after Gabriel has been warned at sunset by Uriel of the presence of an alien Spirit in the Universe, he prepares at evening to set his nightly watch. He gives orders to one of his Angels, Uzziel:

> 'Uzziel, half these (Angels) draw off, and coast the South
> With strictest watch; these other wheel the North,
> Our circuit meets full West.' As flame they part
> Half wheeling to the Shield, half to the Spear.
>
> —Book IV:782-785.

Gabriel then selects two scouts 'from these . . . that neer him stood.' It is here evident that these scouts were selected from the group which he himself was to command—the group that turned 'to the spear,' or to the right. This was the direction in which this group was to move, and as we know that Gabriel had taken the North as the direction in which he and his band of Angels were to patrol, Uzziel, with the group that had turned left, was to move to the South. We thus have a very definite idea of the directions connected with the point at which Gabriel and his Cherubim now stood when

> from thir Ivorie Port the Cherubim
> Forth issuing at th' accustomd hour stood armd
> To thir night watches in warlike Parade,
>
> —*ibid.* 778-780.

Gabriel's orders, together with the description of the division of forces and how they wheeled, make it possible to discover not only the directions to be taken by the two bands, but also the location from which they set out, or the location of Gabriel's station. On Gabriel's right was north, and south was on his left. He was therefore facing due west. His order to his two bands of troops 'our circuit meets full West' can only have one meaning. It is clear that what he intends is that the two bands of Angels, one coasting to the south and the other to the north, shall circumvent the Universe. They will then meet at what in the Ptolemaic cosmology was one of the four fixed points of the compass, the West. It is a little difficult for us to think of points of the compass as having objective existence in space, but in the system of which Milton was now thinking, there was no such difficulty. The location of Gabriel, at his station in the Universe when these orders were given, is made doubly certain by his further orders concerning the disposal of Satan if he is found,

'Such, where ye find, seise fast, and hither bring.'
                                        —*ibid.* 796.

'Hither' is the place from which the orders were given, the opposite of 'due west' on the other side of the Universe at which point the 'coasting' bands of Angels were to meet.

Gabriel's station is thus seen to have been the other of the four cardinal compass-points, the East. But why should Milton have placed Gabriel at this point?

The answer is contained in the Jewish notion of Gabriel's station. Buxtorf's lexicon contains one account of this station, and as I have already suggested this work as a source for certain aspects of Uriel, it may again be invoked in connection with Gabriel. As a matter of fact, the information the lexicon yields about Gabriel is found in the same entry that contains the information already

248 *Milton's Rabbinical Readings*

noted in connection with Uriel. The Gabriel material contained in that entry follows:

Gabriel stat ante conspectum ejus ad vexillum tribus Jehudae, juxta Mosen et Aharonem versus orientem. Quare dictum est nomen ejus נבריאל? De Jehuda scriptum est: Nam Jehuda נבר praevaluit fratribus suis, 1 Paral. 5. 2. Et de Mose scriptum est: ויקרא אל משה Et vocavit ad Mosen, Levit. 1. 1. Ulterius scriptum est, Et vocavit nomen ejus פלא יועץ אל נבור Jesa. 9. 6. Ecce hinc est nomen נבריאל.

This suggestion in Buxtorf that Gabriel is *juxta Mosen et Aharonem versus orientem* has also been taken from the Jewish במדבר ר' מ' *Midrasch Rabba to Numbers*. In this work we find the following description of the position and station of the Angel Gabriel, who is one of the Four Angels of the Presence:

גבריאל מלפניו כנגד מלכות יהודה ומשה ואהרן שהיו במורח

Gabriel stands before him towards the kingdom of Judah, and Moses and Aaron, which was in the East, (towards the sunrise).

In being so precise about his description of directions connected with Gabriel's station, it seems to me that Milton shows another vestige of his original intention to make much of the various traditions, originally Jewish, that employ and explain the great Archangels of the Presence. But all that remains in the finished poem of this idea is the description of Uriel and the details of Gabriel's station and its position in the Universe.

MICHAEL

Another Angel all of whose functions in the poem have never been sufficiently explained is Michael. It has been noted by many commentators that this Angel was, on the basis of Revelation 12, the leader of the embattled Angels in the Warfare in Heaven. The conception of him as the 'great Prince' has likewise been pointed out as originating from Daniel 12:1.[1] But none of the commentators have much to say of him as Adam's mentor after the Fall. Milton provided detailed instructions and definite orders for this mission, at the close of the conclave in Heaven to determine man's punishment for his sin. Closely following Genesis 3:22-24 in its opening, Milton's full statement of God's decision concerning Adam's punishment contains the charge to Michael:

> '. . . . Man is become
> To know both Good and Evil, since his taste
> Of that defended Fruit; but let him boast
> His knowledge of Good lost, and Evil got,
> Happier, had it suffic'd him to have known
> Good by itself, and Evil not at all.
> He sorrows now, repents, and prayes contrite,
> My motions in him, longer then they move,
> His heart I know, how variable and vain
> Self-left. Least therefore his now bolder hand
> Reach also of the Tree of Life, and eat,
> And live forever, dream at least to live
> For ever, to remove him I decree,
> And send him from the Garden forth to Till
> The Ground whence he was taken, fitter soile.
>   *Michael*, this my behest have you in charge,
> Take to thee from among the Cherubim
> Thy choice of flaming Warriours, least the Fiend
> Or in behalf of Man, or to invade
> Vacant possession som new trouble raise:
> Hast thee, and from the Paradise of God
> Without remorse drive out the sinful Pair,
> From hallowd ground th' unholie, and denounce
> To them and to their Progenie from thence
> Perpetual banishment. Yet least they faint
> At the sad Sentence rigorously urg'd,
> For I behold them soften'd and with tears
> Bewailing thir excess, all terror hide.

[1]Verity, *op. cit.*, p. 509 note.

If patiently thy bidding they obey,
Dismiss them not disconsolate; reveale
To *Adam* what shall come in future dayes,
As I shall thee enlighten, intermix
My Cov'nant in the womans seed renewd;'

—Book XI:84-116.

Newton's explanation of Michael in this capacity still passes current among most modern commentators, and although Newton's notes are often better than later ones, in this case he is inadequate. He said of Michael in connection with XI:99:

Our author has with great judgment singled out *Michael* to receive this charge. It would not have been so proper for the sociable spirit Raphael to have executed this order: but as Michael was the principal Angel employed in driving the rebel Angels out of Heaven, so he was the most proper to expel our first parents too out of Paradise.

Verity has added to this that Raphael had been sent down to Adam while man was still innocent, and now it was logical that for poetic reasons of proportion Michael should have been used. Both remarks are, perhaps, true enough; but there is more to be said of such an employment of Michael, and perhaps better reasons for employing him.

First of all, it was especially fitting that Michael should have been chosen (XI:99) to carry out the decree of banishment of the human pair from the garden. Not only did the orthodox conception of this Angel give him charge of the garden of Eden (cf. Bonaventura, *loc. cit.* 'praepositum paradisi etc.') but likewise made of him the embodiment of the principle of God's Justice ('venire in adjutorium populo Dei' and Rashi). In addition to having him pronounce the decree of banishment, Milton has also had him, according to other traditions, point out to Adam not only his own future life outside of the Garden, but also the whole future of the race. Milton, for this purpose, might have selected any one of a large number of Angels for each of whom as the expounder of a vision he would have had a precedent in Jewish apocalyptic literature. But Milton chose Michael for this function chiefly, I believe, in view of the fact that Adam saw principally a cyclorama of Hebrew history. The proper Angel to have used for such a purpose is determined by Exodus 23:20-23:

Behold, I send an angel before thee, to keep thee by the way, and to bring thee into the place which I have prepared. Take ye heed before him, and hearken unto his voice; provoke him not; for he will not pardon your transgression: for my name is in him. But if thou shalt indeed hearken unto his voice, and do all that I speak; then I will be . . . For mine angel shall go before thee, and bring thee in unto (the promised land)
    —(American R. V.)

In this passage, it will be noted that the austerity of the Angel is stressed, as it is in Milton; his voice is to be heeded, and he is not to be provoked. If his voice is heeded, then will his capacities as mentor or guide be revealed, and he would lead or show the way to the promised land. Of course, to Christians, this passage in the Pentateuch was taken to mean that this Angel would watch over God's chosen people 'mine angel shall go before thee' and lead them until the coming of the Messiah. In *Paradise Lost*, therefore, the whole vision of Adam is an expansion of these verses in Exodus into the history of the Hebrews from Adam's Fall to the coming of the Christ.

Although the Biblical text itself does not name this Angel, to the rabbis he was specifically Michael. In Buxtorf's Bible, both Ibn Ezra and Rashi, commenting on the verse quoted above, declare the Angel to have been Michael, the great Prince over Israel (Daniel 12:1). Rashi says definitely of the name of the Angel in Exodus 23:21,

כי שמי בקרבי' מחזר לראש המקרא השמר מפניו כי שמי משותף בו' ורבותינו אמרו
זה מטטרון ששמו כשם רבו מטטרון בגימטריא

'for my name is in him.' Partner to the Almighty. The text
hides him from us, (i.e., does not give us his name) for the name of
the Partner is in him. But our rabbis say that this (Angel) is
Metatron, that his name is [the same] as the great *Metatron* in the
Gematria (i.e., *Michael*).

Ibn Ezra is equally as explicit when he says of the same
verse:

כמו היושבים ראשונה במלכות וזה המלאך הוא מיכאל

So it is settled (or they *settled*) that (this refers to) the chief of the
Angels, and this is he. The Angel is Michael.

Thus, it was not by bare chance, neither was it by accident
that Milton gave each of the quadrumvirate of great
Angels an important task to perform in the poem. It
would not be exactly true to say with Newton or with
Verity, from Dunster, that the function of Michael in the
poem rested upon wholly aesthetic considerations. The
fact of the matter is that Milton knew the proper traditional functions of his Angels much better than have any
of his subsequent commentators. For the various tasks
he assigned each of his individual Angels, he had excellent
authority in each case. In the case of Michael, as with
Gabriel and the others, rabbinical tradition was the ultimate basis on which the great Prince of the Angels was
made to function, not only in the Warfare in Heaven, but
in his dismissal of the human pair from the Garden as well.

Before leaving the subject of the Loyal Angels, there is
one other whom Milton apparently drew directly from
Jewish sources. The Angel Uzziel, to whom Gabriel
issued his orders when he set in the fourth Book to find
Satan, is another of Milton's Angels who has received inadequate explanation in the past. Hume explained the

name and the conception by saying of Uzziel, 'The next
commanding Angel to Gabriel; his name in Hebrew is
the strength of God, as all of God's mighty Angels are.'[1]
Keightley says of the same name, 'Uzziel (עזיאל Might of
God), a frequent proper name in Scripture: see Exod. vi.
18; Numb. iii. 19.'[2]

Masson followed these two commentators entirely, saying of Uzziel only 'Strength of God.'[3] Verity also follows
the same general tradition, saying only '*Uzziel*, "strength
of God." The name occurs in the Bible (e.g. in Exod.
vi. 18), but not as that of an Angel.'[4]

There were, however, warrants enough for Milton to
have used the name *Uzziel* as that of an Angel. Nor need
we in any way assume that the name was invented for the
occasion. Just why Milton used it in the way he did, is
not clear. But the use of the name as that of an Angel was
justified by its occurrence in such a usage in several places.
Perhaps the most natural place to look for the name and
what it signified in Milton's day would be in the same
lexicon in which the names of Uriel and Gabriel have been
found together with certain material connected with them
which Milton used from this source or a similar one.
Buxtorf says of Uzziel,

עזיאל Usiel, nomen angeli, cujus socius Samchasai, qui deciderunt
ex coelis, et commixti hominibus, genuerunt gigantes, Genes. 6.
v. 4. in Jonathane.

The reference Buxtorf cited in this statement is to the
same Targum used in connection with Uriel, the Targum

[1] P.[atrick] H.[ume], *Annotations on Milton's Paradise Lost* (London, 1695),
p. 163.
[2] Thomas Keightley, *An Account of the Life, Opinions, and Writings of John
Milton*, (London, 1859), p. 470.
[3] David Masson, *The Poetical Works of John Milton* (London, 1896, 3 vols.)
vol. III, p. 356.
[4] Verity, *op. cit.*, p. 470.

of Jonathan Uziel, found in Walton's *Polyglotta*. This work yields the following for the passage cited by Buxtorf:

הנפילים שמחואי ועוזיאל הינון נפילין מן שמיא והוו בארעא ביומיא האינון ואוף בתר
כן דעלון בני רברביא לות בנת אינשא וילידן להון והינון מתקרין גברין דמעלמא
אינשי שמהן

Schamchazai & Uziel, qui cadebant ex coelis, erant in terra in diebus illis: & etiam postquam ingressi sunt filii magnatum ad filias hominum, & pepererunt illis; & hi sunt qui vocantur Viri qui a seculo, Viri nominum.

Uzziel, then, was a well-authenticated Angel in Milton's day, and there is no reason longer to speculate on his origin for the poet. Why Milton used him as he did in the poem, I should not venture to say. But *Uzziel* as the name of an Angel must have been wide-spread in Jewish, if not in Christian angelological literature. Perhaps other accounts of him besides those just noted were known to Milton which would have provided a basis for having employed this Angel as he did.

It is by no means my intention completely to scrutinize all of Milton's Angels in order to discover how much or how little each of them owed to Jewish and more particularly to rabbinical influences. In the treatment of Uriel and, to a lesser extent, in the very brief and relatively unimportant treatments of Gabriel and Uzziel, I have sought rather to proceed in such a way as to make apparent the possibilities of investigation of such material in *Paradise Lost* from the point of view of Milton's rabbinical readings. The material presented above is a fair cross-section of what may be expected from such investigation. Sometimes, as in the case of Uriel, much new light may be thrown on Milton's basic conceptions, even of his composition of an idea found in his poetry. Then again, as in the case of Uzziel, investigation may result in very little being learned of any importance. But even when there is as little return as in the case of Uzziel, that little is actually new knowledge, and, in connection with other bits, such as Gabriel's station, may result in contributing its little strength to the little strengths of those other bits until an important result is achieved. In this case, the putting of the rather slight Uzziel material with the also rather slight Gabriel material, results in the discovery when attached to the Uriel material of a new and hitherto unknown tool that Milton quite evidently employed, which was the Buxtorf lexicon. But this is not the most important result of examining Milton's use of these particular Angels. The important point in the work of this entire chapter is that Milton has obviously used rabbinical material in developing his conceptions of individual Angels and in his whole idea of the order and arrangement of the Angels. His use of the quadrumvirate of Jewish angelology instead of the triad of Christian angelology is an indication of how greatly he depended upon rabbinical sources for his whole treatment of Angels.

CHAPTER VII

SOME REBEL ANGELS

Although Milton's general scheme of angelology in *Paradise Lost* is a fairly conventional one, some of the names he used for the individual Angels are not easily explained as names of Angels. If the names of the two Archangels, Michael and Gabriel, have scriptural and other obvious warrants for the manner in which he used them, the names of many of his lesser Angels cannot be found in Scripture or in kindred sources as the names of Angels at all.

Some of the names of Angels which Milton used, as a matter of fact, have been extremely difficult to account for as names of Angels. In truth, because of lack of knowledge of the origins and meanings of their names, some of Milton's lesser Angels have been, I think, almost misunderstood.

For instance, in the account of the Warfare in Heaven in the sixth Book, occur the names of three of the angelic combatants, Ariel, Arioch, and Ramiel. Milton says of them:

> 'Nor stood unmindful *Abdiel* to annoy
> The Atheist crew, but with redoubl'd blow
> *Ariel*, and *Arioc*, and the violence
> Of *Ramiel*, scorcht and blasted overthrew.'
>
> —Book VI:369-372.

Satisfactory treatments or discussions of these names, particularly the last three, Ariel, Arioch, and Ramiel, are and always have been lacking. Such discussions as occur are inadequate and perplexing.

Of the three names, perhaps the most interesting is Ariel, although all three are fascinating. But to Ariel, the first named of the three, I shall first turn my attention.

The name *Ariel* is familiar to all of us because of its occurrence in Shakespeare's *The Tempest* and in Goethe's *Faust*. But it is at once apparent that there is little if any of Shakespeare's conception of it in Milton's use of the name. The dainty, ethereal creature depicted by Shakespeare whose name is indeed thought of as an embodiment of the adjective *ethereal*, is not to be found in Milton's conception. The latter is very apparently the conception of a warrior possessed of terrific prowess, and any comparison of the two conceptions at once shows that they are wholly unconnected.

Milton seems to have selected the name *Ariel* as being indicative particularly of mighty fighting and passages at arms by champions in battle. At least, in the lines of *Paradise Lost* in which the name is involved, it is clearly a symbol of terrific fighting, and noisy, violently heroic feats of arms. But why should Milton have so used the name, and what did he understand by it? Why should the name *Ariel* have been used to suggest terrific fighting such as is implied in the passage in which the name occurs? And more particularly, why should it have suggested heroic if violent feats of arms? Why should Milton have selected this name for an Angel in connection with mighty deeds of warfare, and to what kind of an Angel did he apply it?

Commentators on *Paradise Lost* have uniformly failed to offer adequate explanations for the use of this name, indeed, many commentators have been entirely silent about it. The earliest explanation of the name occurs in Hume's notes to his edition of *Paradise Lost* of 1695. He said of it, '*Ariel*, Hebrew, *the lion of God*, or *a strong lion*.' This or less has sufficed for all editors and commentators since, the four principal editors, Todd,

Keightley, Masson, and Verity, following Hume almost *verbatim*.[1]

No other explanation of the name or of its use has been heretofore presented, and Hume's is inadequate. He made no attempt whatever to explain why Milton used *Ariel* as the name of an Angel, loyal or rebel, nor did he adequately explain why Milton used this particular name to indicate the terrific nature of the battle between the Loyal and the Rebel Angels. The meaning which Hume found in it, *lion of God*, is an entirely permissible explanation of the Hebrew word אריאל whose first syllable ארי means *lion* and whose second syllable אל means *God*. This meaning of the name would somewhat explain the fighting characteristics attached to it, at least sufficiently to account for its use in connection with battle. But such an explanation leaves unanswered the larger portion of the questions we have already raised about the name and its occurrence in the poem.

In order fully to understand and appreciate all that Milton's use of the name *Ariel* implied as he has used it, it is necessary to know something of the origin of the name. The word has a curious history, and, like many other Hebrew proper names, its original meaning is at least partly a mystery. It is undoubtedly, as Hume stated, of Hebrew origin. As a proper name, it occurs unmistakably but once in the Old Testament; as an indeterminate term, it occurs several times; but never as the name of an Angel, good or bad.

The one place in the Old Testament in which the form אריאל *Ariel* occurs as an unmistakable proper name is in the sixteenth verse of the eighth chapter of Ezra. Here the

---

[1]It seems unnecessary to cite the notations of these editors and commentators here, even in a footnote. Their explanations of *Ariel* may be found in the notes to the respective editions by these editors referred to previously.

name is clearly *Ariel* (אריאל) a masculine proper name of a chief man among the returning exiles: *Then I sent for Eliezer, for Ariel, etc.* (ואשלחה לאליעור לאריאל).

The same form אריאל occurs again in the twenty-second verse of the eleventh chapter of first Chronicles. But what it actually means there is uncertain. The Revised Version reads, *he slew the two (sons of) Ariel of Moab* (הוא הכה את שני אריאל מואב). The phrase *sons of* is not in the original. The same strange statement occurs again in the twentieth verse of the twenty-third chapter of second Samuel, in this case using the form אראל. The Revised Version reads precisely the same here as in Ezra although the Hebrew is slightly different, הוא הכה את שני אראל מואב. As to what this *Ariel* was or these *Ariel* were, the best authorities are uncertain.[1]

The form אריאל occurs again in the first verse of the twenty-ninth chapter of Isaiah, for which the Revised Version reads *Ho, Ariel, Ariel, the city where David encamped!* (הוי אריאל אריאל קרית חנה דוד). Here the meaning seems to be that of a special appellative for Jerusalem. Here the word is clearly feminine, and probably a proper name of some kind. The word here has passed through a complicated process of poetic transmutation. It is evidently connected with the word אראיל in the Massoretic text for the fifteenth verse of the forty-third chapter of Ezekiel, for which the Revised Version reads, *and from the #altar hearth and upward* (ומהאראיל ולמעלה) the marginal note reading, *Heb. Ariel, see Is. 29:1.* In the Hebrew, the word ומהאראיל carries the *qere*, or marginal reading sign. In the margin, instead of the form ומהאראיל as in the text, the form והאריאל is found, pointed precisely like the other forms of the apparently proper name אריאל *Ariel* al-

[1] Cf. Brown, Driver, & Briggs, *A Hebrew and English Lexicon*, p. 72a.

ready cited above. In Ezekiel, the word is clearly masculine again.

These are all of the occurrences of the word in the Old
Testament, and certainly so far as the text of any of them
is concerned, we can learn nothing of how Milton came to
use the term as the name of an Angel. But however the
meaning of the name *Ariel* be construed or denied by com-
petent modern lexicographers, the important consideration
in the present investigation is what the name meant in
Milton's time and to him. Here we are on much less uncertain ground. And if we find that modern lexicographers
and commentators are perplexed and uncertain of how to
explain the word, we may be sure that the commentators
of Milton's time and before must have exerted their best
efforts in attempts to explain it properly. In fact, the
examination of the various occurrences of the word in the
text of the Old Testament having explained nothing connected with Milton's use of it, suggests that his usage and
understanding of the term must have come from some
other source than the scriptural text itself.

Milton's use of the name *Ariel* was due to a syncretic
conception of it derived from various sources, chiefly from
commentaries on Scripture, including the rabbinical, indeed, primarily from the latter. Tremellius's text and
notes, however, for the various occurrences of the name in
the Old Testament are very informative.

His text for the passage in second Samuel reads

is percussit duos valentissimos Moabitas

He has translated the Hebrew אראל Ariel by the word *valentissimos*, which carries the marginal note: *Heb. ariel,
id est, duos leones fortissimos.* That is, he has taken the
word *Ariel* as a plural meaning *strong lions*, used figuratively for *valiant men*, or *mighty men*. Tremellius's text

for the passage in Chronicles reads the same as his translation of the Samuel text; but the word *valentissimos*
carries no note in the Chronicles passage.

The next passage that contains the name *Ariel* is that in
Ezra, and as the name here occurs as an unmistakable
proper name, Tremellius neither changes the text nor
glosses it with a marginal note, but accepts the form that
occurs in the Hebrew.

His treatment of the name in Isaiah is interesting and
curious. He makes no change in the text, his translation
reading *Vae Arieli, Arieli*, but to the word *Arieli*, he
appends the following long note:

Arieli, id est, altari, ac proinde templo synecdochice; est autem
Ariel vox composita, significans de verbo ad verbum leonem Dei
fortis: quo nomine intelligitur sive focus ingentis illius altaris aerei,
de quo 2 Chronic. 4. 1. quia velut immanis leo holocausta allata
consumebat igne perpetuo, cujus mentio est in fine hujus pro-
phetiae infra 31. 9. sic etiam accipitur Ezek. 43. 15. & 16. Est
autem in priore hujus versus membro prolepsis sive propositio
summa utriusque calamitatis, quam sequentia verba ex ordine
interpretantur.

This note connects the word as it occurs in Isaiah with the
occurrence in Ezekiel.

Tremellius also furnishes us with another textual reading, which adds another Biblical occurrence of the name to
those already noted. In the seventh verse of the thirty-
third chapter of Isaiah, a word occurs that is somewhat
like אריאל *Ariel*, and which Tremellius takes to be the same.
There is no hint of this in the reading of the Revised Version, which reads *Behold their valiant ones cry without*, for
the Hebrew הן אראלם צעקו חצה. It is the word אראלם that has
been translated *valiant ones* by the Revised Version.
Tremellius anticipated this translation, but he also connects it with אריאל *Ariel*. His text reads *En valentissimi*

horum clamaverant foris.   The word *valentissimi*, as in his
text for the Samuel passage, carries a marginal notation,
in fact, it carries two marginal notes, one explaining the
meaning of the text, and the second providing the reading
of the Hebrew. The second note reads: *Heb. Ereel, quod
dicitur Ariel, 2 Sam. 23. 20.* The first is as follows: *id est,
praefecti Judaeorum, missi a rege Chizkija ut audirent lega-
tionem Rab-schakis 2 Reg. 18. 37.*

The one remaining passage that contains the name
Ariel, the passage in Ezekiel, reads in Tremellius's text,

Ita ipsum Hareel quatuor cubitorum est: ab ipso denique Ariele
sursum versus cornua sunt quatuor.

In this text, the word *Ariele* carries no note; but the word
Hareel carries one which is interesting because of the
cross-references. It reads:

Hareel, id est, ἐσχάρα sive focus altaris holocausti & spatium illud
vacuum in quod indebantur ligna atque holocausta imposita crati
sive reticulo, ex analogia legis Exod. 27. 4. vide Is. 29. 1.

Tremellius connects the word הראל *Hareel* with the word
Ariel as it occurs earlier in Isaiah, and assumes that both
refer to the altar, as they probably do.

It will be noticed from this survey of Tremellius's treatment of the word *Ariel* in his text and in his notes, that he
supplies the idea that the name implies *strength* or *might*.
He does this because of the first syllable of the word ארי
lion. But he has nowhere suggested that the word means
Angel or has any connection with Angel, even his discussion of the אראלם in the thirty-third chapter of Isaiah
failing to make any connection between *Ariel* and Angel.
That is, so far as Tremellius was concerned, *Ariel* was
not the name of an Angel in the Old Testament, nor, in his
full annotation of the text did he at any time attempt to
make it appear so.

If Tremellius yields little of consequence in connection with Milton's idea of Ariel as an Angel, the reverse is true of the rabbinical commentaries in Buxtorf's Bible to the various Old Testament texts in which the name occurs. These commentaries are very suggestive in connection with Milton's use of the name, and because the name *Ariel* appears in several different forms in the Hebrew, the rabbinical commentary on these various forms is especially diverse. For certain of its occurrences, one aspect of the name is stressed; and for other occurrences, other aspects are stressed. But in order to obtain a true idea of how Milton drew on these commentaries for his use of the name in *Paradise Lost*, a full examination of the texts in which it occurs and of the commentaries accompanying them is necessary.

Because the rabbis in their commentaries so often refer to earlier occurrences of the same words they are explaining, we shall begin with the earliest use of the word *Ariel* regardless of the form in which it occurs. This is the passage in Samuel in which the name occurs in the form אראל. In Buxtorf, three rabbis, Rashi, Ralbag, and Kimchi, comment on the text of Samuel. Their comments on the verse in which the name *Ariel* occurs are somewhat unequal in amount and in significance to us. But they are much more informative than was Tremellius of the implications of the name here. The idea of *Ariel*, singular or plural, as mighty fighter or fighters is fully brought out in these commentaries, and impressively presented. Surely no one who read them would ever forget that the name *Ariel* stood for powerful fighters. The reading of the clause containing the name will be recalled, *and he slew two (sons of) Ariel of Moab*, in which *sons of* was inserted by the translators. Rashi says of this:

את שני אריאל מואב' ית' תרין רברבי מואב ורבותינו אמרו שלא הניח כמותו לא
במקדש ראשון ולא במקדש שני

two Ariel [of] Moab, the Targum reads רברבי מואב *great men, princes of Moab*, and our rabbis say that their like [in size] was not allowed either in the time of the first or of the second Temple. (Rashi means that such mighty men as were the *Ariel* have long since disappeared from the earth, no longer being 'allowed').

Ralbag is the second rabbi commenting upon this verse and the word *Ariel*. He says

הוא הכה את אריאל מואב' הנה המגדל החזק יקרא אריאל ולזה נקרא בית המקדש
אריאל והרצון בו שהוא הכה אנשי המגדלי" החזקים ההם שהיו במואב והמלה מורכבת
מארי ומאל ועניני ארי תקיף כי הארי הוא רב הגבורה ואפשר גם כן שהיה בהם צורת
אריה להורות על התוקף והחוזק':

he slew two Ariel [of] Moab. Behold the mighty and powerful the author calls אריאל. And the Temple [in Jerusalem] is called the same. And the meaning of this verse is that he killed the two mightiest and strongest men of Moab. And the word (*Ariel*) is made up of ארי (*lion*) and of אל (*God*). And we say a lion seizes, for the lion is the mightiest of the mighty. And it is possible also that there is in the word [the idea of] the shape of the lion to show power and strength. (Ralbag in this last sentence is probably referring to the Temple and its shape).

These two commentaries, therefore, begin to attribute to the word *Ariel* various characteristics all of which are concerned with terrific fighting qualities, even the derivation of the word from *lion* and *God* stressing the fact that the lion is the mightiest of all mighty beasts. The third rabbi to comment here, Kimchi, adds little to what Rashi and Ralbag have already said. Kimchi says:

את שני אריאל מואב' כתרגומו ית תרין רברבי מואב והיא מלה מורכבת מן ארי ומן
אל וארי יש לו גבורה ואל הוא לשון חוזק

The Targum reads *he slew two mighty men of Moab*. And the word (*Ariel*) is derived from ארי (*lion*) and from אל (*God*). And ארי (*lion*) signifies *strength*, and אל (*God*) signifies חוזק (*power*).

The corresponding passage in Chronicles, identical with the Samuel passage except that it uses the form אראל where Samuel uses אריאל, carries the commentaries of Rashi and Kimchi only. What they have to say of this passage in Chronicles is but a duplication of their comment on the passage in Samuel.

Kimchi says

שני אריאל מואב' שני גבורי מואב וכן אמר המתרגם בשמואל תרין רברבי מואב וכנה הגבורים אריאל לפי שארי גבור וחזק' וכן אל לשון חזק

two mighty men of Moab as the Targum to Samuel reads. And these mighty men (heroes) were called אריל because ארי (*lion*) means *mighty* and *strong*, and אל (*God*) means *power*.

Rashi's comment is very similar to this,

אריאל' גבורי' בעלי כח ארי גבור וגם אל לשון אילי הארץ

אריאל *Heroes;* men of strength (power); ארי *lion* is mighty, as is אל in the expression אילי הארץ (Ezekiel 17:13.) *the mighty of the land.*

The occurrence of the word *Ariel* in the book of Ezra calls forth comment from but a single rabbi, Ibn Ezra, who comments as follows:

לאריאל' הם היו שלוחים ולמ״ד היא המורה על העצם וטעמו לעצם אליעזר והנוכרים

to Ariel, These (Eliezer and Ariel) were messengers. And the ל *lamed* (the preposition attached to the name *Ariel* in the Hebrew) causes difficulty, as it will be remembered it did with [the name] *Eliezer* (the name occurring in the text before *Ariel*).

The only point of importance in this comment is the statement that *Ariel* was one of the שלוחים *messengers.* This explanation will be used later in connection with another occurrence of a form very similar but not identical with *Ariel.*

The first occurrence of the word in Isaiah is in the passage beginning with *Ho, Ariel, Ariel, the city where David encamped!*   Three rabbis comment on the passage and on the word *Ariel*.   These rabbis are Rashi, Ibn Ezra, and Kimchi.   Rashi says:

הוי אריאל' תירגם יונתן מדבחא דיי' ואף יחזקאל קראו כן שנאמר והאריאל שתי'
עשרה על שם אש שלמעלה שהיתה רובצת כארי על גבי המזבח כמו ששנינו בסדר
יומא ורבותי' פירשוהו על ההיכל שהיה צר מאחריו ורחב מלפניו

Ho, Ariel etc.   The Targum Jonathan [reads] *altar of God*.   And likewise Ezekiel called it so when he said *and the altar-hearth twelve* (Ezekiel 43:16) [meaning] that the fire of the steps was crouching like a lion at the base of the altar, so also the two places in *Yoma* (Mishna).   And our rabbis explain that this was the Temple, which was narrow behind and wide in front [like a lion].

That is, Rashi's comment here, like that of the other two rabbis, emphasizes the derivation of the word *Ariel* from the root ארי meaning *lion*.

Kimchi's comment is very much like Rashi's:

הוי אריאל אר' המובח נקרא אריאל' וכן בספר יחזקאל ומהאריאל ולמעלה קרנות
ארבע' וכן תרגם יונתן ווי מדבחא מדבח' דבני בקרתא דשרא בה דוד ורבותינו ז"ל
אמרו שההיכל צר מאחריו ורחב מלפניו ודומה לארי' שנאמר הוי אר' מה הארי הזה
צר מאחריו ורחב מלפניו וכו' וכפל אר' כדרך הנוהים שכופלים דבריהם כי הנביא
היה נוהה עליו' ואמר עליו הוי

The altar-hearth was called *Ariel*.   And so it is in the book of Ezekiel (43:16) and so in the Targum Jonathan. . . .   And our rabbis, may their memory be blessed, say that the Temple was narrow behind and wide in front like a ארי *lion*.   That was why it was said, *ho, Ariel* for the lion is broad in front and narrow behind.   And the word *Ariel* is repeated because there were two Temples.

All of this connection of the altar-hearth and the Temple was done of course to supply the idea of the *strength* of the Temple as implied in calling it, or the altar, *Ariel*, with the lion-like implications of strength in that word. Ibn Ezra's comment is aimed directly at explaining this point:

הוי אריאל' יש אומר כי נקראת ירושלם כן על שם המזבח כמו וההראל והאר' כי
אותיות יהו"א מתחלפות ויש אומר' שנקראת כן בעבור שמזלה אריה וזה רחוק

Ho, Ariel. This is explained by virtue of the fact that Jerusalem
was called by the name of the altar-hearth [as in Ezekiel]. For the
letters י and ר are here transposed. And the explanation of its
being so-called (by the name *Ariel*) is that the constellation Leo
was referred to, and this represents power.

The connection of the name *Ariel* with the city of Jerusalem and the Temple, because of the similarity of the name
with הראיל *Hareel* which meant the altar-hearth, is exhibited in the further comments of the rabbis to the same
chapter. These are only important because they help to
explain what the rabbis were talking about when they
mention the Temple and the altar so many times in explaining *Ariel*.

Rashi says of another and later use of *Ariel*,

כאריאל' תהא מוקפת חללי חרב כמזבח המוקף וזבחי בהמה

as Ariel. This is connected with the burnings round about as the
altar is connected with sacrifice.

Kimchi explains this still further and in greater detail as
follows:

לאריאל' קרא שם העיר ירושלם אריאל על שם המזבח אשר בה' ואמר שיציק לה'
כן היה כי כל סביבותי' תפש מלך אשור... כאריאל' ירושלם תהיה לי כמו המזבח
שמוקף זבחים כן תהיה היא מוקפת הרוגים בערים אשר סביבותיה

to Ariel, The name of the city, Jerusalem, is called אריאל *Ariel* because of the altar which was in it. And this has reference to the
affliction of the city. That is, it means that the king of Assyria
would burn all that lay round about it. . . . *As Ariel* means that
all about Jerusalem would be slaughtered and burnt as sacrifices
are burnt about the altar.

The same rabbi also says that *Ariel* means the city in
which the altar was found:

על אריאל' על העיר שהמזבח בתוכ' כמו שפירשנו

Ibn Ezra explains the word in about the same manner when he says

כאריאל שהמזבח שמם מהעולות או כאריאל שיובחו כלם

fight against Ariel. As the altar consumes the burnt-offerings, or כאריאל *as Ariel* sacrifices all of them.

All of the commentaries thus far examined have supplied only one direct idea for the name *Ariel* that Milton has used, and that is the idea of strength, power, or fighting qualities. Nothing in any of the comments thus far suggests anything of an Angelic nature. But the later occurrence of a similar word in the thirty-third chapter of Isaiah, *Behold their valiant ones cry without*, is the obvious origin of *Ariel* as the name of an Angel. The same three rabbis, Rashi, Ibn Ezra, and Kimchi, comment here as on the earlier passage. Rashi says only

הן אראלם צעקו חוצה' היה הנביא מתנבא נחמות ואומר שהפורענות כבר אכלוהו
מעתה אקום ואנשא לגאלם: הן על אר' שלהם הוא המזבח כבר צעקו וספדו בחוצותם
ברחובותם בבכי ונהי

behold אראלם *cry without.* This is the prophet prophesying consolations, and he says that great retributions shall consume him. And then the אראלם are appointed and brought to redeem. *Behold* אראלם refers to the altar, meaning already they cry and lament outside and in the market-place with weeping and lamentations.

This comment is unlike Rashi, for it is not particularly clear as to just what he had in mind. But if his words are taken literally, as they probably should be, he certainly adds little to the verse as it reads in the text, and nothing whatever to the word *Ariel* as the name of an Angel.

However, Ibn Ezra's comment begins to supply the idea that the אראלם were angelic messengers. He says:

הן אראלם' יש אומר' מגזרת אריאל כאילו אמר על אראלם ואיננו נכון בטעם
הפרשה ויש אומרים שהן שתי מלות אראה להם גם זה רחוק והנכון בעיני שמלת

אראלם כמו מלאכיהם והעד מלאכי שלום וכמוהו את שני אריאל מואב והטעם כי
מלאכי כל גוי שיבקשו שלום בעולם יבכי וגו'

Behold אראלם.   There are sayings connected with אריאל *Ariel*, as if
it said *to the* אראלם.   And we might determine the meaning as if it
said אראה להם as if there were two words, and this is different.   But
the meaning of the word אראלם is as their מלאכיהם *messengers* (*Angels*).
And the meaning then is *their messengers* (*Angels*) *of peace*, which
is like (2 Sam. 23:20) *two Ariel of Moab*.   And the meaning of this
is that the messengers (Angels) of all the nations ask peace for the
world, and lament etc.

This explanation by Ibn Ezra is characteristic—the explanation is more complicated than the original expression.
We need give but little attention, however, to any of his
comment except his implication that the word אראלם, which
he apparently takes to mean *their Ariel*, being the same as
their messengers.   When he says that אראלם is the same as
מלאכיהם, he makes use of the word that is used throughout
the Old Testament for *Angel*.   But he fails to inform us
further on the subject.

The third rabbi, however, Kimchi, clearly points out the
angelic nature of the אראלם *Ariel*.   Kimchi says

ואראלם' מלאכים' כי אר' שם למלאך' וכן רבותינו ז"ל זכרו המלאך בזה השם' ואמרו
נצחו אראלים את המצוקים ונשבה ארון הקדש' כי כמו שמלת מלאך יאמר על שליח
נופני ועל שליח רוחני כן מלת אר'

and אראלם.   These are מלאכים *Angels* (*messengers*) for אראל is the name
for *Angel* (*messenger*).   And thus our rabbis of blessed memory
remember the Angel in this name when they say *the* האראלים *Ariel*
(*Angels*) *conquered the* המצוקים *mortals, and the Holy Ark was taken*,
(cf. *K'thuboth, Talmud*, and Jastrow, M. *Dictionary*, p. 113b).
For the word מלאך means *agent of my essence and agent of my spirit*,
and so with the word אראל'.

In this comment, the connection between the *Ariel* and the
Angels is clearly made, Kimchi even referring to a passage
in the Talmud in which the word אראלם is used specifically
of Angels.

With the complete rabbinical comment on the various forms of the name *Ariel* which occur in the Old Testament before us, we are now ready to determine how these comments contributed to Milton's conception of that name.

The treatments of the name by the rabbis fall into three chief categories. The first is made up of those discussions that conceive of the name *Ariel* as being a symbolic name for the Holy Altar, or altar-hearth. These are found in the comments to the passages in Isaiah and in Ezekiel.

Perhaps beginning with the *strength* of the Altar or of the City of the Altar, suggested by the principle of the inviolability of Mount Zion or Jerusalem, or perhaps suggested by the first syllable of the word which means *lion* being confused with another root, ארה, which means *hearth* from a root that clearly means *to burn*,[1] the second class of meanings for the word was indicated. In this sense, the meaning is taken to be in some manner indicative of *might*, and, in the identical passages occurring in Samuel and Chronicles, the word is taken by the rabbis to mean *heroes* or *mighty men*, *champions* of the Moabites. These passages of the rabbinical commentaries do not fail to indicate that it was precisely the heroic nature of the *Ariel* which makes the Biblical passages containing the word important and difficult. But the meaning of the word from these comments is *men of heroic fighting prowess*. The rabbis suggest the derivation of the name by its syllables, *lion* and *God*, in order to explain how the word *Ariel* actually means *heroes* or *champions*.

The third class of treatment of *Ariel* by the rabbis occurs in the comments to the passages in Ezra and in the thirty-third chapter of Isaiah. These commentaries make of the *Ariel* messengers or Angels, Kimchi even going so

---

[1]Cf. Brown, Driver, and Briggs, *op. cit.*, p. 72a.

far as to point out that the word *messenger* means
Angel, or one to whom is delegated God's essence and
spirit.

In the rabbis, moreover, the two meanings *strong-fighter*
or *hero* and *Angel* are intermixed throughout the discussions of the name. This was common knowledge in Milton's day so far as the rabbinical writings were concerned,
as is attested by the entry under אראל in Buxtorf's lexicon.
He says of it 'אראל, *Valens, Praevalidus:* Sumitur & pro
Angelis: ut אראלים ומצוקים אחזו בארון Angeli & Homines justi,
(qui vocantur מצוקי ארץ 1 Sam. 2:8) tenuerunt arcam ejus,
Ketubh. fol. 104. 1.'[1]

Combining the three meanings of the word found in the
rabbis, (and Buxtorf saw in the various forms only differences of roots and not differences of meaning), the result
is informative in connection with Milton's use of *Ariel* as
the name of an Angel in a passage in *Paradise Lost* which
sought to convey the idea of terrific fighting between the
Heavenly forces. The name *Ariel*, with its two meanings,
hero, mighty warrior, champion, and *Angel* or *messenger*,
was precisely the kind of conception Milton wanted and
presented. He had no direct authority for so doing from
Scripture itself; but from the rabbinical explanations of
those texts that carry the name, he secured ample warrant
for, and explanation of, the use he made of it.

So far in this discussion of this Angel, I have deliberately
confined the investigation of conceptions of *Ariel* to those
rabbinical works which Milton certainly knew. Of course,
in the rabbinical literature in general, and in the Talmud
in particular, are to be found those conceptions of the
spirit or Angel *Ariel* which ultimately produced the water-
spirit of the Middle Ages, best known to us through Shake-

[1] Buxtorf, *Lexicon Chaldaicum*, col. 207. Buxtorf's reference is to the Talmud
and is the same as was quoted by Kimchi.

speare's *Ariel* of *The Tempest*.   But this is a different spirit from Milton's.

There is, however, another stream of tradition in which the name is found.   The earliest, or one of the earliest and basic works in this tradition which has been as yet only partially connected with Milton, and then in a most fragmentary form, contains *Ariel* and the אראלם unmistakably as Angels.   This is the apocryphal *Book of Enoch*, which, as M. Saurat has pointed out, Milton knew through a fragmentary redaction of it made about the twelfth century by the Byzantine chronographer, Syncellos.[1]   It should perhaps be noted here that the אראלם, the form of *Ariel* from the thirty-third chapter of Isaiah that we have considered above, occur twice in the *Book of Enoch* as a class of Angels. It should be noted that their occurrences fall within the fragment of the work to be found in Syncellos.   These are in the fourteenth and thirty-ninth chapters respectively.[2]

I have nothing to contribute here to the Enoch-Milton connection, but wish only to call attention to the probability of the whole Enoch angelology having affected the angelology of the rabbis.   Perhaps Milton knew of an even fuller account of the Angel *Ariel* than any I have listed in some rabbinical work that has not yet been connected with him.[3]

---

[1]D. Saurat, *op. cit.*, pp. 254-258.   But the connection of the Enoch literature with Milton is not yet complete.   The *Book of the Secrets of Enoch* also contains many angelological suggestions that appear also in *Paradise Lost*; but how could Milton have known of them?   The necessity for confining one's self to works that can be directly connected with Milton is nowhere more clearly apparent, perhaps, than in dealing with his Angels.

[2]Cf. text in Hugo Odeberg, *3 Enoch, or the Hebrew Book of Enoch* (Cambridge, 1928), p. 36 (text) and note, and p. 124 (text) and note.   Scholarship owes a debt to Dr. Odeberg for having so fully assembled the elements which go to make up the Enoch literature, and to the Cambridge University Press for the admirable manner in which the work has been produced.

[3]A conception of Ariel very similar to Milton's occurs in a work that cannot possibly have been directly known to him.   This is the Coptic *Pistis Sophia* in which

But most important from the standpoint of the student of Milton is the observation of what Milton actually did with this rabbinical glossing of the name *Ariel*. In fact, it seems to me that the whole value of the notation of rabbinical treatments of the name is the opportunity thus afforded us of seeing what Milton did with such material.

With the various commentaries spread before us, it will be noted that no particular one of them supplies precisely the conception that Milton presented. Some of the comments emphasize the idea of strength, might, and fighting prowess of the *Ariel*, while others dwell on the idea that the name meant *Angel*. But there is not a single one of the commentaries that gives to Milton a clear-cut idea of the warrior-Angel Ariel, either as a Loyal or a Rebel Spirit. Rather the significant point here is to notice how Milton has seized upon the rabbinical embroidery of various Biblical passages in such a way as to secure from the suggestive commentaries the different parts of his complete idea. He then synthesized these elements into his finished conception, and employed it directly as a detail in those lines of the sixth Book of *Paradise Lost* which so greatly contribute to giving to the Warfare in Heaven that tone of fierce, desperate, and titanic fighting for which it is noted. Milton's use of the name owes, therefore, a great

---

Ariel is a demon (i.e. a Fallen Angel) in the Lower World in charge of the punishments (of the Dead). The name *Ariel* occurs in a number of passages in the *Pistis Sophia*, usually in the following manner, 'Say unto them, Renounce litigiousness, and be worthy of the mysteries of the Light, and be delivered from the punishments of Ariel.' Ariel also has 'rivers of flame,' evidently for punishment, and 'seas of fire.' (cf. George Horner's English translation, *Pistis Sophia*, London, 1924., pp. 128, 129, 195, 196; and Carl Schmidt's German text, *Die Griechischen Christlichen Schriftsteller der ersten drei Jahrhunderte*, vol. 13, Leipzig, 1905, pp. 165, 166, 247, 249, 250.) The *Pistis Sophia* was almost certainly unknown to Milton or to his age, but traces of it are to be found in the Hermetic writings that *were* known to the Middle Ages and later centuries. The important point to keep in mind here is that the material in the *Pistis Sophia* is made up largely of rabbinical treatments of Greek ideas.

deal to the rabbinical suggestions to which he had access in Buxtorf's Bible.

Returning now to the trilogy of Warrior-Angels in which Ariel appears in *Paradise Lost*, the second of the three is the name *Arioch*. The full explanation of the reasons which led Milton to use this name as that of a Warrior-Angel of terrific fighting strength is much less complicated than in the case of Ariel. The name *Arioch*, like the name *Ariel*, occurs in the Old Testament a number of times, but never as the name of an Angel.[1] Unlike Ariel, the name Arioch is not in any of its Biblical occurrences commented upon by Tremellius in his notes to the various passages in which it occurs. Milton, therefore, could scarcely have begun his conception of this Warrior-Angel from Tremellius's notes.

The first explanation of the name Arioch, again like Ariel, was furnished by Hume, and similarly, little has been added to this explanation since. Hume's explanation was '*Ariel*, Hebrew, *the lion of God*, or *a strong lion*. . . . *Arioch*, of the like signification, *a fierce and terrible lion*.'[2] Keightley has added but little to this explanation when he says of it, 'Arioch (אריוך), a Chaldean proper name (Daniel 2:14). It was probably used by the Rabbin (*sic*)

---

[1] The name occurs twice in the Pentateuch, Genesis 14:1 and 9; and in Daniel 2:14, 15, 24, 25, in all of these cases as the name of a man. In Genesis the name is that of one of the kings of the East who warred against the kings of Sodom and Gomorrah. He is presented as one of four Eastern kings, and is usually identified with *Rimsin* or *Eri-aku* son of *Kudur-mabug*, a king of Larsa of Elamite descent, contemporary of Hammurabi. Names bearing some similarity to Arioch, Tidal, and Cheoorlaomer have been found on a cuneiform tablet written not earlier than the fourth century B.C., or about 1800 years after the time of Hammurabi. (cf. L. W. King, *Letters and Inscriptions of Hammurabi*, I. xxvii.) Cf. the discussion of the name in Century Bible, W. H. Bennett's *Genesis*, p. 187.

The name occurs also in Old Testament apocryphal literature, in Judith 1:6 and in the Book of Jubilees 13:22. The latter is a midrasch on Genesis and part of Exodus.

[2] Hume, *Annotations*, p. 200.

as the name of an evil spirit. "As also great Arioch, that is termed the spirit of revenge." Nash, Pierce Pennilesse, p. 78.'[1] His reference to Nash and the quotation seem to imply that there was an Elizabethan meaning of the name which attached to it a meaning involving some kind of *daemon*. Such a meaning has never, to my knowledge, been further elaborated from Elizabethan sources. But Keightley's suggestion might, with search in Elizabethan writings, bear fruit. Masson in his notes follows Hume completely,[2] while Verity has also followed the same annotator, but he includes Keightley's suggestions.[3]

However, the name *Arioch* as Milton used it, may have been suggested to him by rabbinical explanation of it. Of the various Biblical passages in which it occurs, only one has attached to it a rabbinical comment that attempts to explain the name, and this explanation is indirect. No comment bearing on the meaning of the name or the nature of the person to whom it belonged appears for its occurrence in Genesis. Of the Daniel passages, only one has a comment in Buxtorf which is connected with the explanation of the name, and this is indirect. Rashi has explained, not the name, but Arioch's office, which the Revised Version calls 'captain of the king's guard' (רב טבחיא). Rashi says:

---

[1]Keightley, *op. cit.*, p. 472.

[2]Masson, *The Poetical Works*, vol. III:365. '*Arioch* (Lion-like) from Daniel ii. 14., where it is the name of a man.'

[3]Verity, *op. cit.*, p. 518, '*Arioch*, lion-like; cf. *Gen.* xiv. 1, *Dan.* ii. 14 (where Nebuchadnezzar's "captain of the king's guard" is so called). That the name was applied, possibly in rabbinical writings, to some evil spirit, seems proved by Nash's *Pierce Pennilesse*, "great Arioch, that is termed the spirit of revenge" (Keightley, *Life of Milton*, p. 472).' Nash's reference was one which he himself did not understand. He referred to no particular source for the tradition he expressed, and it is doubtful if his statement can be relied upon so far removed is it from contact with an authentic use of the name Arioch in a learned sense. But the Elizabethan meaning of the word, as suggested above, needs more attention.

רב טבחיא' שר ההורגים המחויבים הרינה

chief of the guardsmen, chief in charge of the executions or slayings of those condemned to official execution. (In the *Talmud*, *Kiddushin* IV, 14, the word טבחים apparently means *butcher*. Cf. Jastrow, *Dictionary*, p. 516b).

Certainly, the brutality of Rashi's conception of the office of Arioch is suggestive of Milton's Fierce Warrior. But there is no suggestion in the rabbinical commentaries to the scriptural passages in which the name occurs of its being in any way connected with an Angel.

However, it does so occur in early rabbinical writings. For instance, a clear-cut use of the name as the name of an Angel occurs in the *Book of the Secrets of Enoch*, an apocryphal work that is in reality a midrasch on Genesis and part of Exodus. In this work, Arioch is referred to as an Angel in the following statement:

I have instructed My Two Angels, Ariukh and Pariukh, whom I have put upon the earth as their guardians.

Another text for this same passage reads:

(Because these) will not be required etc. I have ordered my Angels, Oriokh and Mariokh, to give orders to guard in season the writings etc. that they should guard the writings etc.

In these passages, the connection between the Angel and the office of guard is very clear.[1]

I would not suggest that Milton knew or had direct access to this apocryphal work, but he might well have encountered the use of the name *Arioch* in some other rabbinical work than the commentaries in Buxtorf's Bible. However, Rashi's suggestion of Arioch as chief of the slaughterers has quite evidently added to Milton's conception of the fierce Warrior-Angel, taking part in the

[1] Cf. R. H. Charles, *The Book of the Secrets of Enoch* (Oxford, 1896), p. 48, and note for Sok. or B text.

terrible Warfare in Heaven. The idea of using Arioch as the name of such an Angel may or may not have come to him indirectly from the *Book of the Secrets of Enoch*. At any rate, Hume's derivation of the name from ארי *lion* is, it seems to me, pointless. The ferocity of Arioch in *Paradise Lost* may well have been based on Rashi's commentary and some other rabbinical source that made an Angel of this terrifying creature.

The third name in this group of fighters is *Ramiel*. The name of this Angel has unfortunately suffered a complete misunderstanding, it seems to me, because of Hume's gloss of so many years ago. He said of it, '*Ramiel*, Hebrew, a name well suited to one of the proud Angels that exalted themselves against their Maker.'[1] Todd quotes this, and subsequent commentators have for the most part followed him. Keightley says, 'Ramiel, (רמיאל, *Exaltation of God*) is apparently one of the names coined by the poet, for it does not occur in Scripture.'[2] Masson says only, '*Ramiel* does not occur in Scripture,' apparently using only Keightley's note.[3] Verity also depended almost wholly upon the same annotator, saying, '*Ramiel*, "exaltation of God"; whence Milton took the name (or whether he coined it) is not known.'[4]

Hume's statement concerning this name was perhaps responsible for the manner in which it has been treated since his day. His statement to the effect that the name does not occur in Scripture is true; but, I think, Keightley was misled, despite his great learning, by what Hume earlier had said of the name. The form of the word in English might be from either of two Hebrew roots. Milton's use of the name in the phrase 'the violence of

---

[1] Hume, *op. cit.*, p. 200.
[2] Keightley, *op. cit.*, p. 473.
[3] Masson, *op. cit.*, p. 365.
[4] Verity, *op. cit.*, p. 518.

Ramiel' is not particularly clarified by deriving Ramiel from the root רום (*be high, exalted, rise*) as Hume obviously derived it. Keightley in following Hume overlooked the other possibility in the name which is much more effective as Milton has actually used it. The other possible root for the form of the name that occurs in *Paradise Lost* is רעם *thunder*. The Hebrew form of the proper name *Ramiel* would then be רעמיאל *thunder of God*, or *God's thunder*. Not only would deriving the name from this root give meaning to Milton's 'violence,' but a form corresponding to this and with that meaning actually occurs in Scripture. This is a form parallel to *Ramiel*, but whose final syllable is יה *Jah* instead of אל *El*. The meaning *thunder of Jah* is of course precisely the same in translation as *thunder of El*, *Jah* and *El* being only different names for Deity in Hebrew. The form *Ramiah* occurs in the seventh verse of the seventh chapter of Nehemiah; in the ninth verse of the first chapter of first Chronicles; and in the twenty-second verse of the twenty-seventh chapter of Ezekiel.[1]

In addition to this, it seems almost certain that Milton intended the name to mean *thunder of El* when he spoke of Ramiel's violence, for the name appears as the name of an Angel appointed over the thunders in the *Book of Enoch*, and, what is more important, in that portion of the book contained in Syncellos's *Chronographia*.[2] The phrase used in Enoch is, 'Ramiel, who is appointed over the thunders,' or in the original רעמיאל שממנה על הרעמים. It seems to me, therefore, that Milton's *Ramiel*, in all his violence, is an Angel of the thunder, and as such is much more comprehensible in the midst of the terrific fighting that surrounds him in the poem than as an 'Exalter of God.'

[1] Cf. Brown, Driver, and Briggs, *op. cit.*, p. 947b.
[2] Cf. also Odeberg, *op. cit.*, 14:4, p. 38 (translation of text) and p. יט of original.

Thus various rabbinical treatments of the three names *Ariel*, *Arioch*, and *Ramiel*, aid greatly in supplying us with a better idea of why Milton used these names to indicate the terrible nature of the fighting that took place in the overthrow of the Rebel Angels. Even more important, however, than merely supplying us with new sources for these Angels, is the opportunity afforded by knowing more of the sources to discover how selective and syncretic Milton was in his use of the rabbinical material.

AZAZEL

In conclusion, I wish to speak of one other Fallen Angel whom Milton has used in *Paradise Lost*, and on whose use therein the rabbis throw some light. Perhaps there is no more perplexing name in the poem than the one selected for the standard-bearer of the Rebel Angels, Azazel. When Satan had finally rallied his Fallen Troops, and again had begun to marshall them into some kind of order, as soon as he saw that they were surely beginning again to assemble, he commanded:

> that at the warlike sound
> Of Trumpets loud and Clarions be upreard
> His mighty Standard; That proud honour claim'd
> *Azazel* as his right, a Cherube tall:
> Who forthwith from the glittering Staff unfurld
> Th' Imperial Ensign, which full high advanc't
> Shon like a Meteor streaming to the Wind
> With Gemms and Golden lustre rich imblaz'd,
> Seraphic arms and Trophies:
> —Book I:531-539.

The conception here is of one of the Fallen Angels of very high rank, apparently, at least that of the order of Cherubim. This Cherub, tall and dominating in appearance, claims the right to the position of standard-bearer to the thronging Troops of Satan. This, clearly enough, is Milton's conception of Azazel, who appears nowhere else in the poem. This is all of the information Milton supplied about him.

The origin of this conception of Azazel for Milton has been more or less of a mystery to commentators from Patrick Hume to Verity. Hume turned to the Biblical origin of the name, the eighth verse of the sixteenth chapter of Leviticus, and said only that the name meant 'scapegoat.' But such a note does not help much in explaining why Milton used Azazel as the name of one of the Fallen Angels, and is of no benefit whatever in explaining why Azazel was made standard-bearer to the Rebel Hosts.

Hume's explanation was first attacked and controverted by Bishop Newton, in the latter's edition of the *Poetical Works*. Newton was the first editor, I believe, who attempted to explain why Milton used the name *Azazel* as the name of a Fallen Angel who could claim the right to bear the standard of Satan's cohorts.[1] Newton drew upon the work of John Spencer to show that Azazel was the name of an Evil Spirit.[2] That is, he found an authority for the use of the name *Azazel* as that of a Fallen Angel or Demon, but contributed nothing to the understanding of the name which would explain why Milton selected Azazel

[1]Thomas Newton, *Paradise Lost, with Notes of Various Authors* (London, 1749, 2 vols.), vol. 1, pp. 53-54. '*Azazel* is not the *scapegoat* as it is commonly call'd, but signifies some Demon, as the learned Dr. Spencer hath abundantly proved in his dissertation *De hirco emissario*. He shows that this name is used for some Demon or Devil by several ancient authors Jewish and Christian, and derives it from two Hebrew words *Az* and *Azel* signifying *brave in retreating*, a proper appellation for the standard-bearer to the fall'n Angels. We see Milton gives *Azazel* a right to be standard-bearer on account of his stature; he had no notion of a dapper ensign who can hardly carry his colors.'

[2]John Spencer, *De legibus Hebraeorum*. Hagae-Comitum, 1686. The final dissertation in this work, entitled *De hirco emissario*, is a 54-page (pp. 450-504) work of twelve chapters on the meaning of the name Azazel as it appears in Leviticus 16:8. Spencer points out that the word is sometimes taken to mean the goat sent into the wilderness, sometimes the name of a mountain in the wilderness, and sometimes the name of an Evil Spirit. He prefers this last meaning.

as a standard-bearer. Except in the elaborate notes of Callander, the eighteenth century made no further contributions to the question, nor was there any other departure from Newton's explanation, Todd following him entirely on the name *Azazel*.[1]

Callander, however, went so far as to point out that the name *Azazel*, or *Azalzel*, appears as the name of a chief of the demons in the Enoch fragment known to the seventeenth century and earlier times as part of the *Chronographia* of Syncellos.[2] No later commentator ever made use of Callander's suggestion, but as we shall see, the point he made about the name occurring in Syncellos has been rediscovered very recently.

The nineteenth century added little to what Hume and Newton had previously contributed to the subject. Keightley did, however, accuse Milton of having used Azazel as a standard-bearer because of a misunderstanding of the derivation of the name. But it is doubtful if this could be held to constitute a variation from the eighteenth century commentary.[3]

---

[1]Todd, *op. cit.*, vol. 1:342. Todd merely quotes Newton's note, with proper acknowledgment.

[2]John Callander, editor, *Paradise Lost, Book I* (Glasgow, 1750), p. 110. His note reads: 'This (Azazel) is the name of one of the Εγρήγοροι, or Angels, who, according to the Jewish tradition, fell in love with the daughters of men before the flood, and having polluted themselves with them, were cast out of heaven by God, as a punishment of their crime. The author of the fragment under the name of the Patriarch Enoch, calls one of their chiefs Azalzel, Αξαλξελ.' Cf. Kathleen Hartwell, *Lactantius and Milton* (Cambridge, Mass., 1929), pp. 158 ff.

[3]Keightley, *op. cit.*, p. 473, 'Azazel (עזאזל). In Leviticus (xvi. 8, 10, 26) we find that on the day of atonement the high priest took two buck-goats and cast lots on them; the one to be for Jehovah, and to be offered in sacrifice, the other for Azazel, and to be let go in the wilderness. The question then is, who or what was Azazel? a name which occurs nowhere else. The most current opinion, that which Milton follows, is, that it was the name of an evil demon, supposed to dwell in deserts and to be appeased by victims. Others think it was the goat itself, as signifying the *averter* or *remover*, deriving the name from the Arabic verb *'azala*, to remove. It is one of those points on which certainty is hardly to be attained. Milton's motive for making Azazel the infernal standard-bearer, and styling him a cherub

Masson added nothing to these discussions, merely citing the notes of Hume and Newton with mention of the annotators themselves.[1]

In the twentieth century, Verity, in his immense edition of *Paradise Lost*, suspects that Milton followed some medieval tradition in making use of Azazel, but makes no suggestions of what its source may have been.[2]

Only very recently has there been any further contribution to the matter. Perhaps the most distinct advance made in the discussion of the reason for Milton's having used Azazel as one of the Rebel Angels and having made him their standard-bearer is to be found in the work of Saurat. This writer, in the most ingenious and in many ways the most stimulating work on Milton of this century, has strongly suggested, quite independent of Callander, that Milton derived his whole conception of Azazel from the Enoch fragments contained in the *Chronographia* of the Byzantine historian, Georgius Syncellos.[3] Professor

(i. 534), was perhaps an erroneous derivation of the name from '*azaz* (עזז), to be strong.'

[1] Masson, *Poetical Works*, vol. III, p. 339, 'The name, according to Hume, signifies in Hebrew "the scape-goat" (Levit. xvi.); but Newton translates it "brave in retreat." '

[2] Verity, *op. cit.*, p. 390, '*Azazel*, from Leviticus xvi. 8, where the A.V. has "the scapegoat," while the margin has *Azazel*, which the R.V. adopts. That the word was the title of some demon is now generally held; and I suspect that in making him one of the fallen angels M. simply followed some tradition of the medieval demonologists.'

[3] D. Saurat, *op. cit.*, pp. 255 ff. 'Azazel has always been a hard angel to explain with Milton's commentators. Newton, who was perhaps the most qualified to speak on such questions, writes, "The name is used for some demon or devil by several ancient authors," and translates the Hebrew as a sneer—"brave in retreating." But Milton certainly never thought of his devils as cowards. Now, it is only in the Book of Enoch that Azazel is mentioned as one of the leaders of the fallen angels. The word is in Leviticus 16:8, but it is rendered by "scapegoat." Jonathan and Raschi (sic) in Walton's Bible make of Azazel the name of a place in the desert where the goat is sent. Milton, had he thought about the subject at all, would probably have adopted either sense—but for the Book of Enoch. I suggest, therefore, that Milton got his Azazel from the Book of Enoch. One special phrase in the Miltonic text that has particularly exercised the commentators is

Saurat's suggestions and his method are sound and of great value in such discussion as this. His progress in the explanation of the name Azazel is in the right direction. His connection of the Enoch fragments in Syncellos with Milton is especially valuable. But Professor Saurat has not spread before us a sufficiently complete treatment of the name *Azazel* in Milton's day, although he has made it clear that what is needed in connection with the name is to arrive as nearly as possible at sources that Milton certainly used and which contain conceptions of Azazel from which he might have drawn.

We now have before us a survey of the various treatments by Miltonic commentators of the name Azazel as it occurs in *Paradise Lost*. We have seen that, aside from Callander's note and Saurat's suggestions, no definite reasons for Milton's having used the name as that of a Fallen Angel have been advanced. Saurat has shown that the name was to be found so used in a work, that of Syncellos, actually used by Milton. None of the earlier commentators have succeeded in pointing out any reasons for Milton's having made Azazel the standard-bearer to the Rebel Hosts, and here Saurat succeeds least. That Azazel was an important Angel in the system of angelology found in the fragment from the Book of Enoch in Syncellos, even with the specific description of his talents found therein, is no particular reason for having designated him the rightful standard-bearer. Saurat's chief contribution to the problem of Azazel is to have connected Milton definitely with the Enoch tradition as found in Syncellos,

"as his right." Milton must have meant it, to risk the inelegant jingle, "Azazel as his right." Now we have, in Enoch (in Goar's text): (quotes Latin from Dindorff's Syncellos) Azazel evidently was the chemist, jeweller, and goldsmith of the infernal band; he dealt in women's ornaments, but also in men's weapons. So I further suggest that he was the maker of the "imperial ensign," and that this was the reason why he carried it "as his right."'

which made of Azazel an important Fallen Angel.   But it is extremely doubtful if the Enoch fragment in Syncellos alone was the basis for Milton's having used Azazel as a Fallen Angel; it is even more doubtful if this passage formed the basis of the 'standard-bearer' idea.

It seems to me that the solution lies in another direction pointed out by Professor Saurat. It is only by a reconstruction of the various treatments of Azazel which were available to Milton, a reconstruction of the seventeenth century ideas about and treatments of Azazel, that any adequate conception of what Milton was doing with and how he was using the name can be formed. In order to secure such a reconstruction, a brief survey of the growth and origin of the name is necessary, and then a glance at some of the standard seventeenth century treatments of the name must be made.

The origin of the name will probably never be fully known, and need not detain us here further than to remark that it is Hebraic. Whatever it may originally have meant, there very early developed a conception of it which became incorporated in post-exilic angelology. By the beginning of the Christian era, or by the time that Jewish angelology had become almost completely formed, the name had come to have certain well-recognized meanings. It is found in many authors of the early centuries of the Christian era, Christian as well as Jewish. Saurat has mentioned its occurrence in two early Christian writers. Irenaeus and Origen. I am not sure that Origen's statement indicating his conception of the nature of Azazel can be so shortly dismissed in connection with Milton as Saurat would have us believe. Origen seems to have known Azazel as a Spirit of Evil dwelling in the wilderness, who was equivalent to Satan. This is an early Christian form of the tradition, derived from the Jewish form, that

Azazel was the name of an Evil Spirit. To equate him with Satan certainly would be to make of him a Fallen Angel. But equally certain is the fact that Origen's conception and statement are inadequate as a complete basis for what Milton has made of Azazel.[1]

The name also occurs in Irenaeus's *Against Heresies*, where it is unmistakably the name of a Fallen Angel.[2]

[1]For the Greek of this passage, cf. Paul Koetschau, *Die Griechischen Christlichen Schriftsteller der ersten Drei Jahrhunderte* (Leipzig, 1889), vol. 3, vi:43, pp. 113-114. I quote here the English translation by Roberts and Donaldson, revised by A. C. Coxe, in the *Ante-Nicene Fathers* (New York, 1907), vol. IV:592.

'Mark now, whether he who charges us with having committed errors of the most impious kind, and having wandered away from the (true meaning) of the divine enigmas, is not himself clearly in error, from not observing that in the writings of Moses, which are much older not merely than Heraclitus and Pherecydes, but even than Homer, mention is made of this wicked one, and of his having fallen from heaven. For the serpent—from whom the Ophioneus spoken of by Pherecydes is derived—having become the cause of Man's expulsion from the divine Paradise, obscurely shadows forth something similar, having deceived the woman by a promise of divinity and of greater blessings; and her example is said to have been followed also by the man. And further, who else could the destroying angel mentioned in the Exodus of Moses be, than he who was the author of destruction to them that obeyed him, and did not withstand his wicked deeds, nor struggle against them? Moreover (the goat), which in the book of Leviticus is sent away (into the wilderness), and which in the Hebrew language is named Azazel, was none other than this; and it was necessary to send it away into the desert, and to treat it as an expiatory sacrifice, because on it the lot fell. For all who belong to the "worse" part, on account of their wickedness, being opposed to those who are of God's heritage, are deserted by God. Nay, with respect to the sons of Belial in the Book of Judges, whose sons are they said to be, save his, on account of their wickedness? And besides all these instances, in the Book of Job, etc.'

[2]For English translation, *ibid.*, vol. 1:340.

'With good reason, therefore, and very fittingly, in reference to thy rash attempt, has that divine elder and preacher of the truth burst forth in verse against thee as follows:—

"Marcus, thou former of idols, inspector of portents,
Skill'd in consulting the stars, and deep in the black arts of magic,
Ever by tricks such as these confirming the doctrines of error,
Furnishing signs unto those involved by thee in deception,
Wonders of power that is utterly severed from God and apostate,
Which Satan, thy true father, enables thee still to accomplish,
By means of Azazel, that fallen and yet mighty angel,—
Thus making thee the precursor of his own impious actions."
Such are the words of the saintly elder.'

The name largely disappears from Christian angelology after these early centuries, appearing again, it is true, in the work of Syncellos, who cited a fragment from the apocryphal Book of Enoch.[1] But if in Christian literature the name Azazel almost disappeared as that of an Angel, Fallen or otherwise, the same statement is not true of Jewish literature. It is unnecessary to speak here of the earlier Jewish treatments of the name, whether in Talmud, Targum, or Midrasch. But it is important to mention and perhaps quote some of the Jewish treatments of the name which would have been available to Milton. Especially important are those medieval treatments of the name, whether they appear as new contributions to the subject or as repetitions of older material. In both cases, the discussion of the name Azazel by the medieval rabbis became of increasing importance in Christian treatment of the passage in Leviticus. There is a trace of the influence of the rabbinical tradition in the text and margin of the Authorized Version. All modern Christian expositions of the Leviticus passage include an almost complete digest of the medieval rabbinical treatment of it.[2] This process by which the rabbinical treatment of the name Azazel became of increasing importance in the Christian understanding and explanation of it, had begun early enough to have affected the whole direction such understanding eventually took.

[1] Too much must not be made of the often repeated statement that the Book of Enoch and other 'lost' Apocrypha were unedited and unprinted for centuries. Various manuscripts of them existed and were relatively widely circulated, as well as other manuscripts, which contained excerpts from these 'lost' Apocrypha.

[2] Cf. especially Chapman & Streane, *The Book of Leviticus* in the Cambridge Bible for Schools (1914), Appendix v., pp. 185-189. And also D. Hoffmann's *Das Buch Leviticus* (Berlin, 1905), vol. 1, pp. 442-445. These works are representative of the modern exposition of the passage, and the amount of rabbinical material they cite is large.

Let us now turn, therefore, to a discussion of the rabbinical material connected with Azazel that was available to Milton and endeavor to discover its influence. The great difficulty in such a discussion is to keep it confined to rabbinical writings that actually are connected with Milton in some form or another. There is so much rabbinical material available dealing not only with the scapegoat and Azazel, but also with what for the Jew is the more important matter connected with the whole passage in Leviticus, the account of the ritual of atonement, that it is necessary to make certain of not including too much. Much of the rabbinical treatment of the passage cannot be, or has not yet been connected with Milton, and cannot therefore be used. But it is possible to find sufficient rabbinical material that may be directly connected with the poet to make it worth while pointing out the need for taking it into consideration in any discussion dealing with the origin of Milton's Azazel.

The trail begins with the rabbis commenting upon the Biblical text in Buxtorf's Bible. The first of these to be noted is Rashi, although his comment is vague so far as identification of Azazel is concerned. But it needs to be noted here. He says

עזאזל' הוא הר עז וקשה צוק גבוה שנאמר ארץ גזרה התוכה

Azazel, this is a great, rough mountain, a high crag that was called the solitary land, and the land cut off from others.

The other rabbi in Buxtorf commenting upon the Leviticus passage is Ibn Ezra. His comment is characteristically obscure, but notable. After some explanation of the ceremony involved, he says of *Azazel*,

שאחר מלת עזאול תדע סודו וסוד שמו כי יש לו חברים במקרא ואני אגלה לך קצת
הסוד ברמו בהיותך בן שלשים ושלש תדענו

For it is because of the word Azazel that you know it is a secret. And the secret of the name is that there are similar or related expressions in Scripture. And I shall explain to you the meaning of the secret with a hint: when you are after thirty-three you will know.

This perplexing statement was sometimes taken to be a paraphrastic way of saying that only those who had attained the age of thirty-three, (i.e. years of discretion) or the initiated could understand what Azazel meant. But another, and probably the true interpretation was very early put upon Ibn Ezra's cryptic remark. Nachmanides explained that שלשים ושלש (thirty-three) referred to the thirty-third verse following Leviticus 16:8, the verse in which first occurs the name Azazel.[1] That is, the explanation of the secret to which Ibn Ezra referred is to be found in Leviticus 17:7, where occurs the express prohibition of the worship of the שעירים or demons. Other rabbinical works explain the name Azazel in much the same manner, as Nachmanides pointed out.[2] Ibn Ezra's comment was therefore understood to suggest that Azazel was the name of a great demon. It is not possible to connect Milton directly with this rabbinical treatment of the name Azazel, beyond the suggestion of Ibn Ezra. But there are indications that the further treatment was known to other Christians of his own and even an earlier day. Thus indirectly, it is possible to make out a case for Milton's use of what was originally a rabbinical conception of Azazel, undoubtedly suggested to him by Ibn Ezra's cryptic remark.

However, Milton's conception of Azazel as a leader among the Fallen Angels, so designated by having been made their standard-bearer 'as his right,' is unusual for

---

[1]Nachmanides, commentary to *loc. cit.* (not contained in Buxtorf).
[2]פרקי דר' אליעזר *Pirke of Rabbi Eleazer.*

the time in which it appeared. The least that can be said of such a conception is that back of it must lie a wide range of reading in order to have encountered it. As proof of this statement, it should be noted that the treatments of the name *Azazel* by the lexicons of Milton's day yield practically nothing similar to his conception and treatment of this Angel. In fact, there is no particular lexicographical indication of Milton's time that *Azazel* was the name of an Angel. Pagninus derives the word *Azazel* from the Hebrew עז *capra*, and mentions Rashi's explanation of it in part.[1] Schindler adds nothing to this, in fact his definition is relatively much shorter, although he says practically the same thing.[2] Nor are Buxtorf's two lexicons any more informative than Pagninus or Schindler concerning the nature of Azazel.[3] That is, the standard lexicographers of Milton's day did not supply him with the peculiar conception of *Azazel* that he has employed in *Paradise Lost*. Nevertheless, such a conception as Milton has used was not unknown among Christian Biblical commentators of the time.

There were contemporary accounts of Azazel which made of him the mighty and powerful Fallen Angel he is found to be in Milton's poem, and investigations were going on in Milton's time which were to come as near, perhaps, as we shall ever come to an understanding of what the whole Leviticus passage originally meant. These

---

[1]Pagninus, *op. cit.*, p. 268, 'עזאזל Caper emissarius, D. Hieronym. Leuet. c. 16. 8. R. Dauid componit ex עז, id est capra, et אל, id est Abiit; et vocatur mons sic, eo quod capra vel caper ibat illuc. R. Sal. Mons i. fortis, et difficilis, altus, angustus.'

[2]Schindler, *op. cit.*, col. 1303, 'עזאזל *Azazel*, ab עז caper, et אול abiit: mons its dictus, quod in illum in deserto situm abiret עזאזל caper emissarius.'

[3]Buxtorf, *Lexicon Hebraicum*, p. 537, 'עזאזל Hasasel, nomen hirci in desertum amissi cum peccatis populi, quasi Hircus abiens aut aberrans dictus, ab עז et אול abiit, Levit. 16. v. 8, vel secundum Hebraes nomen loci ab hirco isto sic dicti.' The *Lexicon Chaldaicum, Talmudicum, et Rabbinicum* has no such entry as Azazel.

accounts were at once exhaustive and highly indicative of the rabbinical learning available in England during Milton's life-time. They were not of a popular nature, perhaps, but certainly to the scholar they offered ample opportunity to become familiar with the best contemporary thought on the subject of Azazel.

One of these studies appeared only a few years before the publication of *Paradise Lost*. This was the enormously learned work by Samuel Bochart, entitled *Hierozoicon*, dealing with all the various animals of Scripture, which appeared in London in 1663.[1] Bochart set forth the three possibilities for the explanation of the word *Azazel*, and, like Milton, for Milton had the same possibilities to select from, Bochart selected and substantiated his selection of *Azazel* as the name of a great Demon.[2] The greater part of Bochart's discussion is of little or no significance here, but much of the earlier part of his entry under the title *De Hirco Azazel, qui vulgo emissarius dicitur* is pertinent to the whole discussion of Azazel as the name was used during the seventeenth century. The more important of Bochart's references to various conceptions of Azazel on

---

[1] *Hierozoicon, sive bipertitum opus de Animalibus Sacrae Scripturae.* Auctore Samuele Bocharto (Londoni, 2 vols.), MDCLXIII.

[2] Bochart, *op. cit.*, vol. 1, col. 650, (introductory sketch of the material which follows)

'vox Azazel ignota. In ea mysterium. Nonnullis montis nomen. Vox composita, ut multis placet, qui refelluntur. Aliis Azazel emissarius tanquam ex Graeca versione. In qua tamen aliud nempe averruncus, depulsor malorum. Hesychius emendatus. Sors una Domino, id est, averrunco Daemoni, juxta julianum Apostatam. Ita Hebraeis Azazel Daemon, cui hircus oblatus die propitiationum. Hoc uno die cur Satan in homines nihil possit, ratio Cabalistica. Valentinianis etiam et Magis Azazel Daemon. Qui omnes confutantur. Etiam hircus Azazel Deo devotus. Azazel neque mons est, neque hircus emissarius. Nova vocis explicatio ex Arabismo. Tityrus, et musimon, quid proprie. Victimae, Dei cibus. Etiam hircus Azazel coram Deo sistitur. Lingua coccinea, capiti hirci Azazel imponi solita die propitiationum exalbescebat in signum propitiationis. A Christi morte desiit hoc miraculum, et Templi valvae sponte apertae sunt. Cur manus etc.'

which he drew for his discussion of the name follow:

"Locus postulat, ut discutiamus quid sit עזאזל *Azazel* Levit. xvi. ubi legitur versu 8. *Aaron sortes jaciet super duos hircus, sortem unam Domino et sortem unam* לעזאזל *Azazeli*. Et versu 10. *Et hircus, in quem ceciderit sors, Azazeli stabit vivus coram Domino, ut per eum fiat propitiatio, et mittatur ad Azazelem in desertum.* Et versu 26. *Et qui miserit hircum ad Azazelem, lavabit vestes suas, etc.* In iis locis quid proprie sit *Azazel*, magno molimine quaerunt interpretes, neque dum id constat satis. Prudentiores vocem Hebraeam relinquunt, ut e multis interpretationibus lectori libera sit optio. Ita Jonathan, Onkelos, Samaritanus, et plerique recentiorum. Aben Ezra in hac dictione magnum aliquod mysterium subesse significat, quod nemo possit capere ante annos virilitatis. Multis Azazel est nomen montis, in quem hircus deducebatur. R. Selomo,

עזאזל' הוא הר עז וקשה צוק וגביה שנאמר ארץ גזרה חתוכה

Azazel est mons asper, et confragosus, angustus, et celsus, qui versu vigesimo secundo dicitur terra גזרה *id est, ab aliis divulsa et excisa.* Quod ex Jonathane sumptum, qui cum alibi vocem עזאזל, Azazel, invariatam retineat, tamen in fine decimi versus Hebraea verba, לשלח אותו לעזאזל למדברה *ad mittendum eum ad Azazelem in desertum*, ita reddit לשדרא יתיה במתת באתר תקיף וקשי במדברא דצוק דהוא בית הדורי

ad mittendum eum ad mortem in locum asperum, et confragosum, in deserto Tsuk, qui est locus flexuosus . . . . Et R. Saadias Gaon putat esse vocem compositam ex עז et אל, ut mons עזאזל *azazel* dicatur pro עזאל *azazel* id est, mons asper Dei. Quo sensu celsos montes David appellat הררי אל *montes Dei* Ps. xxxvi. 7. Idem sensisse videtur Syrus, qui hic . . . . Sed R. Levi merito rejicit hanc originationem; quia Moses non scribit עזאל *azazel*, sed עזאזל *azazel*, litera *Aleph* inserta inter duo *Zajin*. Quod esset divellere literas Sacri nominis monosyllabi, et biliteri. Itaque Hebraeorum alii, Kimchius, Pomarius, Acquinas etc. literarum ordine servato, vocem עזאזל azazel, constatam esse dicunt ex עז, ez, *caper*, et אזל azal, *abiit*, et inde nomen inditum monti, in quo caper oberrabat, eo missus a Sacerdote. Quae originatio priore nihilo est melior. Nam עז non est *caper*, aut hircus, sed *capra*. Nec genere conveniunt עז et אזל. Illud Foemininum est, hoc Masculinum. Proinde vox non potuit ex utroque conflari.

Tamen id ipsum sequuntur, quotquot volunt עזאזל *azazel* fuisse nomen hirci in desertum emissi: in qua sententia est magna pars recentiorum. Itaque ex illorum mente verba Mosis sic reddenda sunt, *Aaron jaciet sortes super duos hircos, sortem unam Domino*, id est in hircum Domino mactandum; *et alteram in Azazelem*, id est, in hircum in desertum abiturum, et dimittendum . . . . (There follows a list of Greek commentators with quotations.) Nec est, quod quis hic dicam scribat Graecis interpretibus, quasi ambigua versione huic errori ansam dederint, cum ex Hebraeis etiam in hunc eundem lapidem multi impegerint. Ita *Menachem* in Leviticum ex hoc loco colligit עזאזל *Azazel* unum esse ex quatuor Daemonem antesignanis, quorum haec sunt nomina, si recutito credimus, מחזאל,עזאל,עזאזל,סמאל *Sammael, Azazel, Azael*, et *Machazeel*. At in *Capitulis* R. Eliezer *Azazel* Daemon idem, qui Sammael, cui cur Israelitae hircum obtulerint die propitiationum, prout concludere se putat ex verbis Mosis, en tibi jocularem rationem capite quadragesimo sexto: *Die, quo data fuit Lex, Deum Sanctum, et Benedictum ita compellavit Sammael, Domini mundi, cur in reliquos totius orbis populos mihi dedisti potestatem praeter solos Israelitas? Respondit Deus, Etiam in illos habebis potestatem, si die propitiationum peccatum in illis inveneris. At, si peccati sunt expertes, nihil erit tibi juris in illos.*

לפיכך היו נותנין שוחד ליום הכפורים לסמאל שלו יבטל קרבנם שנאמר גורל אחד ליהוה וגורל אחד לעזאזל גורלו של הקב״ה הוא קרבן העולה וגורל עזאזל שעיר חטאת כל עונות של ישראל עליו

Ideo Sammaeli dant munus die propititiationum, ne irritam reddat illorum oblationem. Hinc dicitur, Una sors Deo, altera Azazeli. Sors Sancti et Benedicti Dei est oblatio holocausti, et sors Azazelis est hircus peccati, super quem sunt omnes iniquitates Israelis. Hinc legas in libro Capthor pag. 71. prout citat Buxtorfius Synag. cap. 21. *Judaeos ideo Satanae dedisse munus, ut illius oculos praestringerent, ne ab illo accusarentur, quia scriptum est*, Exod. xxiii. 8. *Munus excoecat oculos videntis.* Alii Satanam asserunt hoc uno die nihil posse, atque inde esse, quod literae numericae nominis, השטן, id est, Satanae, valent CCCLXIV, quia per anni dies totidem imperium suum exercet in homines, nec ullus excipitur in toto anno praeter diem, quem diximus. Valentinianos quoque Azazelem pro Daemone habuisse suadent veteris Poetae Christiani carmina in Marcum, Valentini discipulum, qui praestigiis suis credebatur spectatoribus illudere: (Greek verse concerning Azazel already quoted above in

English) Hos versus ex Irenaeo citat Epiphanius Haeresi trigesima quarta, et vir doctus ita reddidit, (Latin translation of the same verse) Quin hodieque in Magorum libris Azazel inter Daemones, qui elementis praesunt. . . . Cum nihil quidquam fingi potuerit absurdius, quam Deum ex duobus hircis alterum sibi, alterum Diabolo destinasse, et offerri jussisse. Cum sequentis capitis versu septimo sacrificare daemonibus vetet disertis verbis. Et ille ipse hircus, qui servabatur vivus, *coram Domino* sisti jubeatur Levit. xvi. 10. Itaque hircus uterque Deo fuit ex aequo devotus, et solum differebat in offerendi modo. Unus enim super altare mactabatur, alter in desertum vivus emittebatur. Quid igitur haec sibi volunt, *sors una Domino, altera Azazeli?* An ibi Azazel est montis nomen, ut statuunt Arabes, et non pauci ex Hebraeis? Non videtur verissimile; quia in regione toties peragrata, et tam accurate descripta, nemo est, qui meminerit montis Azazel. Itaque nemo situm indicat praeter anonymum in *Aben Ezra*, qui admovet monti Sinai. Quo hircum ab urbe quotannis Israelitas deduxisse non facile illis persuadebitur, qui norunt quam vastae sint interjectae solitudines. Praeterea, si Azazel est nomen montis, cur id tacuisset Moses? Quidni dixisset הר עזאל, *montem Azazel*, aeque ac montem Abarim, Num. xxvii. 12. etc? . . . . (Follows a list of places in Scripture in which the names of mountains are unmistakably *mountains*). Neque enim id necesse fuit, quia tum erant notissimi, quod de monte Azazele dici non potest. Nihilo magis arrident qui Azazelem dici volunt hircum ipsum emissarium. Nam, ut hanc interpretationem niti taceam falsa originatione vocis Azazel, ut abunde docuimus, haec videntur valde implicata, *Sortes etc* . . . . Fateor interim me de voce עזאל *azazel*, nihil habere satis certum. Sed conjecturam assero, quam doctorum judicio submitto libens. Ea sic habet. Arabice verbum *azala, removere et separare* est . . . . (Follows a long list of citations from the Arabic to substantiate his derivation of the word). Ita hircorum unus recte dicetur Domino fuisse servatus, nempe ut super altare mactatus illi esset in cibum, quod de victimis legitur Levit. xxi. 6. et passim. Alter servatus לעזאל *ad azazel*, id est, ut in locum deserti remotum et separatum deducatur, qui vocatur versu vigesimo secundo ארץ גזרה, *terra excisa*, aut *divulsa*.

Another work which also exhibits the current state of knowledge concerning the name Azazel, appeared about ten years after Milton's death. It would, of course, have been completely unknown to him as a book, although he may have known the author and have been familiar with the whole project of the book in which this discussion of Azazel is a part. This book is that work by John Spencer, entitled *de legibus Hebraeorum*.[1]

Included in this curious collection of various dissertations on Jewish subjects was the dissertation *De Hirco emissario et Praecipuis Expiationis Judaicae Ceremoniis*. This work was, in a way, a culmination of a stream of interest in and information about the Azazel passages in Leviticus. Together with Urim and Thummim, the origin of Sacrifice, Purification, Feasts, the origin of the Ark and the Cherubim, and similar 'mysteries,' the ritual of atonement and the meaning of the strange word עזאזל *Azazel*

---

[1] *de legibus Hebraeorum Ritualibus et earum Rationibus Libri tres.* Authore Joanne Spencero, Hagae-Comitum, M DC LXXXVI. (Cantabrigiae, 1685.)

As this work is in many ways, at least in so far as the treatise on Azazel is concerned, but an epitome of the best current knowledge on that subject, it is needless to attempt to connect its author with Milton. For Spencer was a man who must have been known to nearly every student or alumnus of Cambridge, especially during the period of the Interregnum. He was born near Bleane, Kent, being baptized October 31, 1630. He received his early education at the King's School, Canterbury, and later became a king's scholar there. He was admitted to a scholarship of Archbishop Parker's foundation in Corpus Christi College, Cambridge, on March 25, 1645, almost exactly twenty years after Milton entered Christ's College. From that College and the University he received the following degrees: A.B., 1648; M.A., 1652; B.D., 1659; and D.D., 1665. He was made a fellow of his college about 1665. He then took holy orders and became a University preacher, holding the cures, first, of St. Giles and then of St. Benedict, Cambridge. On July 23, 1667, he was instituted to the rectory of Landbeach, Cambridgeshire, which he resigned in 1683 in favor of his nephew and curate, William Spencer. On August 3, 1667, he was unanimously elected master of Corpus Christi College, and he governed that body for twenty-six years. He contributed verses to the Cambridge University Collection on the death of Henrietta Maria, queen dowager, in 1669. In February of 1671/72 he was appointed a prebendary in the first stall at Ely, and served the office of vice-chancellor of the University in the academical year, 1673-74, and delivered a speech addressed to the Duke of Monmouth on his installation as chancellor of the University. On the 5th of September, 1677, he was admitted on presentation of the king to the archdeaconry of Sudbury in the Church

were perennial causes of curiosity and speculation among
Jews and Christians alike. All of these topics were discussed with more or less satisfactory results by sixteenth
and seventeenth century orientalists all over Europe, coming in for their share in England. It is not so much what
is new in Spencer's discussion that is important here, for
there is very little actually new material therein, most if
not all of his materials being of much earlier origin than
the seventeenth century; but the chief importance of his
treatise to us is that his work represents a collection of the
best available knowledge of the subject to be found at that
time in England. His work appeared just after Milton's
death, and to a man as learned as Milton, most of Spencer's materials would have been already known in one form
or another. Especially informative are his various references to authorities who provide the discussions of the
name *Azazel* which he presents. These authorities are
largely rabbinical, but also, though to a somewhat lesser
extent, patristic and medieval Christian writers.

of Norwich, and a few days later, on the 9th, was instituted to the deanery of Ely.
He died on May 27, 1693. Spencer was a most erudite theologian and Hebraist.
To him forever belongs the honor of having been the first to trace the connection
between the rites and rituals of the Hebrew religion and those of other Semitic
religions. In 1669 he published a *Dissertatio de Urim et Thummim*, later incorporated in the *de legibus*, in which he connected those mystic emblems with an
Egyptian origin. In 1685 the *de legibus* appeared at Cambridge, and the following
year at The Hague (1686). In this work Spencer bravely left the paths ordinarily
followed by Biblical commentators. Robertson Smith has said of this work, 'it
may justly be said to have laid the foundations of the science of comparative
religion. In its special subject, in spite of certain defects, it still remains by far the
most important book on the religious antiquities of the Hebrews.' (*Rel. of the
Semites*, 1894, Preface, p. vi.) The work is a remarkable compilation of data from
classical and patristic writers of Greece and Rome, from the works of Josephus,
from rabbinical works, and from the Bible itself. Spencer stated that his object
was 'to clear the Deity from arbitrary and fantastic humor;' but it was inevitable
that his work should have been attacked as unorthodox, and the late 17th century,
together with the early 18th, resounded with the clamor of supporting and attack-
ing theologians. But his work remains as a marvelous epitome of the Biblical
learning of his own and of an earlier day.

Spencer's conclusions are especially interesting. He begins his whole discussion with a survey of the material from Bochart, already quoted. Then, after another survey of the various rabbinical contributions, he proceeds to center his efforts on making a case for the name *Azazel* being the name of a great demon. The second section of his first chapter is devoted entirely to the support of this point. The following extract will make clear his position.

Ne quaeram ambages, Vocem *azazel*, si ad primariam vocis intentionem respectus habeatur, Diabolum significare, multis inductus argumentis (artificialibus et inartificialibus) me persuasum habeo. Nam Primo: Diabolum *Azazelis* nomine hac in Lege venire, perique Judaei et Christiani veteres existimasse videantur. Judaeos antiquiores ita censuisse, documento est fragmentum illud (a) Judaicum quod *Enochi* nomine circumfertur, (in the margin is the reference to *Ap. Georg. Sincel. Hist. p. 11, 12.*) et ante Christi tempora traditione perantiqua scriptum creditur; quo *Azalzel* (corrupte, pro *Azazel*) inter Angelorum lapsorum principes numeratur. Ab iis hoc nomen ad Cabbalistas transiit, qui, docente (b) Mercero, *Daemones in sepulchris maxime versari* dicunt, *et hujusmodi daemonem Azazelum vocant.* (In the margin is the reference, *Praelect. in Genes. p. 88. C.*) Christianos etiam antiquos hoc nomine Diabolum intellexisse, ex Origene non obscure discitur. Nam ut probet, Diabolum ipso Mosis aevo innotuisse; inter alia, (c) inquit, (quotes Origen's Greek) *Ille in Levitico dictus quem Scriptura Hebraica Azazel nominat, non alius erat nisi Diabolus.* (in the margin, the reference is to *Lib. 6. contra Cels. p. 305.*) Haec probabiliora faciunt antiqui poetae Christiani carmina in Marcum, Valentini discipulum, qui miraculis ejus mendacibus illusit populo: (quotes the Greek verse) Hos versus, inter alios, ex Irenaeo citat Epiphanius haeresi trigesima quarta, quos etiam (d) vir doctus sic Latinos fecit;

> Haec tu illa, Satanae fretus auxilio patris,
> Azazelique, mira designas ope.

(in the margin is the reference to *Ap. Bochart. de animal. col. 653.*) A Judaeis aut Christianis antiquis (quod obiter noto) nomen hoc ad Magos transitum fecit, qui in classe Daemonum, quos elementis praefectos asserunt, Azazelum collocant. Cum itaque significatio jam dicta, Judaeorum et Christianorum veterum patrocinio se tueri possit, non est quod eam suspectam habeat quispiam, aut novitatis nomine rejiciendam censeat.

Secundo: Jonathan, Onkelos, Samaritanus, et Interpretes alii bene multi, nomen *azazel* relinquunt . . . . Quis autem opinari potest, interpretes tam doctos *azazel* meris tenebris involutum relinquere voluisse, si nomen illud appellativis accensendum esse, et *hircum abeuntem sonare*, credidissent? Fidei multo propius est, eos *azazel* Diaboli nomen proprium existimasse, et ideo illud (uti propria solent alia) sine interpretatione praeteriisse.

Tertio: In veteris Testamenti scriptis, nomine propria frequenter, appellativa rarissime, composita reperiuntur. Horum equidem exempla tam pauca sunt, quod facili opera (uti statim constabit) enumerari possint. Cum itaque nomen עזאזל e vocibus duabus constatum esse, doctorum omnium suffragio confirmetur; linguae Hebraicae consuetudini congruum est, ut illud nominibus propriis potius quam appellativis annumeretur.

Quarto: Ipse legis hujusce contextus opinari cogit, vocem *Azazel* de Diabolo tantum intelligendam esse. Nam 1. Sors una ליהוה *pro Domino*, et sors altera לעזאזל *pro Azazele*, supra duos hircos, Lege jubente poni debuere. Cum itaque Jehovah persona sit, cui hircorum unus sortito cedere debuerit; oppositionis ratio postulat, ut Azazel aliquis esset, cui hircorum alter sorte tribuendus erat. Hunc autem Angelum bonum, aut hominem aliquem, esse potuisse, ne suspicari fas est. 2. JEHOVAH ET AZAZEL, hac in Lege, tanquam partes extremae et oppositione maxima ab invicem separatae, statuuntur. Cum itaque distantia et oppositio maxima inter Deum et Daemonem semper intercesserit, consentaneum est ut Azazel Daemonem (non montem aut hircum) notare censeatur. 3. Lege praeceptum est, ut e duobus hircis, quis Jehovae, quis Azazeli, destinandus esset, sorte decerneretur. Antiquitus autem sortitio fieri solebat, tantum cum respersonarum ageretur. Haman, ... 4. Expiationis Lege cautum est insuper, *ut hircus in quem cecidit sors pro Azazele dimittatur ad Azazelem in deserto.* Horum autem verborum sensus implicatus et incommodus erit, si Azazelem de hirco emisso; sed facilis et expeditus, si de daemone, vocem eam intelligamus. Tunc enim hunc sensum apertum et cohaerentem dabunt: 'Hircus ille cui sorte obtigit, ut Daemoni tradatur, mittatur ad *azazelem*, vel Daemonem, in deserto ubi praecipue versari solet.' Hic sensus eo probabilior est, quod loca deserta et ab hominum commercio remota, Daemoni gratiora, et illius habitacula maxime familiaria, olim haberentur. Christas enim in desertum, utpote Daemonis provinciam, ductus est, ut a Diabolo tentaretur: Mat. 4. 1. Luc. 8. 27. saepius a Diabolo in desertum impellebatur. Hac de re statim fusius et opportunius acturi sumus.

Quinto: Si vocem *Azazel* sensu jam dicto capiamus, *Lamed*, Jehovae et Azazeli praefixum saepe, casum eundem, nempe Dativum, semper denotet, nec opus sit ei significationes aut usus diversos, eodem in commate nonnunquam, attribuere. Hoc argumentum ab exemplis aliquot in hac Lege, lucem petat: ver. 8. *Ponat sortes duas,—unam* ליהוה *Jehovae, et unam* לעזאל *Azazeli:* ver. 10. *Et hircus super quem ceciderit sors* לעזאל *Azazeli* (ut cederet Azazeli) *mittatur* לעזאל *Azazeli.* vers. 26. *Qui miserit hircum* לעזאל Azazeli,—Exemplis hisce liquet, omnia belle cohaerere et sine salebris fluere; nec opus esse, ut *Lamed*, nunc *ab* vel *propter*, nunc *ad*, nunc hoc nunc aliud, notare putetur; modo vocem illam vexatissimam de Diabolo dictam intelligamus. His argumentis ostensum arbitror, Diabolum Azazeli nomine designari. Praesentis instituti ratio jam postulat, ut nominis illius originem et imponendi causam, pro facultatem mearum modulo patefaciam. Ut itaque ad provinciam meam recta veniam: ambigere non habeo, quin AZAZEL *fortem abeuntem*, aut cito *fugientem*, denotet, et inde vocis origo et imponendi ratio derivetur. Hoc eo constantius assero, quod haec etymologia, Voci Azazel, Legi praesenti, Diabolo denique, maxime convenire videatur.

Primo: Voci ipsi: nam lippienti clarum est, עזאל a עז *fortis* et אזל *abiens, cito recedens, fugiens, conflari*, et hac etymologia nihil coacti vel violenti contineri. Nec peccat in leges Grammaticae, voces duas generis diversi jungens, aut voci עז genus masculinum in vocabulo tantum *Azazel* tribuens. Haec etiam etymologia Hebraea tota est, adeoque voci *Azazel* apprime convenit; cum inter vocabula plurimum Hebraica reperiatur, et ad legis hujus essentiam spectet Hebraeorum genti traditae.

Secundo: Haec etymologia, cum praecipuo Legis illius instituto, qua vox *Azazel* toties occurrit, maxime consentire putetur. Cum enim Deus praeceptum dederit, ut hircorum alter in Desertum ad Diabolum amandaretur; consentaneum erat, ut Diabolus העזאל *fortis ille fugiens* aut *abiens* appellaretur. Sic enim illius instituti mentem, paulo apertius explicandam censeo: 'Cum hircus ille piacularis, peccatis Gentis totius oneratus, summam inde foeditatem et impuritatem hauserit, et prorsus indignus evaserit ut in hircorum vulgarium gregem et censum admittatur; abeat quo dignus est, ad impurum Daemonem nempe, cujus Angeli שעירים *hirci* vel *hirci-formes* appellari solent. Cum autem Daemon עזאזל sit, *fortis abiens*, et in desertum (habitaculum sibi quasi relictum) perpetuo *fugiens;* eo hircum illum immundum amandari velim, ut cum Azazele tantum et Angelis ejus hirci-formibus, ibi plerumque commorantibus, societatem habeat.'

Tertio: Si ad voces eas (עז et אזל) e quibus *Azazel* conflari dictum est, attentius advertamus, appareat facile, nomen illud ad amussim Diabolo convenire. Nam,

1. Diabolus עז *fortis* aut *potens* erat, et sic a Gentibus olim habebatur. Eam enim fortitudinis et potentiae famam apud Ethnicos acquisivit, quod prout Deus verus יהוה צבאות *Dominus Exercituum*, sic et ille (Dan. 11. 38.) אלה מעזים *Deus fortitudinum*, inter suos, appellatus est: Et prout summus Deus (Psal. 24. 8.) עזוז וגבור *fortis et potens* audiit; ita Diabolus, apud Phoenices nomine 'Aζιζος, id est, *fortis aut validus;* apud Arabes antiquos nomine ALOSSA vel ALUSSA, *summe potentem* notante, colebatur. Et ita tandem potentiae suae fides hominum animos occupavit, quod eum titulis illis, מלך et אלה, potentiam eximiam indicantibus, ubique gentium insignirent. Sed nil opus est ut hoc Argumentum nos diutius moretur, cum Diabolus (Luc. 11. 21.) in Scriptura, et Angeli ejus (Ephes. 6. 12) signanter appellentur.

2. Nomen Azazel, *fortis abiens* aut *recedens*, in Diabolum quadrat maxime. Sic enim non injuria vocari possit, si ad Deum, Angelos bonos, Homines, aut ipsos Diaboli mores, respectus habeatur. *Respectu Dei*, a quo celeriter abiit et defectionem fecit in aeternum. Inde Diabolus, in scriptis Rabbinorum מרוד, *apostata*, *qui a Deo defecit*, per eminentiam quandam appellatur. Id nominis etiam *Respectu bonorum Angelorum*, Daemonibus attribui potest. Cum enim Angeli boni, (Zach. 6:5. Luc. 1:19) עזים עומדים *fortes stantes* essent, et in statu integro permanerent; Daemones עזים אזלים *fortes abeuntes* erant, utpote (Jud. 6) et statum primaevum minime retinentes. Non minus *Hominum respectu* nomen azazel Diabolo quadrare censeatur: quod nempe Daemones locos et aedes frequentes plerunque fugiant, et ad locos desertos et ab hominum commercio remotos abeant. Ideoque spiritus illi (Deut. 32:17)

שדים *solitarii, agrestes,* dicti sunt, quod se locis agrestibus et soli-
tariis oblectent, et humanorum coetuum inimici sint, *insociabiles,*
sine jure, et sine lare. Postremo, *Morum suorum respectu,* Diabolus
azazel aut *fortis abiens* appellari meruit. Nam in Scriptura describitur tanquam spiritus de loco in locum semper abiens, nec
uspiam moram faciens, praesertim si repulsam patiatur. Job. 2. 2.
Dixit Dominus ad Satan unde venis? etc. Mat. 12. 43.; 1 Pet. 5. 8.
Jacob. 4. 7. Hisce libentius immorati sumus, quod inde nominis
hujus origo, simul et significatio, non parum confirmentur. Cum
enim e jam dictis appareat, nomen *azazel* Daemoni exacte convenire; suadet Ratio, ut illud Daemonem significare censeamus.

Milton's conception of Azazel as 'standard-bearer' to the
Rebel Angels is perhaps due more than Saurat thought to
the quotation from Irenaeus through Epiphanius. Milton
has cited both Irenaeus[1] and Epiphanius[2] a number of
times, besides citing Petavius, the Jesuit-commentator on
Epiphanius, who turned the Greek verses against Marcion
into Latin.[3] I am inclined to believe that the tenor of
these verses had more to do with the 'standard-bearer'
idea than has been supposed.

From the mass of material presented or indicated above,
Milton constructed his conception of the Fallen Angel,
Azazel. The rabbinical authority for using Azazel as a
Fallen Angel is to be found in the hints of Ibn Ezra. The
'cherub tall' indicative of the importance of the Angel,
is derived from the statements concerning him as a great
demon to be found in the *Pirke* of Eliezar of Worms.
Thus, authority for Azazel being treated as a Fallen Angel,
and one of considerable rank, is rooted in rabbinical works,
whether we turn to *Enoch* or to the medieval rabbis, the
details being known through the many references supplied
by Bochart and Spencer.

[1] *Of Prelatical Episcopacy,* Mitford, vol. III, pp. 78, 81, 83, 86, 89. *Areopagitica,*
vol. IV:413. *Pro populo,* vol. VI., pp. 66, 68.
[2] *Areopagitica,* vol. IV:413. *Tetrachordon, ibid.,* p. 266.
[3] *Pro populo,* vol. VI:66.

CHAPTER VIII

CONCLUSION

I

Because the investigation of Milton's rabbinical readings is a relatively new field for study and research, it is not possible as yet fully to evaluate its significance. So far as the present work is concerned, it has no more than opened the way, or more properly speaking, a way into the whole field of his rabbinical readings. Perhaps its value lies as much in its method as in its results. But, in so far as the results obtained have been found to provide authentic sources for many of Milton's images and ideas which the investigation of no other source material has ever provided, it is important to summarize the chief effects of such a study as this.

Milton's rabbinical readings grew naturally out of his interest in Semitic study in general, which in turn was an outgrowth of his education and of his affiliation with the humanistic tradition. His entire interest in Semitic studies, and especially the rabbinical readings, was principally the result of his affiliations with the humanism of the Renaissance. The interest in linguistic study, so much a part of the humanistic tradition, is one of the permanent characteristics of Milton's intellectual nature. In addition to this, we must remember that there was another factor directing Milton's great interest in linguistic study in general so that he approached the study of Hebrew and related languages with a special purpose in mind. Whether Hebrew, Aramaic, or rabbinical Hebrew, Milton attacked them all because they belonged to, indeed were a necessary part of a whole realm of study in which he was enormously interested. His attention to Semitic languages and their

literature, while derived from the general humanistic tradition, specifically came about because these languages
were essential to the study of the Bible. It was for this
reason that Milton became so absorbed in their study that
he made himself proficient in Hebrew and Aramaic, and
fairly familiar with rabbinical Hebrew. That is, the general humanistic interest in linguistic study of all kinds
centering in Latin and Greek, was in Milton's case given
a greater scope by his great interest in and use of the Bible.
He needed the Hebrew and related languages in order to
make use of the Bible in the way he came to think fitting
and proper, indeed, necessary.

The text of Scripture represented an absolute authority
to Milton. He held that the letter of the text was sacred.
But this authority was only absolute as the authority of a
text to a scholar. That is, it makes considerable difference
as to what text we select that was thus authoritative to
him. The only authoritative text to Milton was the original Hebrew of the Old Testament, and the original Greek
of the New. So far as these texts were concerned, and
especially the Hebrew of the Old Testament, when he
came to say anything about them or to cite them in any
way, he was, of course, forced to use them in some other
form than the original, sometimes Latin and sometimes
English. When it came to such usage, the latitude he permitted himself was very great. He felt, naturally enough,
his own competence to translate the original as he saw fit,
and the result was that he often presented verses in Latin
or English that vary or differ from the text of any and all
versions, allowing himself all the latitude possible so long
as he remained faithful to what he felt to be a fair and
adequate rendering of the Hebrew. In this way, he was
not, in our modern sense, a literalist. His equipment for
using the original texts of Scripture was too large to permit

the use of such a term, for the basic text of Scripture was
to him the original. Thus, whenever he came to use the
text in his work, or to discuss it in the same connection,
and both cases were very frequent, he was often most free
in his adaptation of it to his uses. In this way he may be
said to have been most liberal. But, so far as basic ideas
were concerned, what he found in the text of the original
he accepted fully. Thus we find him constantly and with
remarkable consistency recognizing the need for accepting
the various duplicate accounts of Biblical events, such as
the two accounts of creation in Genesis, the two accounts
of the entry of the animals into the ark, in one account in
pairs and in the other by sevens. Such ideas were fundamental to him, and he never thought of changing them in
any way. On the other hand, matters of interpretation
were to him matters of opinion, and we find him setting
himself against many current and conventional interpretations as when he pointed out that the eighth chapter of
Proverbs referred, not to Christ, but to an allegorical
presentation of Wisdom as the Spirit of God.

Thus, I see no need of saying with Professor Tillyard
that 'when we come to the Bible and the kind of authority
Milton allowed it the difficulties are great.'[1] Such difficulties as he mentions arise chiefly, perhaps, from a mis-
apprehension of what the Bible meant to Milton. Certainly he is frequently found employing Scripture to
support strange arguments; but he is rarely if ever found
attaching Biblical texts however particular for the first
time to the support of arguments he wished to further.
A dozen or more medieval or Renaissance authorities may
be found for every one of Milton's employments of Scriptural texts. This scarcely seems possible to the present
age that actually uses the Bible so little, but to Milton's

[1] E. M. W. Tillyard, *Milton* (London, 1930), p. 217.

age it was a commonplace matter. Professor Tillyard is right in charging Milton with partisanship in his use of Scripture, and he certainly did 'disregard the plain sense of a passage or altogether omit what is for the Biblical author of the first importance.' However, we need to recognize clearly that Milton was never being particularly original when he did this but was almost invariably depending upon the original reading or some commentator whom he had read. It was difficult, even three centuries ago to suggest new meanings for the text of Scripture. In his use of the Bible in the *de doctrina*, Milton's greatest inconsistency is more apparent than real. He was honest enough in stating that he was going to set forth a system of theology based *solely* on Scripture. But for a man who had read as much critical Biblical material as he had, such a procedure was actually impossible, although he himself may have been and no doubt really was completely unaware of the fact. After all, Milton's worst offense in the use of Scripture was his many times repeated practice of employing the same verse or verses of Scripture under varying circumstances to support utterly different ideas or positions. But in doing this he was in a large company of illustrious fore-runners conspicuous among whom were the medieval rabbis in their Biblical commentaries.

Milton's rabbinical readings belonged largely with his reading of Biblical commentaries. They rank in importance with his reading of the other critical apparatus of Scripture. That is, Milton's rabbinical readings were not isolated and independent parts of his reading, but were integrally part of a whole system of reading in which he engaged, perhaps not primarily for the writing of his great epic, but which culminated in that achievement. It is a significant fact that the rabbis we have connected with Milton must be examined as if they were a separate and detached source for him when actually they could not have been. They were part of the material connected with the Biblical text that Milton read, and after they have been examined in detail, for which purpose they must be detached, they must be recognized as for him a part of the critical apparatus connected with the text of Scripture. This aspect of them may often be noted in Milton's use of such apparatus. When he referred to the various interpretations of the passage in Judges connected with the basic reasons for divorce, he very naturally cited various interpreters of the passage, among others, the rabbis. Such citation of authoritative commentators is found throughout his work, sometimes varying with an appeal to a particular version, and may be seen in the appeal to the Syriac in the *Areopagitica* and in the *de doctrina*, or to the Targums and even other versions of Scripture, as well as references to Calvin, Luther, Perkins, Ames, Paraeus, and other Christian divines. The result in all such cases is the same, and is a recognizably conventional procedure in the use of Scripture of his day—he only followed his contemporaries when he cited various commentators or versions as the bases for his difference from the orthodox or best known interpretation of the text.

II

Another important aspect of this investigation of Milton's rabbinical readings lies in the light it has shed upon his mental activities and capacities. Beginning with the relatively less important information it has afforded as to the wide range of his intellectual interests and activities, this study has more or less followed him through some of his wanderings in learned by-ways, lying far from the beaten path of ordinary knowledge. The extent of his intellectual curiosity, judged by the rabbinical readings, has been found to have been colossal. The enormous mass of material that he in some manner drew on is staggering. This is the more remarkable in him when it is recalled that, in any modern sense, this particular field, the rabbinical, was virtually uncharted in his day. Such activity as he displayed meant the reading of a few more or less standard works that most sketchily outlined the field, and then the hit-or-miss collection of books and manuscripts, chiefly from the Continent, or from the private collections of his friends. Most of the aids, in fact all of the bibliographical helps to the efforts of a modern student who may wish to work with the rabbis were lacking, and only the enormous ambition and unflagging enthusiasm of the individual so engaged could in Milton's time make at all possible any headway in such reading and study.

There were, it is true, as we have seen, a certain number of lexicons and grammars from which one could begin to explore the field. The references found in such works to the literature of the rabbis in a way blocked out the compass and extent of the whole; and large masses of the material were to be found in such single works as Buxtorf's rabbinical Bible. In addition to this, a certain amount of rabbinical material was slowly being translated, and attention was being called to various branches of the whole field by the best of the Biblical commentators. First-hand acquaintance with many rabbinical works was not at all impossible; but any individual who became acquainted with such works necessarily possessed a certain toughness of intellectual stamina that definitely set him apart from ordinary intellects. Actual exhibition by a Christian scholar of the seventeenth century of a knowledge of rabbinical literature is not so much a mark of an unusual form of intellectual activity as it is a mark of the high quality of his educational training and of the great range of his intellect. The very best Christian scholars of the time made an attempt at an acquaintance with the rabbis, indeed, in the Buxtorfs, father and son, in Pococke, in Lightfoot, and in many others of the century, we have some of the greatest Gentile rabbinical scholars who ever lived. So far as Milton is concerned, one very important aspect of this investigation of his rabbinical readings is the manner in which there is set in sharp relief his eager capacity for study and intellectual pursuits by the observation of his use of rabbinical and other material in his writings.

Specifically, the most important point established in the present work is the fact that Milton actually made use of certain rabbinical materials. The proofs of this point are his own references to such materials as we have found those references in the *Divorce* tract and in the *Apology*. There, we have found unmistakable references to rabbinical writings which constitute direct proof of his use of the rabbis. Added to this is the indirect evidence afforded by the appearance in *Paradise Lost* of rabbinical material, which was unquestionably taken direct from the rabbis, since it is not found elsewhere than in their writings.

III

All of the material of a rabbinical nature that Milton actually referred to in his prose works and which we have here examined is of a single nature, that of rabbinical commentary on Scripture. In so far as we have examined the rabbinical material found in *Paradise Lost*, we have confined ourselves to the examination of the appearance in the poem of the same kind of material. Rabbinical commentaries on Scripture therefore constitute the first considerable body of rabbinical literature to be definitely connected with Milton. This is important to notice, for it

has permitted us to be very specific and direct in considering what rabbinical material we should examine in connection with him.

In addition to this, Milton's references to the rabbis are
of such a nature that it has been found possible to recognize and to determine the form in which he used this rabbinical commentary on Scripture. Both in the *Divorce*
tract and in the *Apology* the references to the rabbis clearly
fit and agree with the rabbinical commentary and other
apparatus found in the Buxtorf edition of the rabbinical
Bible. It has therefore been possible to connect Milton
definitely with this edition of the rabbinical Bible as distinguished from other and earlier editions such as those of
Bomberg.

We have examined this Buxtorf Bible and its commenting rabbis, discovering that such a work afforded Milton
rabbinical commentaries on the whole of the Old Testament, with full textual apparatus, including the excellent
Hebrew text Buxtorf printed, and the Targums found
therein. The rabbinical commentaries that Buxtorf
printed included the best of such commentaries ever written. Rashi appears on almost the whole canon, and Ibn
Ezra, David Kimchi, and Ben Gerson add their contributions to the more important Old Testament books. Other
rabbinical commentators also appear, but the above four
make up the great mass of commentaries found in Buxtorf's Bible. This is an enormous amount of rabbinical
material to connect with Milton all at one time; and the
importance of connecting him with a rabbinical Bible must
be recognized as of the greatest significance in the investigation of his rabbinical studies, because such a connection
affords him contact with so large an amount of rabbinical
material within the covers of a single book. In addition to
this, when we connect him with Buxtorf's Bible, we con-

nect him with a definite text, not only for the Old Testament canon in Hebrew and for the Targums in Aramaic, but also for the rabbinical commentators who appear therein. All of these texts may be examined for any peculiarities that appear in them. We have succeeded, therefore, in opening up not only a new field of source material for Milton, but have at the same time established the definite and particular text from which he secured such material as he took from that field.

Now there is one point in connection with Milton's use of the rabbis that must be constantly kept in mind and which cannot be too greatly emphasized. This point is that his knowledge and use of the rabbis must not be thought of as particularly unusual in a man of his education and attainments during the seventeenth century. His use of the rabbis marks him of unusual but not unique learning. Every scholar who could, used rabbinical material to a greater or lesser extent, depending upon his ability to do so, largely because in the development of Protestantism, rabbinical commentaries on Scripture had become part of the critical apparatus connected with the study of the Biblical text, and all the best scholarship of the time arranged itself about that text and its study. To be sure, not all rabbinical commentaries were known to all Christian scholars, but the commentaries found in such a Bible as Buxtorf's were known in varying degrees of completeness to European men of learning. Milton's interest in such commentaries arose from his splendid education and from the demands of his own eager spirit, demands that were inaugurated by his sympathies with Humanism and by his connections with Protestant learning in general, centering in Biblical study. The fact that the most learned Christians generally were, throughout the sixteenth and seventeenth centuries, more and more

making use of rabbinical materials, and especially the
scriptural commentaries, must be recognized constantly
in connection with Milton in order to understand that his
knowledge and use of such materials were unusual chiefly
as indicating his remarkable educational attainments.
Otherwise, pointing out his connections with rabbinical
works might unduly emphasize the importance of his rabbinical readings. For Milton's use of rabbinical materials
is by no means the most important fact concerning either
his so-called theology or his poetry. It is rather an important fact among others, equally to be reckoned with,
but in no way superseding, for instance, his use of classical
material, of orthodox or heterodox Christian theological
ideas, or of all the other literary and intellectual influences
of his time to which he was heir. I am certain that when
the time comes for a final accounting of the many influences at work upon him, his rabbinical readings will take
their place, perhaps a lowly one, among the whole mass of
his various studies, which are so interrelated and connected that to invoke one is to invoke them all.

IV

Rabbinical commentaries supplied Milton with many details connected with or supplementing what is to be found
in the Bible concerning Creation and other materials or
ideas Milton took therefrom. On the whole, the rabbinical commentaries furnished him with embellishments
only, and they were not, I think, primarily responsible for
many of Milton's fundamental ideas, although the rabbis
may well have supported some of his more noticeably
Jewish notions, such as the soul's non-survival of bodily
death, his strong anti-Trinitarianism, and his support of
polygamy based on the Old Testament accounts of it.
However, his interpretation of Scripture often reflects very
strongly the influence of his reading of rabbinical com-

mentaries, especially in his treatment of and attitude toward such portions of Scripture as the eighth chapter of Proverbs, the Song of Solomon, and the book of Job. Equally notable is the influence of the rabbis on his whole treatment of Creation, but on the whole this influence is best seen in Milton's use of rabbinical details connected with and supplementing the Biblical material.

For the most part, these details appear in his poetry, chiefly in *Paradise Lost*, rather than in his theological prose discussions. His poetical treatment of Biblical material in the epic is highly colored by his use of many details and embellishments culled from rabbinical commentaries on Scripture. On the other hand, the direct proofs of his acquaintanceship with such rabbinical commentaries occur entirely in his prose works. Specifically, the *Divorce* tract passage and that in the *Apology* actually and unmistakably, as has already been pointed out, cite passages from the rabbinical commentaries and indicate Milton's use of a rabbinical Bible. Milton's connection with and use of the material to be found in such a Bible, including the commentaries of the rabbis, is no longer a matter of conjecture or speculation. My present work has definitely settled not only the fact that he used such a Bible, but also the actual text of which he made use. There may be considerable difference of opinion regarding the influence of such commentaries on his work, and even regarding the appearance of specific details in *Paradise Lost* which to me seem to have come from the rabbis. But there can no longer be any hesitation over the matter of his use of rabbinical commentaries to Scripture in their originals, or over the form and text in which he knew them.

As sources for poetical material, and at present this appears to me to have been the most important use Milton

made of the rabbinical commentaries, the work of the
rabbis was valuable to him for several reasons. As already
stated, they supplied him with many additional details not
to be found in the text of Scripture itself; or in the form of
embellishments of the scriptural material they furnished a
more fully rounded account of what was barely indicated
in the Bible. For much of the Biblical material used in
Paradise Lost, such enlarged treatment and additions to
Scripture were very welcome to him, and were used in
great profusion, whether he took them from the rabbis or
from more accessible and better known sources. Milton's
use of such material in general is well known, and was the
common practice of his day in all treatments of scriptural
topics. In addition to the extra details and embellishments the rabbis furnished him, they also provided explanations of textual discrepancies to be found in the Bible,
and in the case of Milton's treatment of the Creation of
plants for instance, whether or not he drew directly on the
rabbis, there is provided in their commentary an explanation of the process Milton employed as a means of recon-
ciling what to him were two otherwise inexplicable and
conflicting accounts of plant Creation. In other words,
the rabbis often provided him with an explanation of what
they refused to allow to be a discrepancy between different
portions of the biblical text dealing with the same material
or idea in different ways.

Furthermore and lastly, especially from a poetical
standpoint, the rabbinical commentaries were often highly
imaginative and suggestive. The whole idea of Creation
as a birth-process, although much older and more primitive in origin than the Middle Ages, was treated by the
medieval rabbis, especially by Ben Gerson, with considerable imagination and with suggestion of a very high order.
The same is true of the rabbinical treatments of the per-

sonification of Wisdom in Proverbs, especially in connection with Creation, making her at once an idea in the mind of God, and a sort of separate aspect of his Spirit emanating from God's will to create, if not thrown off by it. All of these various aspects of rabbinical commentaries to Scripture have left their impression upon Milton, and in a manner their appearance in his work serves as an indication of his use of the particular material from the rabbis in which they originally are to be found.

V

The most remarkable aspect of the present study is, perhaps, its suggestions of Milton's manner of working, especially in his poetry. All of the material presented here has a bearing upon the poet's modes of composition. Much might be said of the enormous amount of time he must have spent in accumulating and sorting material; the thought and judgment expended upon it after it was assembled; and then the alchemy that transmuted it often into extremely marvelous poetry. It is salutary to note while mentioning this aspect of the work that the entire study has reaffirmed most strikingly a principle on which Milton invariably worked, and that was the principle of using authentic material. Especially in the details of his work is he accurate. Every point he makes or uses has its own *raison d'être*, often, unfortunately, in an unknown or forgotten source. It is, it seems to me, much more remarkable to find Milton thus using authority for even the smallest details of his work than it would be to discover that he created such details from his own imagination. Often, the poetic element is submerged in this adherence to authority; but we must marvel at a mind that could and did hold so many authentic details in solution.

INDEX OF BIBLICAL PASSAGES CITED
OR QUOTED

BIBLIOGRAPHY

The following works, arranged under appropriate headings, represent a selected, working bibliography. No attempt has been made here to be in any way exhaustive, only those works providing an introduction to the various subjects indicated, or those texts actually employed being listed.

The Works of Milton

Editions of the Poetry Edited by Milton

Poems of Mr. John Milton, etc. London, 1645. [British Museum, E. 1126.]

Paradise Lost/ a/ Poem/ Written in/ Ten Books/ . . . London . . . 1667. [B. M. 6. 14. a. 9.]

Paradise Regain'd/ a/ Poem/ In IV Books./ to which is added/ Samson Agonistes./ . . . London,/ . . . 1671./ [B. M. 684. a. 33.]

Poems Upon Several Occasions. London, 1673. [B. M. 1076. f. 19.]

Paradise Lost/ a/ Poem/ in/ Twelve Books./ The Second Edition/ . . . London,/ 1674./ [B. M. 1076. f. 20.]

Facsimile of the Manuscript of Milton's Minor Poems Preserved in the Library of Trinity College, Cambridge. Cambridge, 1899.

Annotated Editions of the Poetry by Various Editors

Paradise Lost, with Notes by 'P. [atrick] H. [ume].' London, 1695.

Paradise Lost. Edited by Richard Bentley. London, 1732.

Paradise Lost. Poetical Works. Edited by Thomas Newton. London, 1749-52. 3 vols.

Paradise Lost. Book I. Edited by John Callander. Glasgow, 1750.

Poetical Works. Edited by H. J. Todd, 2nd edition. London, 1809. 7 vols.

The Poetical Works of John Milton. Edited by John Mitford. London, 1851. 2 vols.

The Poems of John Milton. With notes by T. Keightley. London, 1859. 2 vols.

The Cambridge Milton for Schools. Edited by A. W. Verity. Cambridge, 1891-1910. 10 vols.

The Poetical Works of John Milton. Edited by David Masson. London, 1896. 3 vols.

The Poetical Works of John Milton. Edited by H. C. Beeching. Oxford, 1900.

The Poetical Works. Edited by W. V. Moody. Revised edition, Boston, 1924.

The Poems of John Milton. Edited by H. J. C. Grierson. London, 1925-26. 2 vols.

The Prose Works

The Prose Works of John Milton. Edited by Charles Symmons. London, 1806. 7 vols.

The Works of John Milton in Verse and Prose. Edited by John Mitford. London, 1851. 8 vols.

De Doctrina Christiana. Curavit Carolus Ricardus Sumner. Cantabrigiae, 1825.

A Common-place Book of John Milton. Autotype copy for the Royal Society of Literature, 1876.

Commentary, Criticism, and Special Studies

(With the appearance (1929) of Stevens's *Reference Guide to Milton*, it is no longer necessary to list many of the items that have appeared since 1800. Only the most used studies follow.)

E. C. Baldwin, 'Some Extra-Biblical Semitic Influences upon Milton's Story of the Fall of Man,' *Journal of English and Germanic Philology*, xxviii (1929), 366 ff.

H. F. Fletcher, *Milton's Semitic Studies*. Chicago, 1926.

———— *The Use of the Bible in Milton's Prose*. Urbana, 1929.

J. W. Good, *Studies in the Milton Tradition*. Urbana, 1915.

J. H. Hanford, 'The Chronology of Milton's Private Studies,' *PMLA*, xxxvi (1921), 251 ff.

———— 'The Rosenbach Milton Documents,' *PMLA*, xxxviii (1923), 290 ff.

———— *A Milton Handbook*. New York, 1926.

Thomas Keightley, *An Account of the Life, Opinions, and Writings of John Milton*. London, 1855.

S. B. LILJEGREN, *Studies in Milton.* Lund, 1919.

LAURA E. LOCKWOOD, *Lexicon to the English Poetical Works of John Milton.* New York, 1907.

DAVID MASSON, *The Life of John Milton.* Cambridge and London, 1859-94. 7 vols. (vol. 1 revised 1881).

JAMES PATERSON, *A Complete Commentary on 'Paradise Lost.'* London, 1744.

E. K. RAND, '*J* and *I* in Milton's Latin Script,' *Modern Philology*, XIX (1922), 315 ff.

————— 'Milton in Rustication,' *Studies in Philology*, XIX (1922), 109 ff.

DENIS SAURAT, *La Pensée de Milton.* Paris, 1920.

————— *Milton: Man and Thinker.* New York, 1925.

ALFRED STERN, *Milton und seine Zeit.* Leipzig, 1877-79. 2 vols.

D. H. STEVENS, *Reference Guide to Milton.* Chicago, 1929.

E. M. W. TILLYARD, *Milton.* London, 1930.

Hebrew and Rabbinical Lexicons

AVENARIUS, ספר השרשים *Lexicon Ebraicum.* Wittenberg, 1568.

ELIEZAR BEN JUDAH, *Thesaurus totius hebraitatis et veteris et recentioris.* 1908-*ss.*

BROWN, DRIVER and BRIGGS, *Hebrew Lexicon of the Old Testament* (after Gesenius). Boston, 1907.

JOHAN BUXTORF, *Epitome Radicum Hebraicum et Chaldaicum.* Basel, 1607.

————— *Lexicon Chaldaicum et Syriacum.* Basel, 1622.

————— *Lexicon Hebraicum et Chaldaicum.* Basel, 1621.

————— *ibid.* Amsterdam, 1655.

————— *Lexicon Chaldaicum, Talmudicum, et Rabbinicum.* Basel, 1639.

VICTORINUS BYTHNER, *Clavis linguae sanctae.* Cambridge, 1648.

EDMUND CASTELL, *Lexicon Heptaglotton.* London, 1669. 2 vols.

DAVID BEN ISAAC COHEN DE LARA, עיר דוד *sive de convienientia vocabularum rabbinicorum.* Amsterdam, 1638.

HEINRICH HOTTINGER, *Lexicon Harmonicum.* Frankfort, 1661.

DAVID KIMCHI, ספר השרשים (*Book of Roots.*—Hebrew). Venice, 1546.

————— *Radicum liber sive hebraeum bibliorum lexicon.* Berlin, 1847.

JAC. KLATZKIN, *Thesaurus Philosophicus Lingua Hebraica.* Leipzig, 1928. 2 vols.

Elias Levita, ספר מתורגמן (*Meturgeman*) *sive Lexicon Chaldaica*. Edited by Paul Fagius, Isne, 1541.

Sebastian Münster, *Dictionarium Hebraicum.* Basel, (1527) 1548.

——— *Dictionarium Chaldaicum.* Basel, 1527.

Nathan ben Jechoel, ספר מוסף הערוך (Hebrew) *Aruch* (Dictionary). Amsterdam, 1655.

ערוך השלם *Plenus Aruch.* Edited by Alexander Kohut, Vienna, 1878. 4 vols.

Johan Henricius Othonis, *Lexicon Rabbinico-Philologicum.* Geneva, 1675.

Pagninus, קצר אוצר לשון הקדש *Epitome thesauri linguae sanctae.* Antwerp, 1578.

Joh. Plantavitius, *Thesaurus Synonymicus Hebraico-Chaldaico-Rabbinicus.* Lodéve, 1644.

David de Pomis, עמח דוד *Dittionario novo Hebraico.* Venice, 1587.

Valentine Schindler, *Lexicon Pentaglotton.* Hanau, 1612.

Bibles, Hebrew Old Testament with Rabbinical Commentary

מקראות גדולות (Hebrew) The Bomberg III. Venice, 1546-1548.

מקראות גדולות (Hebrew) The Bomberg V. Venice, 1617.

מקראות גדולות (Hebrew) Buxtorf. Basel, 1618-1619.

מקראות גדולות (Hebrew) Warsaw, v.d., 1874-1885. 11 vols.

Biblia Polyglotta Waltoni. London, v.d., 1654 *ss.* (with no commentary, but with Targums).

Qere and Ketiv

Johan Buxtorf, Various Works. *Passim.*

C. D. Ginsburg, *Introduction to the Hebrew Bible, passim.* London, 1897.

——— *Hayyim's Introduction to the Rabbinic Bible.* London, 1867.

Gesenius, *Hebrew Grammar.* Revised by A. E. Cowley, p. 65 and *passim.* Oxford, 1910.

Emil Friedrich Kautzsch, *Grammatik des Biblische-Aramaïschen.* Leipzig, 1884.

Francis Wrangham, *In Biblia Polyglotta Prolegomena . . . Briani Waltoni.* Cantabrigae, 1828. 2 vols.

Bible, Hebrew Old Testament, Pentateuch with Rabbinical Commentaries or Separate Commentaries

Rashi, (on the Pentateuch) תורה (Hebrew Pentateuch) *with Rashi.* Sabbioneta, 1554.

——— *Der Raschi-Kommentar zu den fünf Büchern Moses*, (Hebrew text with German translation, the Hebrew now superseded by Berliner's text, and the translation by Bamberger's) edited and translated by Julius Dessauer. Budapest, 1887.

——— *Raschi, der Kommentar des Solomo ben Isak über den Pentateuch*, (Critical text edition of the Hebrew) edited by A. Berliner. Frankfort a/M, 1905.

——— *Raschis Pentateuchkommentar*, (German translation without Hebrew) by Selig Bamberger. Hamburg, 1922.

——— *Rashi on the Pentateuch*, (Hebrew text with very full English translation) by J. H. Lowe. London, 1929.

Ibn Ezra, אבן עזרא על התורה (Ibn Ezra on the Pentateuch, Hebrew) Stanislau, 1927.

——— באור על ספר שמות (Ibn Ezra on Exodus, Hebrew, Shorter Commentary) Prag, 1840. (*Editio princeps.*)

——— *ibid.* Vienna, 1926.

——— Decalogus. (Hebrew-Latin with Ibn Ezra's Commentary) Basel, 1527.

Levi ben Gerson, רלבג פירוש על התורה (Ralbag on the Pentateuch, Hebrew) Venice, 1547.

Bible, The Prophets with Rabbinical Commentaries

Prophetae hebraicae (Hebrew) with Kimchi on the Twelve Minor Prophets. Stephanus, Paris, 1539-1540.

Samuelis libri ebraice et latine, ad usum academiarum. (Hebrew) Leyden, 1521 (i.e. 1621). (Hebrew, Prophets and Hagiographa with Rashi) Amsterdam, 1699.

Bible, Hagiographa

Psalms ספר תהלים (Hebrew text with Kimchi) Isne, 1541.

Psalmorum Davidis. (Beza's translation, with some use of rabbinical commentaries) London, 1580.

Psalmi Davidis. (Tremellius's translation, with much use of rabbinical commentaries) London, 1580.

A Commentarie upon the 15 Psalmes called Psalmi gradum translated into English by Henry Ball. Martin Luther (from the Latin, but with some attention to the Hebrew). London, 1615.

Lectiones in CL Psalmos Davidis. William Ames. Amsterdam, 1635. (Ames was one of Milton's favorite theologians, and in this work Ames devotes some attention to the Hebrew text and to rabbinical commentaries upon it)

Job

Job Expounded by Theodore Beza. Cambridge, 1589.

The Book of Job. Expounded by Hermann Hedwig Bernard, edited by Frank Chance. vol. 1, (all issued) London, 1864. (Although a modern work, this book is an excellent opening to the rabbis for the beginner)

Proverbs

Proverbis Solomonis. (Hebrew-Latin) Basel, 1524.

Commentar zu den Sprüchen Solomon's. (Hebrew, Ibn Ezra) Frankfort, 1884.

Ecclesiastes

Ecclesiastes. (Hebrew-Latin) Basel, 1525.

Commentary on Coheleth. Hugh Broughton. London, 1605.

Canticles

Canticles. (Hebrew-Latin) Basel, 1525.

Lamentations

(Hebrew-English) translated by Hugh Broughton with some commentary. London, 1608.

Bible Concordances, Hebrew, English, Latin

Concordantiae Bibliorum Hebraicae. Compiled by Buxtorf. Basel, 1632.

A Complete Concordance. Clement Cotton (A very early, if not the first concordance to the A. V.). London, 1635.

Concordantiae Bibliorum sacrorum vulgatae editionis. F. P. Dupripon. Paris, 1838.

Veteris Testamenti Concordantiae Hebraicae atque Chaldaicae . . . Editio minor. Solomon Mandelkern. Leipzig, 1896.

Rashi (Rabbi Solomon ben Isaac)

SELIG BAMBERGER, *Raschis Pentateuchkommentar*. Hamburg, 1922.

A. BERLINER, *Raschi, der Kommentar des Salomo ben Isak über den Pentateuch*. Frankfurt, 1905.

A. DARMSTETTER, 'Les Glosses françaises de Raschi dans la Bible,' *Revue des Etudes Juives*, LIII (1907), 161 ff.; LIV (1908), 1 ff. and 205 ff.; LV (1909), 72 ff.; LVI (1910), 70 ff.

JULIUS DESSAUER, *Der Raschi-Kommentar zu den fünf Büchern Moses*. Budapest, 1887.

M. GRÜNBAUM, *Zum Raschi-Jubiläum*. Berlin, 1905.

NEHEMIAS KRONBERG, *Raschi als Exegete*. Halle, [1879.]

M. LIBER, *Rashi*. Philadelphia, 1906.

———— Article 'Rashi' in *Jewish Encyclopedia*.

J. H. LOWE, *Rashi on the Pentateuch*. London, 1929. vol. I.

FELIX MASCHKOWSKI, 'Raschi's Einfluss auf Nikolas von Lyra in der Auslegung des Exodus,' *Zeitschrift für die alttestamentliche Wissenschaft*, XI (1891), 268 ff.

A. T. MICHALSKI, 'Raschi's Einfluss auf Nikolas von Lyra in der Auslegung der Bücher Leviticus, Numbers, und Deuteronomy,' *ibid.*, XXXV (1915), 218 ff.; XXXVI (1916), 29 ff.

A. S. ONDERWYZER, *Raschi's Leven en Werken*. Amsterdam, 1901.

WINTER and WÜNSCHE, *Die Jüdische Litteratur seit Abschluss des Kanons*. Berlin, 1894-97. 3 vols. *passim*.

LEOPOLD ZUNZ, 'Salomon ben Isaac, Genannt Raschi,' *Zeitschrift für die Wissenschaft des Judenthums*, I (1823), 277 ff.

Abraham ben Meir Ibn Ezra

WILHELM BACHER, 'Abraham Ibn Ezra's Einleitung zu seinen Pentateuch-Commentar,' *Sitzungsberichte der Philosophisch-Historischen Classe der kaiserlichen Akademie der Wissenschaften, Wien*, LXXXI (1876), 361 ff.

———— *Ibn Ezra als Grammatiker*. Strassburg, 1882.

———— *Varianten zu Abraham Ibn Ezra's Pentateuch-Commentar*. Strassburg, 1894.

———— in Winter und Wünsche, *Die Jüdische Litt.*, II (1895), 185 ff.; 289 ff.

MORITZ EISLER, *Vorlesungen uber die jüdischen Philosophen des Mittelalters*. Vienna, 1876, 1870, 1883. (3 vols. in 2.) vol. I (1876), 113 ff.

M. FRIEDLÄNDER, *Essays on the Writings of Ibn Ezra.* London, 1877.

ISAAC HUSIK, *A History of Medieval Jewish Philosophy.* New York, 1916.

RAPHAEL LEVY, *The Astrological Works of Abraham Ibn Ezra.* Baltimore, 1927.

S. MUNK, *Mélanges de Philosophie Juive et Arabe.* Paris, (1857) 1927.

DAVID NEUMARK, *Geschichte der jüdischen Philosophie des Mittelalters.* Berlin, 1907. 2 vols.

S. OCHS, *Ibn Ezras Leben und Werke nebst den hergestellen Kommentaren zu Jeremias, Ezechiel, Proverbia, Ezra, und Chronicles.* Breslau, 1916.

DAVID ROSIN, 'Die Religionsphilosophie Abraham Ibn Ezra's,' *Monatschrift für Geschichte und Wissenschaft des Judenthums,* XLII (1898), and XLIII (1899).

M. STEINSCHNEIDER, 'Abraham Ibn Ezra,' *Abhandlungen zur Geschichte der Mathematischen Wissenschaften mit Einschluss ihrer Anwendungen, Leipzig,* XXV (1905), 28 ff.

Levi ben Gerson

NIMA ADLERBLUM, *A Study of Gersonides.* New York, 1926.

LEON ALÉGRE, *Lévi ben Gerson.* Paris, 1880.

ISAAC BROYDE, Article 'Levi ben Gerson' in *Jewish Encyclopedia.*

MORITZ EISLER, *Vorlesungen über die jüdischen Philosophen des Mittelalters.* Vol. III.

ISAAC HUSIK, *A History of Medieval Jewish Philosophy.* Pp. 328-361.

———— 'Studies in Gersonides,' *Jewish Quarterly Review,* N. S., VII (1916-17), 553 ff.; VIII (1917-18), 113 ff.; 231 ff.

M. JOEL, *Lewi ben Gerson als Religionsphilosoph.* Breslau, 1862.

DAVID KAUFMANN, *Geschichte der Attributenlehre in der jüdischen Religionsphilosophie des Mittelalters von Saadia bis Maimuni.* Gotha, 1877.

BEN ZION KELLERMANN, *Die Kämpfe Gottes von Levi ben Gerson.* Berlin, 1914. 2 vols.

S. MUNK, *Mélanges.* Pp. 497-501.

ERNEST RENAN, *Averroes et l'Averroïsme.* 4th edition. Paris, 1882.

RENAN ET NEUBAUER, *Les écrivains juifs françaises du xive siècle.* Paris, 1893. Pp. 240-298.

ISADORE WEIL, *Philosophie religieuse de Lévi-Ben-Gerson.* Paris, 1868.

David Kimchi

WILHELM BACHER, in Winter und Wünsche, *Jüd. Litt.,* vol. II, 191 ff.

EPPENSTEIN, 'Studien über Joseph Kimchi,' *Monatsschrift für Geschichte und Wissenschaft des Judenthums,* XLI (1897), 165 ff.

P. F. FRANKL, in Ersch und Gruber, *Allgemeine Encykolpädie der Wissenschaft und Kunst,* sect. II, XXXVI (1850), 56 ff.

GIOVANNI BERNARDO DE ROSSI, *Historisches Wörterbuch der jüdischen Schriftsteller und ihrer Werke, übersetzt von C. H. Hamberger.* Leipzig, 1839. 164 ff.

J. TAUBER, *Standpunkt und Leistung des Rabbi David Kimchi als Grammatiker.* Breslau, 1867.

JOHANN CHRISTOPH WOLF, *Bibliotheca Hebraea.* Hamburg, 1715-33. 4 vols.

Jacob ben Asscher (Baal Ha-Turim)

P. BUCHHOLZ, 'Historischer Überblick über die mannigfachen Codification des Halachastoffes, von ihren ersten Anfängen bis zu ihrem letzten Abschlusse,' *Monatsschrift,* XIII (1868), 241 ff.

H. GRAETZ, *History of the Jews,* IV, 87 ff.

Saadiah

PORGES, *Monatsschrift,* XXXIV (1890), 63 ff.

ROSIN, *ibid.,* XXXII (1888), 230 ff.

LEOPOLD ZUNZ, *Zur Geschichte und Literatur.* Berlin, 1845. 71 ff.

Angelology and Demonology

ABELARD, *Sic et non,* in J. P. Migne, *Patrologiae cursus completus, Series Latina,* CLXXVIII, 1404; 1412 ff.

ACQUINAS, *Summa,* I. q. 50-62; 106-108; 110-113.

ANSELM, *De Casu diaboli. Pat. Lat.,* CLVIII, 325 ff.

V. APTOWITZER, 'Les noms de Dieu et des anges,' *Revue des Etudes Juives,* LX (1925), 39 ff.

G. Bareille, 'Le Culte des Anges à l'epoque des Pères de l'Eglise,' *Revue Thomiste*, VIII (1900), 41 ff.

G. A. Barton, 'The Origin of the Names of Angels and Demons in the Extra-Canonical Apocalyptic Literature to 100 A.D.,' *Journal of Biblical Literature*, XXX-XXXI (1911-12), 156 ff.

F. Bechmann, *De angelorum loquela.* Jena, 1661.

J. A. Becker, Article 'Engel' in Wetzer und Welte, *Kirchenlexikon oder Encyklopädie der Katholischen Theologie und ihrer Hülfswissenschaften*, vol. IV, 503 ff.

Jacob Behm (sic), *Mysterium Magnum, or An Exposition of the First Book of Moses called Genesis.* London, 1656.

Billuart, *Tractatus de angelis*, in *Cursus theologicae*, vol. II. Paris, 1852.

G. Brecher, *Das Transcendentale, Magie, und magische Heilarten im Talmud.* Vienna, 1850.

Caspar Brochmand, *De angelis.* Hafn., 1629.

Buxtorf, *Lexicon Talmudicum, passim.*

Benjamin Camfield, *A Theological Discourse of Angels, and their Ministries, wherein their Existence, Nature, Number, Order, and Offices, are modestly treated of.* London, 1678.

R. H. Charles, *The Book of Daniel.* Oxford, 1929. (See 'Daniel')
———— *The Book of Enoch.* Oxford, 1912. (See 'Enoch')

S. Clotz, *De angelographia.* Rostochi, 1636.

P. de Comitibus, *Tractatus de angelis.* Petavium, 1684.

Cremer, Article 'Engel' in *Realencyklopädie fur protestantische Theologie und Kirche*, vol. V, 368 ff.

[Daniel] *A Critical and Exegetical Commentary on the Book of Daniel.* R. H. Charles. Oxford, 1929.

[pseudo]-Dionysius, *De caelesti hierarchia. Pat. Graec.* III, 333 ff.

Walter Eickmann, *Die Angelologie u. Dämonologie des Korans im vergleich zu der Engel und Geisterlehre der Heiligen Schrift.* New York, 1908.

[Enoch] *The Book of Enoch*, R. H. Charles. Oxford, 1912. (The standard German editions of this apocryphal work should be consulted for details in addition to Charles.)

O. Everling, *Die Paulinische Angelologie und Dämonologie.* Göttingen, 1888.

J. Fromme, *De Cherubim et Gladio Flammante.* Wittenberg, 1670.

J. M. FULLER, 'Angelology and Demonology.' Excursus to Tobit in Wace's *Apocrypha* (London, 1888. 2 vols.) Vol. II, 171 ff.

JOH. GERHARD, *Angelologia sacra*. Jena, 1637.

J. HAMBURGER, Article 'Engel' in *Real-Encyclopädie für Bibel und Talmud*, vol. I (Strelitz, 1884), 305 ff.

THOMAS HEYWOOD, *Hierarchie of the Blessed Angels*. London, 1635.

HUGO OF SAINT VICTOR, *De hierarchia caelesti*. *Pat. Lat.* CLXXV, 923 ff. *De sacramentis*, CLXXVI, 245 ff. *Summa sententiarum*, tr. II. CLXXVI, 79 ff.

ISIDORE OF SEVILLE, *Etymologiarum*. *Pat. Lat.* LXXXII, 272 ff.

JEROME, *Opera, passim*. Especially *Commentarius in Danielem Liber*.

LEO JUNG, *Fallen Angels in Jewish, Christian, and Mohammedan Literature*. Philadelphia, 1926.

E. KAUTZSCH, *Die Apokryphen und Pseudepigraphen des Altes Testament*. Tübingen, 1910. 2 vols. *passim*.

A. KOHUT, 'Die jüdische Angelologie und Dämonologie in ihrer Abhängigkeit von Parsismus,' *Abhandlungen für die Kunde des Morgenlandes*, (Deutsche Morgenländische Gesellschaft) IV (1866). (Also reprinted separately the same year)

L. LANZONE, *Gli angeli nelle divine scritture*. Turin, 1891.

H. LECLERCQ, article 'Ange' in *Dictionnaire d'Archéologie chrétienne et de Liturgie*, vol. II. 2080-2161.

PETER LOMBARD, *II Sentences, Pat. Lat.*, CXXI. 655 *sq*.

MARTIN LUTHER, *Predigt von den Engeln*, 1531, and *Drei Predigten von guten Engeln*.

J. T. MAIOR, *De nature et cultu angelorum, facta collatione Paganorum, Judaeorum, Mahaummedanorum, et Christianorum*. Jena, 1653.

HENRY MORE, Ψυχωδια *Platonica; or, a Platonicall Song of the Soul*. [Cambridge] 1642. [B. M., E. 1108.]

J. ODE, *Commentarius de angelis*. Tra. ad Rhenum, 1739.

HERMANN OEHLER, *Die Engelwelt*. Stuttgart, 1898.

ORIGEN, *Opera, passim*, especially *de principiis*, and *in Matth*.

J. A. OSIANDER, *De jubilaeo angelis*. Tubingae, 1670.

J. H. OSWALD, *Angelologie, die Lehre von den guten und bösen Engeln im Sinne der Katholischen Kirche*. Paderborn, 1883.

PETAVIUS, *De theol. dogma. III. De angelis*, lib. 1-2.

D. PFEFFINGER, *De cultu angelorum*. Argentorati, 1708.

ROBERT PULLUS, *Sententiae, Pat. Lat.*, CLXXXVI. 719-726.

E. Reusch, *De cultu angelorum.* Helmstadt, 1739.

Roland Bandinelli (Alexander III) *Sentences.* (*Die Sentenzen Rolands*, Freiburg-im-Brisgau, 1891. pp. 85-103.)

J. W. Rothstein, 'Die Bedeutung von Gen. 6:1-4 in der gegen-wärtigen Genesis,' *Zeitschrift für alttestamentliche Wissenschaft, Beiträge*, 1920, 150 ff.

Rupert, abbe of Deutz, *De victoria verbi Dei, Pat. Lat.* CLXIX. 1218-1244. *De operibus S. Trinitatis, Genesis.* CLXVII. 206-209 *De glorificatione Trinitatis*, CLXIX. 54-74. *Comment. in Matth.* CLXVIII. 1627.

Martin Schultze, *Handbuch der Ebräischen Mythologie.* Nord-hausen, 1876.

Moïse Schwab, 'Vocabulaire de l'Angelologie d'àpres les Manu-scripts hébreux de la Bibliothèque Nationale,' *Mémoires pre-sentés par divers savants à l'Academie des Inscriptions et Belles-Lettres*, 1re Serie, 2de Partie, x. 113-430, Paris, 1897.

Strack und Billerbeck, *Kommentar zum Neuen Testament aus Midrasch und Talmud.* Munich, 1924 ss. *passim.*

G. Stuhlfauth, *Die Engel in der spätjüdische und altchristliche Weltanschauung.* Freiburg, 1897.

———— *Die Engel in der altchristliche Kunst.* Tübingen, 1897.

Suarez, *Opera Omnia*, II. *De Angelis*, lib. 1-6.

Syncellos, Enoch Fragment.

Targum of Jonathan Uziel in Walton, *Biblia Polyglotta, passim.*

Vigouroux, article 'Ange' in *Dictionnaire de la Bible.*

A. Vittorelli, *De angelorum custodia.* Patavii, 1605.

Paul Volz, *Jüdische Eschatologie.* Leipzig, 1903, *passim.*

A. Wabnitz, article 'Anges' in *Encyclopédie des Sciences Relig-ieuses*, vol. I. 310-315.

Michael

J. B. Bernhold, *De Michaele archangelo.* Altorf, 1725.

J. Dornfeld, *De pugna draconis cum archangelo Michaele.* Leip-zig, 1708.

J. W. Gobel, *De certamine inter Michaelem archangelum et diabolum de corpore Mosis.* Helmstadt, 1738.

F. D. Haeberlin, *De S. Michael archangelo, ejus festis et cultu.* Helmstadt, 1758.

S. A. Horodezky, 'Michael und Gabriel,' *Monatsschrift für Ges-chichte und Wissenschaft des Judenthums*, LXXII (1919), 499 ff.

W. Lueken, *Michael.* Gottingen, 1898.

J. B. Maius, *De Festi Michaelis.* Cologne, 1698.

A. G. Mirus, *Michaelis archangeli cum diabolo certamen de corpore Mosis.* Helmstadt, 1766.

E. F. Neubauer, *De Michaele archangelo.* Giessae, 1733.

Programm. Helstd. *De S. Michaele archangelo tutelari imperii romani.*

G. Stengel, *De S. Michaele archangeli principalis, apparitionibus, templis, cultu et miraculis.* Vitteburgi, 1629.

E. F. Wernsdorf, *De originibus solemnium S. Michaelis.* Viteburg, 1773.

Uriel

F. Cancellieri, *De Urieli nomine, una cum aliis trium Archangelorum.* In *De secretariis basilicae Vaticanae.* (Rome, 1876), vol. II (1800), 1002 ff.

Gabriel

R. H. Charles, *The Book of Daniel.* Oxford, 1929.

S. A. Hordezky, 'Michael und Gabriel,' *Monatsschrift, loc. cit.*

Azazel Bibliography

(The literature on this subject is very large; the following items represent a working but not an exhaustive bibliography.)

Joseph Bergel, *Mythologie der alteren Hebräer.* Leipzig, 1882.

Samuel Bochart, *Hierozoicon, sive bipertitum opus de Animalibus Sacrae Scripturae.* London, 1663. 2 vols.

R. H. Charles, *Apocrypha and Pseudepigrapha of the Old Testament.* London, 1913. 2 vols.

T. K. Cheyne, 'The Date and Origin of the Ritual of the "Scapegoat,"' *Zeitschrift für alttestamentliche Wissenschaft,* xv (1895), 153 ff.

Natalis Comes, *Mythologiae, sive Explicationem fabularum libri decem.* Venice, 1568.

Diestel, 'Set-Typhon, Asahel, und Satan,' *Zeitschrift für die historische Theologie,* xxx (1860), 159 ff.

Hans Duhm, *Die bösen Geister im Alten Testament.* Tübingen, 1904.

R. Dussaud, *Notes de mythologie syrienne.* Paris, 1903-5.

EERDMANNS, *Das Buch Leviticus*, in *Alttestamenliche Studien*, IV. Giessen, 1912.

GILBERTUS GAULMYN, *De vita et morte Mosis*. Paris, 1629.

LILIUS GREGORIUS GIRALDUS, *De Deis gentium varia et multiplex historia, in qua simul de eorum imaginibus et cognominibus agitur, ubi plurima etiam hactenus multis ignota explicantur et pleraque clarius tractantur*. Basel, 1548.

M. GRÜNBAUM, 'Beiträge zur vergleichenden Mythologie aus der Hagada,' *Zeitschrift der Deutsche Morgenländische Gesellschaft*, XXXI (1879), 183 ff.

THEODICORUS HACKSPAN, *Fides et leges Mohammaedis exhibitae ex Alkorani manuscripto duplici, praemissis institutionibus arabicis*. Altorfii, 1646.

J. HAMBURGER, Article 'Azazel' in *Real-Encyclopädie für Bibel und Talmud*, vol. I, 120 ff.

D. HOFFMANN, *Das Buch Leviticus*. Berlin, 1905-6. 2 vols.

ANTON JIRKU, *Die Dämonen und ihre Abwehr im Alten Testament*. Leipzig, 1912.

LEO JUNG, 'Fallen Angels,' *Jewish Quarterly Review*, n.s., XVI (1925-26), 326.

J. KATWIJK, 'Azazel, sien Gereform,' *Theologisch Tijdschrift*, XLVII (1913), 79 ff.

KAUFMANN KOHLER, *Origins of Synagogue and Church*. New York, 1929.

SIMON LANDESDORFFER, *Der βααλ τετραμορφος und die Kerube des Ezechiel*. Paderborn, 1918.

S. H. LANGDON, 'The Scapegoat in Babylonian Religion,' *Expository Times*, XXIV (1913), 9 ff.

H. J. LAWLER, 'Early Citations from the Book of Enoch,' *Journal of Philology*, XXV (1905), 164 ff.

MARK LIDZBARSKI, *Ephemeris für semitische Epigraphik*. Giessen, 1902. vol. I. 201 ff.

MAIMONIDES (Moses ben Maimon), *Guide for the Perplexed*, (translated by M. Friedländer). London, 1910. p. 359 f.

C. C. McCOWN, 'The Ephesia Grammata in Popular Belief,' *American Philological Association*, LIV (1924), 128 ff.

N. MESSEL, 'Die Einheitlichkeit der jüdischen Eschatologie,' *Zeitschrift für Alttestamentliche Wissenschaft*, Beiträge, 1915, pp. 163 ff.

Hugo Odeberg, *3 Enoch.* Cambridge, 1928.

Abraham Ortelius, *Deorum Dearumque capita ex vetustis numismatibus in gratiam antiquitatis studiosorum effigiata et edita.* Antwerp, 1573. (Also in J. Gronovius, *Thes. Graec. Antiq.* vol. VII.)

Lorenzo Pignoria, *Magnae Deum Matris Ideae et Attidis initia ex vestustis monumentis edente et explicante.* Paris, 1623. (Also in Gronovius.)

Nicholas Remy (Remigius), *Daemonolatreiae Libri tres, ex judiciis capitalibus nongentorum plus minus hominum, qui sortilegii crimen intra annos quindecim in Lotharingia capite luerunt.* Lyons, 1595.

Martin Schultze, *Handbuch der ebräischen Mythologie.* Norhaussen, 1876.

John Selden, *De Dis Syriis*, var. editions, London and Leipzig.

T. A. Spalding, *Elizabethan Demonology.* London, 1880.

John Spencer, *De legibus Hebraeorum Ritualibus et earum rationibus.* Hagae-Comitum, 1686.

Tertullian (Oehlers. Leipzig, 1853, vol. I. 729).

J. T. de Visser, *Daemonologie van het oude Testament.* Utrecht, 1880.

Paul Volz, *Jüdische Escatologie.* Leipzig, 1903.

Gerardus Vossius, *De theologia Gentili, et physiologia Christiana.* Amsterdam, 1641.

L. Wogue, *Le Pentateuque.* Paris, 1860-69, vol. III. 186 f.

Buxtorf

———— *Athenae Rauricae, sive Catalogus Professorum Academicae Basiliensis ab A. MCCCLX. ad A. MDCCLXXVIII. cum brevi singulorum Biographia*, (Basiliae, 1778) pp. 88, 444 ff., 464.

A. J. Baumgartner, *Calvin hebraïsant et interpréte de l'Ancient Testament.* Paris, 1889.

———— *De l'Enseignement de l'hébreu chez les protestants à partir de l'époque de la Reformation.* Geneva, 1889.

H. Baumgarten, *Sleidan's Briefwechsel.* Strassburg, 1881.

Buxtorf-Falkheisen, *Johannes Buxtorf, Vater.* Basel, 1860.

J. Derenbourg, 'L'Edition de la Bible rabbinique de Jean Buxtorf,' *Revue des Etudes Juives*, XXX (1895), 70 ff.

L. Geiger, *Das Studium des hebräischen Sprache in Deutschland vom Ende des* xv. *bis zur Mitte des* xvi. *Jahrhunderte.* Breslau, 1870.

K. R. Hagenbach, *Leben und ausgewählte Schriften des Väter und Begründer reformierten Kirche.* Elberfeld, 1857-62.

────── *Die theologische Schule Basels.* Basel, 1860.

J. C. Iselin, *Neu-vermehrtes historisch- und geographisches allgemeines Lexicon.* Basel, 1726-27. 4 vols.

C. G. Jöcher, *Allgemeines Gelehrten-Lexicon.* (Leipzig, 1750-1819) vol. i, 1523 ff.

D. Kaufmann, 'Buxtorf's Aruchhandschrift wiederaufgefunden,' *Monatsschrift für Geschichte und Wissenschaft des Judenthums,* xxxiv (1885), 185 ff., 225 ff.

E. Kautzsch, *Johann Buxtorf der ältere.* Basel, 1879.

M. Kayserling, 'Richelieu, Buxtorf père et fils, et Jacob Roman.' *Revue des Etudes Juives,* viii (1884), 74 ff.

────── 'Les Correspondants Juifs de Jean Buxtorf,' *ibid.,* xiii (1886), 260 ff.

H. J. Leu, *Allgemeines Helvetisches, Eydgenössisches, oder Schweitzerisches Lexicon.* Zurich, 1745-65. 20 vols.

A. Merx, 'Johan Buxtorf's des Vaters Targumcommentar Babylonia,' *Zeitschrift für wissenschaftliche Theologie,* xxxi (1888), 41 ff.

G. Schnedermann, *Die Controverse des Lud. Cappellus mit den Buxtorfen über das Alten des hebräischen Punctuation.* Leipzig, 1879.

R. Stintzing, *Geschichte der deutsche Rechtwissenschaft,* (1880) in *Geschichte der Wissenschaft in Deutschland,* Band 18.

R. Thommen, *Geschichte der Universität Basel 1532-1632.* Basel, 1889.

H. von Boos, *Thomas und Felix Platter.* Leipzig, 1878.

B. Walde, *Christliche Hebraïsten Deutschlands am Ausgang des Mittelalters.* Münster, 1916.

Works Written, Edited, or Translated by Buxtorf the Elder

Concordantiae Bibliorum Hebraicae. Basel, 1632.
(Also as *Specimen Phraseologiae V. T. Hebraicae.* Basel, 1717.)

De Abbreviaturis Hebraicis liber novus et copiosus.   Cui accesserunt Operis Talmudici recensio . . . Item Bibliotheca Rabbinica nova, ordine alphabetico disposita. Basel, 1613.
Epitome Radicum Hebraicarum. Basel, 1607.
Grammatica Ebraea Martino-Buxtorfiana. Basel, 1625.
Grammaticae Chaldaicae et Syriacae libri III. Basel, 1615.
Institutio Epistolaris Hebraica, cum epistolarum Hebraicarum familiarum centuria. Basel, 1610.
Lexicon Chaldaicum, Talmudicum, et Rabbinicum. Basel, 1639. (Usually referred to as *Lexicon Talmudicum.*)
Lexicon Hebraicum et Chaldaicum. Basel, 1621.   (Frequently reprinted.)
Manuale Hebraicum et Chaldaicum. Basel, 1619. (Occasionally reprinted.)
Synagoga Judaica, hoc est, Schola Judaeorum in qua nativitas, institutio, religio, vita, mors, sepulturaque ipsorum sunt. Hanau, 1604.
Thesaurus Grammaticus linguae sanctae Hebraeae. Basel, 1609.
Tiberias; sive, Commentarius masorethicus. Basel, 1620.

Works Written, Edited, or Translated by Buxtorf the Younger

Florilegium Hebraicum. Basel, 1648.
Lexicon Chaldaicum et Syriacum. Basel, 1622.
Rabbi Mosis Majemonidis liber מורה נבכים *Doctor perplexorum · · · in linguam Latinam . . . conversus.* Basel, 1629.
Tractatus de punctorum vocalium et accentuum in libris Vet. Testamenti Hebraicis origine, antiquitate et authoritate. Basel, 1648.

John Weemse

ROBERT DOUGLAS, *The Baronage of Scotland.* Edinburgh, 1798.
DAVID CALDERWOOD, *The History of the Kirk of Scotland.* [Edinburgh] 1680. (Also in Wodrow Society, 1842-49). 8 vols.
HEW. SCOTT, *Fasti ecclesiae Scoticanae: the Succession of Ministers in the Parish Churches of Scotland, from the Reformation, A.D. 1560 to the present Time.* Edinburgh, 1866-71. 3 vols.
JOHN WEEMSE, *The Christian Synagogue.* London, 1624.

William Schickhard

בחינת הפירושים *Bechinath happeruschim, hoc est Examinis commentarionum rabbinicarum.* Tubingae, 1624.

Horologium Hebraeum. Leipzig, 1624.

Institutiones linguae ebraeae. Jena, 1647.

משפט המלך *Jus regium Hebraeorum.* Leipzig, 1625.

GENERAL INDEX